I Identify as Blind

I Identify as Blind

A Brazen Celebration of Disability Culture, Identity, and Power

∴Lachi

with Tim Vandehey

Tiny Reparations Books®

An imprint of Penguin Random House LLC
1745 Broadway, New York, NY 10019
penguinrandomhouse.com

Tiny Reparations and Tiny Reparations Books with colophon
are registered trademarks of YQY, Inc.

Book design by Kristin del Rosario
Interior art: title page staff © MNP Designs/Shutterstock;
chapter audio waves © Luba Vega

LIBRARY OF CONGRESS CATALOGING-IN-PUBLICATION DATA
has been applied for.

ISBN: 9780593851579 (hardcover)
ISBN: 9780593851586 (ebook)

Printed in the United States of America
1st Printing

The authorized representative in the EU for product safety and compliance is
Penguin Random House Ireland, Morrison Chambers, 32 Nassau Street,
Dublin D02 YH68, Ireland, https://eu-contact.penguin.ie.

To those who have been my community and to those who
will be my community.

To my biological mother, Chief Dr. Marcellina, and to my Disability
mother, Judith Heumann. To my biological ancestors, and to my
ancestors in Disability—including Brad Lomax. To my partner,
Arthur, for diving into this ocean with me.

To my eight-year-old self, who desperately needed this book.
I am honored to finally write it for you.

Contents

I Identify as Blind

I Identify as Blind

I am an expert in exactly one thing. Me. My identity. My mind, my sense of self, and the body in which they are beautifully wrapped. My name is Lachi, she/her, and I'm a Black woman with cornrows. I identify as Blind.

In June 2022, the PBS series *Origins* contacted me about appearing as an expert on Ray Charles in an episode of their show *Historian's Take*. They were looking for someone like me—a Black blind musician—to be an expert on Black blind musicians. While the email didn't open with "Dear Stereotype," I did have to steady myself, saying, "Lachi, this could be your first on-air expert gig for a national broadcast. Let it go." Besides, y'all *know* I was honored. We were just starting to pretend that COVID was over, and a girl needed to keep her platform busy. After working hard to make a name for myself, *of course* I'd be asked to speak about other blind musicians. I didn't consider myself an expert on the subject, but wearing my Blind identity front and center often makes me an instant educator. Like, here's a fun pro tip: As I write this, I'm wearing a faded purple tee, black sweats, and flip-flops, because that's what every millennial wears at the only coffee shop open this late while choosing fonts for the intro of their first big book. I'm hunched over a laptop, inhaling audiobooks at double speed, slowed only by the very real need to refresh my email and DM feeds every nine minutes on the minute.

My point is, if you're blind, that's the vibe, and if you're not blind, that's what some in the blind community call a self-description: a short verbal rundown of one's appearance, including gender, ethnicity, and one pop of visual flair that allows those with vision loss to have access to that information. Now if you're thinking—"Hey, you just taught me something, but you just said you're not an expert"—then yay!

Since I was eight years old, I always wanted to be an expert in something—a guest-sipping-mimosas-with-the-ladies-from-*The-View*-type of expert, respected and even curtsied to. Little did I know how important that PBS interview would become for the trajectory of my life and the realization of my eight-year-old dreams.

Do you remember the first time you were asked what you wanted to be when you grew up? I do. It was in my third-grade class. We were all sitting in a circle on the carpeted floor of a public-school classroom in suburban upstate New York. The teacher asked the room, "What do you want to be when you grow up?" and my mind's eye camera zoomed in on my shocked, excited face. It wasn't every day I had the precise answer to a question asked of the class, but I had *the* answer to this one.

I was going to be a big-time recording artist with a fancy manager and a secretary who said, "Please hold," as soon as she picked up, even if she didn't need to put you on hold. I would be a fancy author with a big-time New York publisher who gave me deadlines that had my fancy friends saying "Girl, I don't know how you do it" over our three-hour lunches. I knew all of this at eight. The teacher encouraged a blonde girl in the circle to answer, and she said, "I want to be an actress like Sandra Bullock!" and we all clapped—good for her, a blonde wanting to be a brunette. A Black kid beside me was next to go, and he said, "I want to be a basketball player like Michael Jordan!" We clapped—we're supposed to be supporting the Knicks, but okay.

My turn. I thought, *I'll say I want to be a singer like Louis Armstrong. No, wait, a female singer like Alicia Keys. No, a blind singer like Ray Charles. Nah, Ray Charles was a dude, and he sang gospel or country or Pepsi jingles, and that isn't me. Ah, I've got it: a Black blind female singer like . . .* Nothing seemed to fit the trifecta, so when my time came and all eyes fell on me in expectant silence, I stood up and said, "I don't know."

But I *did* know. I just didn't want to get laughed out of town for saying I was going to be the first Black blind female anything. Because the truth was, there was no example of future *me* out there in the world tearing it up on the *Billboard* charts, the movie screen, or the TV talk-show circuit. There were no blind women of color I could put on my vision board, and everybody who's ever read *The Secret* knows it ain't gonna happen 'less you put it on the vision board.

So I—a small-town daughter of Nigerian immigrants with a disability—paved my own way through ingenuity, creative thinking, a ton of trial and error, and a hell of a lot of guts. I wasn't going to be Ray Charles. I was going to have to find a way to become an expert in *me* and forge Lachi out of thin air, pure grit, and a touch of golden wit.

So when *PBS Origins* asked me to be their expert on Ray

Charles, I said, "Hell yes!" and jumped into researching him through articles, documentaries, and the 2004 Jamie Foxx blockbuster *Ray*, because I admittedly knew nothing about him other than the Pepsi thing. As I dove into his life, I found that we had much in common. Like me, Ray left his small town for big-city music dreams. Like me, he liked to tour, loved his booze, and was a quick-witted flirt. Also like me, he was fortunate enough to have a mother who prioritized his independence.

By the time the day of the virtual pre-taping came, I was debate-prep-level ready. I was not about to let my momma, grandmomma, and every Black woman on earth down by being even slightly underprepared. Hair? *Check.* Nails? *Check.* I had Alexa blaring Ray Charles classics up until the five-minute mark. I was ready to give *Historian's Take* host Danielle Bainbridge a run for her money. And I think I did, since she ended the interview saying, "I love interviews where I barely have to say anything."

I spouted off everything I knew on the man known as "the Genius" like a text-to-speech Wikipedia article. Our discussion went into well-manicured detail on the trope of the Black blind musician, delving not only into giants like Ray and Stevie but also into pioneers like Blind Tom Wiggins. I took the opportunity to not only share my knowledge, but to amplify my creative projects, my advocacy work, and the up-and-coming blind artists I supported. Meanwhile, Danielle sensed that my taskbar was a bit slow to load on off-the-cuff questions and kindly let me off the hook. I remember thinking, *Please just make me look smart in the final cut*, but not having the chutzpah to voice my wishes aloud.

The interview aired in the second week of July, amid my 2022 Disability Pride Tour—July being Disability Pride month.

Throughout that tour, I'd tweaked my acoustic sets to kick off with a five-to-ten-minute comedic open that included my introduction and self-description for the night, where I mentioned that I identified as Blind. I'd begun using the phrase back in 2021 after stumbling upon the Instagram description of one of the first few prominent blind influencers I'd found, Molly Burke. It read, "I'm a YouTuber. I happen to be blind." In response, I began to introduce myself at shows by saying, "I'm a musician who doesn't just happen to be blind. I am a proud blind woman. Blindness is integral to my identity. All the great opportunities I've enjoyed haven't come despite my being blind, but *because* of it, because of my full identity."

Yeah, as they say in Hollywood, I needed to punch that self-description up a bit. It needed to be short, cheeky, and straightforward. By the time of my *PBS Origins* episode, my segment began with my newly crafted intro: "My name is Lachi, like Versace, she/her, and I'm a Black woman with cornrows. I identify as Blind." After watching the episode on their YouTube channel from the road, I left a cute little thank-you comment and walked away with a smile. That was that, or so I thought. I'm not sure what prompted me to come back to the video days later—maybe it was to check if the view count was still on the rise, like we all do—but I did, and boy was I *not* ready.

The first couple of comments were about Ray Charles, the interview, and blind musicians, with general emoji babble. But as I continued to scroll down, I began to notice a common theme overtake the comments section:

> "WTF does 'identify as blind' mean? You're either blind or you're not."

"Blindness is a medical diagnosis, not an identity you can give yourself."

"Do you need to read Braille or not?"

"We do not need sighted people to start thinking that trans-blindness is a thing."

I was shocked. And like an innocent Dorothy stepping into Oz, I naively broke the one cardinal rule of the internet: I descended into the bowels of the comments section and started responding. I know, I know. But I thought, *If they'd only just hear me out, then everyone will understand and we'll all skip merrily down the yellow brick road into the sunset.* Obviously that wasn't the case, because YouTube is where trolls go to breed, feed, and drink their spiced mead. Needless to say, I had touched a nerve.

What was for me an obvious, everyday reality—disability is a spectrum and an integral part of one's identity, and yes, some blind people have partial vision—was terra incognita to these comment folk. The realization was invigorating. With a few words, I'd gotten scores of internet types asking questions and reflecting on disability in ways they hadn't before. Could I shove even harder against the rigid walls of mainstream thinking and open people's minds to the rich, vibrant, and undercelebrated Disability Culture narratives currently shaping popular culture? What if I could get folks to unmask, bring them face-to-face with their own disability and neurodivergent identities, and help them recognize them not as oddities to be feared or dismissed but as natural attributes and life hacks to be celebrated?

The PBS *Historian's Take* incident was the first—but not the last—time the comments section of a major brand went aggro over my "I identify as Blind" intro. Each subsequent time, my intro sparked new and nuanced conversations, introspective revelation, and heated debate. I was onto something, and that *something* was the seed of this book. It's my celebration of the big-umbrella Disability identity currently coursing through the circulatory system of popular culture, along with the Disability community's many innovations, works of creative genius, legislative wins, and stories of resilience and triumph.

Big-umbrella Disability identity goes beyond the sensory, intellectual, and physical to include chronic conditions like arthritis, asthma, multiple sclerosis, and epilepsy; mental health conditions like generalized anxiety disorder and depression; neurodevelopmental disorders like ADHD and Tourette's syndrome; substance use disorders like those involving alcohol or opioids; learning disorders like dyslexia; and quite a few more conditions, some of which you might identify with. That identity is what we're about to celebrate. This is a book about joy, justice, and radical and collective self-acceptance. That's what you've gotten yourself into. But don't worry. You're in good hands.

⠲ ⠒ ⠶

According to my hairdresser, local corner store clerk, and a neighbor I've said hello to but whose name I still don't know (New Yorkers, amirite?), casual conversations about ethnic identity (miracle hair products and Oscar snubs), gender identity (the very real danger of gender reveal mishaps), and even sexual preference (the ever-growing list of celebrity coming-out stories) are far more commonplace than those about disability. That's because the "average Betty" equates disability with charity, pity, or some form of compliance that nobody got time for.

But like ethnic and gender identity, everyone personally interfaces with Disability identity, whether they are aware of it or not and whether they have an apparent or state-defined disability or not. And while gritty discussions on the hardships and erasure Disability communities continue to endure are relevant and necessary, this book ain't that. Think of our time together here as less Viola Davis and more Maya Rudolph. This is a late-night group chat between you, me, and Disability identity. Like any friendship, there will be laughs, tears, uncomfortable silences, and the eventual flood of heart emoji DMs letting you know we're still cool.

I say all this to make it clear that I am not a proper disability advocate or social justice activist, although I have the utmost respect for them and learn from their awesome examples every day. What I am is a *singer*. I sing songs. I'm a songwriter, an entertainer, a personality, and when I'm feelin' cocky, a rapper. Through music, storytelling, fashion, and a pinch of soul, I work to promote inclusion, to combat the stigma and erasure of the Disability identity, and to amplify Disability Culture and Disability joy.

For a living, I partner with international artists, brands, and cultural outfits to create compelling, impact-driven art, like my 2023 radio-charting alt-pop track "Lift Me Up," which I made in partnership with Google to honor the late Disability rights icon Judy Heumann. I've also hosted the PBS *American Masters* series *Renegades*, highlighting disabled revolutionaries like Brad Lomax and Kitty O'Neil. I've partnered with Amazon Music Studios on my *Mad Different* acoustic concert series celebrating intersectional identity pride. I've met with President Joe Biden and Vice President Kamala Harris at the White House while sporting a white cane decked out in red, white, and blue rhinestones. I've walked Hollywood red carpets, even serving up Blind Barbie eleganza at the global *Barbie* premiere. I've toured around the world, belting out notes and banging on keys, and I've worked on accessibility campaigns with the likes of Meta, Microsoft, and Google.

Many know me from my work with RAMPD. In 2021, while completing my New York University master's thesis on accessibility within the music industry, I founded the RAMPD (Recording Artists and Music Professionals with Disabilities) consulting group and professional network platform. RAMPD has since worked with the Grammy Awards, Live Nation, Netflix, and other media giants to make the music and live entertainment industries safer and more accommodating for patrons, performers, and professionals with disabilities. I serve on several industry boards, including the Recording Academy—where I've served as a board governor and trustee—working to promote inclusion. For my service through RAMPD I've had the honor of being named the 2024 Adcolor Innovator of the Year, a 2024 *USA Today* Woman of the Year, and included in *Forbes's* Accessibility and *Billboard's* Pride 2025 lists.

While I am always humbled and grateful to be recognized for my work, the greater honor is that I get to *do* the work. My team and I frequent plenaries, think tanks, ceremonies, and galas, and we appear at universities, NGOs, culture centers, and corporate outfits from Europe and the Americas to Asia and Africa. At these events, I strut to the podium or piano in a couture outfit, with glammed makeup, nails, and cane, and I perform high-energy songs, prompt thoughtful discussion, or tell raunchy jokes like "I'm not special needs, but I've *got* special needs in the bedroom. DMs are open!" I'm all about letting my audiences know they're gonna be uncomfortable and they're gonna like it, 'cause we're about to crip walk through crip talk the same way Kendrick Lamar wordsmithed America into empathizing with the Black experience.

I try to keep busy.

Through my work, I've come to realize that when you're up against a biased system, you won't win that game with brute force alone. I can't personally fix any system by dismantling it, nor will I accomplish anything more than the tiniest needle shift by attempting to rise through the ranks within that system. I can, however, get the folks who benefit from the system excited to change it with me using music, glamour, and joy.

As a blind, queer daughter of immigrants who grew up working class, I embody *intersectionality*—a framework coined by scholar Kimberlé Crenshaw to describe the unique privileges and biases affecting communities and individuals who identify with multiple groups. As members of many different communities, we carry with us all of the things all of the time. So I'm here to discuss the unique ways Disability identities intersect with the everyday lives of everyday people, from minuscule daily choices to big cultural shifts. I'll celebrate that through my own stories, and through the stories of public and pop culture figures who openly interface with their Disability identity through their art, advocacy, online content, and the media.

You may have clocked that I capitalize the *D* in Disability when referring to it in the context of identity or culture. Folks in the community differ on their preference, but I capitalize the *D* out of pride and respect for our shared history and experience.

What do I hope to do with this book? First, I want to celebrate Disability Culture—to let the world know that disability *is* a culture with its own heroes, contributions, innovations, creative arts, language, histories, and traditions. We'll meet some of those heroes, public figures, and provocateurs, including Illinois Senator Tammy Duckworth, Tony winner Ali Stroker, *Breaking Bad*'s RJ Mitte, Oscar-nominated filmmaker Jim LeBrecht, viral creator Imani Barbarin (Crutches and Spice), comedian Cat Cohen, late Disability Justice cofounder Patty Berne, Microsoft chief accessibility officer Jenny Lay-Flurrie, and many more. We'll learn their unique stories, rock with them as they show up imperfect and authentic, and discover their visions of a future free from conformity.

For the purposes of this book, I refer to people who don't believe they have a disability or neurodivergence (yet) or who don't identify with or acknowledge their Disability identity (yet, perhaps because their condition requires little outside accommodation) as *nondisabled*. I want to welcome the nondisabled public in and show them the powerful influence that different Disability communities continue to exert on mainstream culture. For instance, ever pushed a stroller and thanked God for those curb cuts? That was us. Ever benefit from sending a quick text (because who in their right mind leaves a voicemail post-2016)? Yeah, what we now call text messaging started with us. What about listening to an audiobook to get through a cross-country drive so you can spring up on your ex? You guessed it—all of these started with disabled problem-solvers. We're out here shaping mainstream culture in ways you probably don't even realize. After reading this book, you will know these contributions and a whole lot more.

Second, I want to invite all the folks who "happen to have a disability" to step all the way in. I want people to feel empowered, supported, and proud to identify with these dope stories, messy conversations, and sarcastic non sequiturs jabbing at societal injustices with a smile. I want the big-umbrella, capital *D* Disability community to unite around the joy of our over-the-top, ordinary, extraordinary, resilient, hard, beautiful stories; to come together to tell, highlight, and amplify new stories; and to promote new goals for collective liberation. I hope to provide a framework for you to understand, appreciate, and eventually slide all the way into the DM (that's Disability Movement—yeah, there's gonna be a lot of categorically dad-level jokes, too).

Third, I want to help shift how people view disability. I want to cancel the shame currency that people outside of the Disability community often associate with the word and replace it with identity pride and common understanding. I'm here to let people know it's okay to say the "D-word"—and that it's preferred—but that we may kick you in *your* "D-word" if you call anyone "handi-capable." I want to give folks an amuse-bouche of how powerfully liberating it is to accept an identity that society encourages us to hide—because like it or not, we're all likely to transition into having a full-time disability one day, temporarily or permanently, because of injury, illness, or good old Father Time. If that gives you the heebies, stick with me. I've got you.

Why this book, and why now? Because there's never been a time when humanity has confronted the commandment "adapt or die" with more urgency. From climate change to economic inequality, from pandemics to artificial intelligence, the global shit show is already in act two. We—our governments, businesses, universities, artists, and communities—have to find a way to evolve and survive together without losing our compassion and collective dignity. Who better to teach humanity how to adapt and thrive than people for whom adaptation is our operating system, and for whom creative problem-solving and perseverance are our table stakes?

All this is to say, there's more complexity, nuance, and beauty to Disability Culture and identity than many folks realize. For instance, I'm also diagnosed with ADHD, OCD, and general anxiety. My ADHD powers my one million (and counting) bright ideas. My OCD enables my meticulous follow-through on all those one million (and counting) bright ideas. My anxiety fosters excitement and empathy. My blindness has given me creative problem-solving, drive, and cute-ass Glam Canes. These aren't silver linings. These are just facts. My disabled friends and I aren't sorry to be who and what we are. We're proud entrepreneurs, artists, lawyers, and CEOs, we're sexy as hell when we feel like it, and—this is key—we are *not* the exception.

Y'all, disability isn't something to be afraid or ashamed of, so let's quit whispering about it. Disability is a big, brassy, brilliant party of culture and community that deserves to be celebrated. So let's celebrate. Consider this book your party invitation. If you're comfortable in your Disability identity, this table is for you. If you're a nondisabled person who has a parent, child, friend, or coworker with a disability, get your ass in here, because I saved you a seat. If you don't have disability in your life ("yet," she said knowingly) or you're not sure if that thing you have qualifies, take off your coat, turn the chair backward, and let's talk as we all build this future together.

Come on, it'll be fun. You wouldn't say no to a lady with a Glam Cane, would you?

Chapter One

The Day I Woke Up Blind

Back in the 2010s—the decade of superhero films, fitness trackers, and the fall of the hipster (so, in retrospect, the decade of hope)—I'd gotten to a point in my New York–hustle life where all I needed to feel successful was a song placement with a major brand. So you can imagine how accomplished I felt on June 14, 2016, after turning in my final vocals on a project with my first major client, WWE Music Group. Things were finally starting to turn around for your girl. I slept *good* that night.

The following morning, I woke up blind.

Not just what some folks would call low vision or visually impaired, a diagnosis I'd navigated all of my life, but *blind* blind. Hugging-a-friend-and-realizing-it's-a-tree blind, as if I'd opened my eyes under deep, dark, roiling water. I could perceive lights and darks but couldn't make out any objects. I lay there in my apartment on that sunny Wednesday morning and thought, *Okay, so this is it. It's finally happening.*

It might seem hard to believe how calm I was, especially for an Aries. Most people, if they woke up at what appeared to be the bottom of a murky lake, unable to see, might collapse and curl into a ball, pangolin-style. But I'd never known a time when I didn't have motion sickness, an unhealthy need to eat all the cheese in the fridge—stringed, cubed, wrapped, or shredded, it doesn't matter—and vision loss. I was born with a condition called coloboma, which left me with low and uncorrectable vision, but not total vision loss.

Growing up *blindish*, pretending I could see the chalkboard at the ten different schools I attended from kindergarten through twelfth grade (more on immigrant parents tryna make the American dream work later), I had built up a thick armor of resilience and adaptability around my low vision. While I wasn't quite fully aware of my Disability identity at the time—I navigated through most of my life as *sighted passing*—I did tap into its solutions-oriented energy.

Lying there that summer morning, newly blind, I managed to locate my phone and called my partner, Arthur, at work. I said something all Keanu Reeves–level chill, like, "Hey there! How we doin'? Yeah . . . so, I woke up blind. *Blind* blind."

Arthur instantly perceived that the situation called for heightened stress levels, so he stole the show with an Oscar-worthy outburst. "What?! What do you mean *blind* blind? Are you okay? Don't move! I'll come up during lunch."

"Nah," I said nonchalantly. "I think I'll head down to the Eye and Ear real quick. Get this checked out."

"And take the subway? No way! Whatever you do . . . Do. Not. Leave! Okay?"

"I'll be fine." At this point I was calming *him* down. I ended the call, telling him he could meet me at the clinic. So, the Eye and Ear Infirmary, where I got vision care, was on Fourteenth

Street. I lived on Ninety-Ninth. This was the Dark Ages before the wider reach of Uber and when a Black girl couldn't hail a cab when she *could* see, so I was going to have to navigate eighty-five blocks of Manhattan mayhem on my *first day* of being totally blind.

Back in those days I wasn't big, bad, fearless "Lachi like Versace" quite yet. On a good day, I was more "Lachi like a high-quality Versace knockoff." But that morning, the morning I woke up blind, was big, bad, fearless Lachi's origin story. I wasn't about to sit in my apartment, waiting for someone to save me while hold music played in the background.

Problem-Solving

I managed to brush my teeth—and we all know the struggle of a nearly empty toothpaste tube—so I figured I could do anything. I threw on yesterday's white crop top and, hugging the banister, made my way down four flights of stairs and outside to the streets of East Harlem. In the daylight, I could make out some colors and moving shapes but was still very much swimming underwater. A railing lined a good portion of the block, but I'd have to start using my Manhattan know-how before long.

Ah, New York. The city of big apples, hand-tossed pizzas, and the colloquial adverb *deadass*. A unique dichotomy of children who grow up too fast and adults who never grew up; where, if you get your ass kicked, no one steps in to help, and if you're the one doing the ass-kicking, no one butts in to stop it. I'd originally moved to New York nearly a decade prior, after a rejection letter from NYU dared me to pull up anyway.

By this time I'd lived on my Ninety-Ninth Street block long

enough that we knew each other quite well. I made my way to the sidewalk and ran my hands down the bushes to my right, taking in the brushes-on-snare-drum rustle of foliage. The playground to my left brought the familiar cacophony of rowdy kids and young mothers. With this feedback, I was able to triangulate my position on the sidewalk. Eat your hearts out, bats.*

As I made my way toward the corner, I entered the realm of the daily corner-side catcallers, and I caught the attention of one of them. You know this guy. He wakes up in the morning, showers, shaves, gets dressed, looks in the mirror, gives himself a wink, and thinks, *You got this.* He eats breakfast, hugs his wife and kids, then heads to his spot in front of the local convenience store, where he spends the next eight hours whistling at and asking for the phone number of any woman who walks by. I have no idea how he earns a living.

These guys don't even expect a response; they're just bored, sexist, and lonely. None of which would be my concern, except that on this particular midday, I was newly blind with no cane and needed a bored and lonely Good Samaritan. So I'm sure this particular catcalling charmer practically did a Simone Biles double twist when he dropped his usual "Hey girl, where you goin'? Lemme walk you!" line on me and I responded, "Sure! Walk me to the bodega on the corner."

---

* By the way: Bats aren't blind. Yes, they sleep upside down during the day and yes, there is occasional bloodsucking—for some species—but no, they are not vampires and no, they are not blind. They *do* use nonvisual means to find their way around, just like me, which makes them pretty dope. Also, hi! For those who love footnotes, we're gonna have some fun down here! For those who don't, well, I won't speak ill of you because you're not here to defend yourself. But we will be keeping it popping down here!

Talk about the proverbial dog who caught up to the mail truck. The guy (who we'll call Catcalls) just stood there, like, "Uh, wait, what?" I had him walk me across the street and down two and a half blocks to the corner store right by the subway station.

As we walked, I made conversation, like, "So . . . what do you do?"

Of course, he laughed and said, "I really just hang on the one corner." Employment mystery solved!

At the bodega I asked the store clerk for one of those chia seed kombuchas—because today was the *perfect* day for a difficult snack—and then proceeded to take what felt like a *Lord of the Rings* "Full Boxed Set with Director Commentary" amount of time to locate my debit card among the seemingly identical cards in my wallet.

After I finally managed to pay, Catcalls walked me out of the bodega and offered to help open my kombucha. "You need to shake it, then let it sit," he said, even though everyone on God's green earth knows *you don't shake a kombucha.* You croon to it like it's a newborn you're trying to get back to sleep at two thirty in the morning, then rock it back and forth, patting it gently till it burps.

But Catcalls went on to shake mine like an André 3000 Polaroid picture, right there at the top of the subway station staircase. He handed me the bottle, asked for my number, and walked away content with the ten random digits I spouted. Thank you, sketchy escort, for being my makeshift sighted guide.

I managed to feel my way down the stairwell to the subway station and through the turnstile and swiped my MetroCard—smaller and thinner than my other cards and so easier to identify by touch—and eventually made it to the platform. The train approached, the doors opened, and I found myself a seat on the train bound for Lower Manhattan.

Part One of "Lachi's Perilous Blind Journey" conquered!

Being Adaptable

I adore a good cliff-hanger, so I'll come back to "The Adventures of Lachi, Part Two: The Kombucha Kaper" after these commercial messages. Now, were you expecting me to be dodging rogue taxicabs, running from street criminals, or maybe solving a murder or two along the way? Sorry (not sorry) to disappoint, but from my perspective there was more than enough Tom Clancy–level drama for me to deal with. Even though I had experienced low vision all my life, that was the first time I couldn't perceive anything: no faces, no signs, no bikers who know better than to ride on the sidewalk—nothing.

But the key to the story isn't my odyssey through the streets of Midtown. It's my reaction to waking up unable to see. I was relatively nonplussed—definitely high aura. I had lived with the reality of limited vision for as long as I could remember. I was also pretty well acquainted with my Blind identity. So transitioning from level one to the underwater level was not world-ending stuff.

Every day, people with disabilities improvise ways to board trains, discern street signs, bench-press a rack at the gym (because we're out here trying to look good), and do all the things our counterparts take for granted. Like a good Frank Zappa solo, our improvisational game would leave Wayne Brady slow-clapping in awe. Not all disabled people are fearless, swaggering badasses.

Many of us, however, recognize the ways the world was not built for us, and out of pure necessity, we become masters of adaptability.

When any person confronts a stressful situation, stress hormones trigger our "fight, flight, or freeze" response, causing an inability to adapt and make rational decisions. Whether it's a high-pressure intersection or *Snakes on a Plane*–level turbulence, the effect is the same: Panic prevents us from acting. So the prospect of dealing with the unexpected makes a lot of folks uneasy. But like Jim Rohn says, "If you're not willing to risk the unusual, you'll have to settle for the ordinary."

Ordinary? *¡No soy!*

For those of us who work to navigate, think, and communicate in a world not quite compatible with our bodies and minds, every day comes complete with an evolving to-do list of unexpecteds. Those not yet familiar with Disability identity might be amazed that I kept my cool and navigated the streets of New York City with such grade-A rizz, but any disabled person reading this is going, "Yeah, that's my average Wednesday."

Disabled folks have what author and executive Dr. Paul Stoltz calls a high AQ—adversity quotient. It's the measure of a person's capacity to persevere, adapt, and bounce back from difficult situations. We constantly find option C, and that consistent need for assessment and ingenuity—for turning obstacles into opportunity—hikes up our AQ. We're resourceful, creative thinkers by default, because our problem-solving muscles are as jacked as actor Terry Crews in his thirties, forties . . . or even fifties. You know what? No matter when you read this book, Terry Crews will be very jacked.

Beyond being adaptable, we're also resilient. Let's turn to our cultural history for examples, because it both shapes and reflects how we see ourselves. When it comes to epic disability resilience, I could highlight the grit of late Hawaii senator Daniel Inouye, who lost his right arm to a grenade in World War II and went on to become the only senator to receive both the Congressional Medal of Honor and the Presidential Medal of Freedom. Or African American tap dancer Clayton "Peg Leg" Bates, who lost his leg as a child in 1919 and then went on to tour the world, open for Louis Armstrong, perform for the Queen of England, and own and operate his own country club.

But I want to focus on William Henry "Chick" Webb, an exemplary Black drummer with a spinal cord injury (because as we've established, I am *the* expert on Black disabled musicians). Born in 1905, 1907, or 1909, depending on who you ask, Webb was legendary. From giving Duke Ellington a run for his money in swing competitions to breaking Ella Fitzgerald onto the scene, Chick was one of the most highly regarded drummers of the Big Band Era, influencing the likes of Buddy Rich and Gene Krupa. Chick fell down some stairs as an infant, which injured his spine and left him with a hunched back.

Like me, Webb valued his independence early, taking on a paper route to buy drums after a doctor told his parents that an instrument would be good for him. Also like me, his childhood traumas saw him off to New York as a young adult to chase his big-city dreams. As soon as he touched down, he was playing in house bands, show bands, and touring bands and leading his own orchestra, inventing swing showmanship and syncopation techniques while putting his own health in the "worry about that later" column. The exhaustion of touring took a serious toll on his body, but he pressed on so as to keep making bank for his family and his bandmates' families throughout the Great Depression.

This kind of perseverance in the face of health issues continues across the disabled population to this day. A 2019 study by UK nonprofit Attitude Is Everything found that two in three performers with disabilities had compromised their health for a gig. While I'm not condoning risking one's well-being for a job, resilience and adaptability are woven into the DNA of all doers with disabilities, neurodivergence, and other chronic differences. Just ask jazz guitar legend Django Reinhardt, who influenced major shredders like Black Sabbath's Tony Iommi, Led Zeppelin's Jimmy Page, and Korn's James "Munky" Shaffer; all four of them jammed with missing fingers. Or Les Paul, who shattered his elbow in an auto accident that eventually locked his arm at the guitar-playing angle. Or Def Leppard drummer Rick Allen, who famously lost his left arm mid-career. Rick put it best in a *Greg Hill Show* interview when he said, "All the information that used to go to my left arm kind of went to the rest of my limbs, so I was able to express myself, even though it was in a different way."

The American Psychological Association defines resilience as "the process and outcome of successfully adapting." When I think about someone who embodies adaptability, the ever-optimistic comedian, producer, and TV actor Nic Novicki comes to mind. Nic's appeared in more than forty TV shows and films—*Boardwalk Empire, The Sopranos, The Good Doctor*—and has produced a ton of his own opportunities. Somehow everywhere, yet still going places, Nic and I naturally gravitated toward friendship. While researching for this book, I caught up with him to ask about his experiences building his own empire as a little person actor working Hollywood to the bone.

"I've been a comedian for over twenty-two years," he began. "I've performed on six continents, toured literally every state. When I started, there was no 'it's cool to be a little person' movement. A lot of the acting roles I was getting were very much related to my height—fantasy roles, which I'm not totally against."

I thought about how Peter Dinklage almost turned down the acclaimed role of Tyrion Lannister in *Game of Thrones* because he did not like the stark association of people with dwarfism and the fantasy genre.

Nic went on, saying, "But things have drastically improved in authentic representation for little people."

As he said this, I thought of the character Oberon—played by Warwick Davis—a little person who emcees at a small club in the early part of *Ray*, a role that makes no mention of his height (and yes, I know I'm unironically referencing a film where the namesake blind guy is inauthentically represented by a sighted actor, but more on that later).

I asked Nic about how he adapted on the road as a touring comedian, a lifestyle that can be taxing for anyone. "Travel can be the toughest part of touring," he said. "Long airport lines, so I take my bike. Limited support staff, so I use my charm. If a sink is too tall, I'll turn over a trash can. I find shortcuts and hacks to make it work, because I love what I do, and it's all about getting onto that stage."

I thought back to Chick Webb, who'd ignored telltale signs of exhaustion to keep the shows showing, and asked Nic if all that inaccessibility hurt his set when he finally made it to the stage. "To be honest, it can," he confessed. "If you're in significant pain, night after night, that's in your mind when you're up there."

He then switched to a more playful tone. "Whenever something goes wrong for me, I generally get material out of it."

For further insight, I caught up with good friend Danielle Perez, a wheelchair user who turned her viral moment of winning a treadmill on *The Price Is Right* into becoming a comedian, comedy writer, and TV actress. "There's this idea in stand-up that if you're not grinding, staying out the latest, and constantly working in the way everyone else deems valuable, then you're not a real comedian," she said on our call. "While my profile was rising, I was running myself ragged doing three spots a night, five nights a week. I felt that the minute I got off the merry-go-round, all the balls would drop. Meanwhile, I have a prescription for Klonopin because I'm like, 'Will my wheelchair make it off this flight in one piece, so I can get to my show?'"

I asked Danielle if this was still the case today. "Today, I'm not on the road as much. I focus on writers' rooms and acting jobs, which for me are more lucrative and sustainable," she said. "There's so much out there. Your way of achieving success may not look like mine and that's okay. As long as you're funny and the crowd's into it, you're doing your job."

Ain't that the truth!

Determination

Speaking of on-demand adaptation, let's return to my high-wire trek down the New York City streets while fashionably blind. Safely on the train headed south, cocooned in the embrace of the New York City Transit Authority, it was time to take a deep breath and enjoy my chia seed kombucha. Now, if you drink kombucha, you know you have to tilt the bottle and line up the bubbles when opening it so it doesn't erupt all over you like a seventh-grade science fair volcano. Let's just say on that morning, I had other priorities.

Unable to see, I simply popped the lid . . . and ta-da! Slimy green chia seeds seemed to projectile-vomit all over my white shirt, inside my bra, onto my face, and into my hair. My hair! I was dressed head to toe in a thick, green, globby gown of kombucha. *Great.*

While every New Yorker on the train was serving up a silent *Yep, saw that coming. Shoulda lined up the bubbles,* this sweet, adorable little girl walked over and handed me one of those thin fast-food napkins, like this was a mustard-on-the-collar or dusty-Cheetos-fingers situation. I'm sure I looked like She-Hulk or one of those aliens from *Independence Day,* but I accepted the gesture with grace. I sat there, dripping gooey ectoplasm, until the subway's speakers announced we had arrived at the Fourteenth Street station. I oozed off the train, leaving a trail of slime in my wake, stood on the platform, and took a deep breath to compose myself. Then reality set in. *I'm blind. I look like the Blob. I'm in an unfamiliar place. Time to raise my fast food napkin in surrender.*

I found my way up the stairwell to the street. Upon spotting a woman bedecked in green slime emerging from New York City's underbelly like a Spider-Verse villain, two transit workers rushed over. "Everything okay? You need help?" they asked. I smiled and summarized my situation—I woke up blind, I live on Ninety-Ninth, I'm trying to get to the doctor, kombucha bomb, yada yada. Finally, I said, "I just need a new outfit. Can y'all get me to the Strawberry on the corner?"

I knew the location pin of every Manhattan Strawberry—a women's clothing chain—and there was one right by the Fourteenth Street station. My new transit worker friends walked me over to the store, but as soon as I stepped in, employees flew over from all corners, mainly to keep me from tracking goo any farther than the entrance. Desperate to get out of my slimy top, I picked the closest shirt off of the closest rack with no idea what it looked like, handed someone cash, said, "Keep the change, cowboy," and proceeded to change clothes right there on the store floor in front of God and the crowd forming just outside the store's large windows.

Now that I'd gotten some shopping in, it was time to return to our regularly scheduled emergency. Outside, my transit fam (who'd stuck around to bear witness) hailed me a cab and sent me off with a cheery, "You're alright, kid." And really, I was. The cab driver took me the last few blocks to the clinic, parked the cab, and even walked me to the front desk—skipping the line like a true cabbie—to make sure I got checked into the clinic. Let the world never again slander New Yorkers as rude or callous, because when I needed my city most, she stepped up.

Finally, Arthur huffed breathlessly into the waiting room, rushing in late like the cops in every horror film ever, and sat with me. When I saw the doc, I found out that I'd experienced a complication called corneal hydrops, whereby my corneas erupted and the subsequent fluid caused severely blurred vision and light sensitivity. The doctor gave me eye drops for the hydrops (told you I could rap), and slowly my corneas returned to their former shape. But this new complication was part of my life now. The doctor told me that I would continue to encounter similar eruptions in the future and that my eyesight was on a slow and steady cruise to total blindness. So here I am, still on that journey that started that June morning.

Being Resilient

Because culture keeps getting blindness backward, I want to nip in the bud any notions of "Oh, you going blind must have spiked your other senses like Daredevil, and that's why you were able to navigate so well." My only spiked sense was common sense—and, of course, a very real need to prove to Arthur I could get to the clinic without him, even if I was literally on fire.

Historically, blindness has been portrayed as either divine punishment or divine power. I'm agnostic at best, so that's out. But overcoming obstacles isn't extraordinary work for us—it's ordinary work. Case in point: After attending the 2024 NATO summit, I posted a picture of myself in an evening gown, complete with heels and cane, bearing the caption "I identify as Blind. I eat barriers for breakfast," and the post went viral. A common theme of "She overcame her blindness!" flooded the comments. Nope, still blind. What I overcame was stigma. I just lean away from the social stigma while leaning into the strengths my Blind identity affords me: adaptability and resilience.

In *Forbes*, disabled writer Andrew Pulrang nails this. "Disabled resilience is real. But it's also widely misunderstood," he writes. "People tend to assume that the most significant hardships we endure are our actual disabilities—physical, sensory, intellectual, or mental . . . But it's the way we are treated by others—the social aspects of being disabled—that tend to be the most consistently and deeply wearing."

Bull's-eye. While getting into a rampless office building or navigating a dark and loud nightclub can be challenging, the shame and stigma that mainstream society attaches to disabilities are the real obstacles. I don't succeed *despite* my blindness. I succeed *despite* inaccessibility. Like how Justice Richard Bernstein, a blind Michigan Supreme Court judge, memorizes and internalizes all case materials so as to not slow things down during case conferences. It takes next-level resourcefulness (and no small dose of optimism) to come out swinging every day in a society that often forgets about your basic needs.

Nevertheless, we rise to the occasion, whether we were born with an apparent disability or came to our Disability identity later in life. A 2004 study looked at middle-aged and older adults experiencing vision loss and found that those who managed stress by accepting their new limitations had better mental health than those who didn't. So, essentially, the sooner one accepts their inherent Disability identity, before societal barriers force them to, the more likely they'll be able to wake up blind (or otherwise disabled) and traverse New York like it ain't no thang.

More, you ask? Sure. A University of Kansas study found that students with disabilities handled quarantining, social distancing, and remote learning during COVID-19 with more je ne sais quoi than their nondisabled counterparts. Of course they did! They relied on the strengths, resilience, and self-determination skills hyperdeveloped by the daily demands of being disabled. The irony is that many students and professionals with disabilities had been insisting for years that remote work and school accommodations would allow them to be more productive. Not to throw shade, but it took a global pandemic to bring about remote options, and there go the disabled kids blowing their counterparts out the water.

Okay, maybe just a *little* shade.

This is one of the biggest reasons disabled and neurodivergent folks are so important in a world where disruptive change has become the norm. We bring the high-AQ energy. Want your business to have the chops to pivot in the face of a Superstorm Sandy–type shake-up? While nondisabled employees are running around in circles trying not to get their hair wet, your handful of staff who are confident in their Disability identity will be like, "Okay. Give me the tools I need, and lemme get this handled." That's what we do. We roll with it.

Disability identity is a person's internal sense of self as it relates to big-umbrella disability. It is an identifier—a demographics category heading under which everyone sits—like gender or racial identity. Not knowing your own Disability identity until you're confronted with the concept is natural. For instance, I didn't know I was Black or what my racial identity was until another student told me at around age four or five. Some people's understanding of their gender identity may shift, but the fact that gender identity exists is not under debate.

To recognize your Disability identity, you must recognize any condition of your body, mind, or the way you process emotions that, if unaided, fits under big-umbrella disability. Understand how this part of you informs your choices, shapes who you are, and influences how you navigate the world. Be aware of the ways you overcompensate or adapt and optimize to meet your basic needs in any situation that's incompatible with your unique, natural body-mind. You don't need to call yourself disabled to understand your Disability identity. In evolutionary terms, adversity is a necessary ingredient for growth. Becoming an ace at overcoming adversity comes with a strong Disability identity.

You can strengthen your Disability identity by connecting

with the Disability community, a group of people with disabilities who share a sense of identity and belonging and who view the disability experience from a place of pride, unity, and power building. (This should not be confused with the "disabled population," which includes any human with a disability and is generally referenced in big data statistics. You can be a part of the disabled population without subscribing to the Disability community.)

As a blind woman, I've always had to figure out crafty ways to keep pace with my sighted counterparts. This led me to become fairly skilled at a lot of things: web design, audio engineering, copywriting, video editing, wisecracking . . . I really just have an ability to figure shit out. When I got to the point in my career where I needed a full creative team, I assembled a group of people like me, who specialize in autonomous problem-solving and also have the drive and ability to figure shit out. A team with strong Disability identity—or what I call "Big DIS Energy," the innate ability to problem-solve, innovate, and think creatively, thanks to the built-in drive and sense of self-determination that come from a life of navigating the world differently.

When given the right tools, adequate training, and an encouraging environment with clear goals, people with disabilities go on to become highly productive team members, self-reliant friends, creative and loving parents, jazz drumming legends, or world-touring comedians.

Flexing perceived flaws. Finding and harnessing the power of hidden gems and underestimated treasures. These are the time-tested and history-proven skills of winners. As our ever-changing world continues to throw us fastball challenges, why not look to those who specialize in thriving despite daily adversity as our most promising leaders for charting a path forward? You'll find those innovative, adaptable, resilient, flaw-flexing, challenge-busting leaders in the Disability community.

Postscript

Sitting in the doctor's office, I told Arthur all about my harrowing voyage from Harlem. After taking it all in, he asked, "If you couldn't see, how did you pick out the perfect shirt at Strawberry?"

Apparently, big black text on the shirt read, "Even on my worst day, I'm still killing it."

Message received. The universe was telling me that starting today, I was gonna be a different kind of Lachi.

Chapter Two

Just Say the D-Word

I just took a DNA test. Turns out, I'm 100 percent not "handi-capable." I'm also not "differently abled" or "uniquely abled." I do not have "special needs" (again—except for in the bedroom, DMs open), and I am certainly not "inspirational" just for waking up at 10 a.m., heading down to the corner bakery with my cane, buying a coffee and bag of Doritos, wising up and tossing out the Doritos after one (okay, two) big handfuls, and then hopping back into bed beside a just-waking-up Arthur and acting like I only bought a coffee.

All these euphemisms are straight-up corny, but more important, disability is part of my identity and not something that needs to be euphemized, infantilized, or erased.

Most folks following the Lachi saga know I'm a huge propo-nent of just saying the word *disability*. I trash "differently abled" every time it comes up, and I have no qualms cutting off world leaders mid-sentence like, "I'm sorry, come again?" There is nothing shameful about disability, so why the euphemisms? It's why I and others in the community capitalize the *D* when referring to Disability identity or culture. The word *matters*. Acknowledging the reality *matters*.

That all said, I didn't pop out of the womb a "Say the word" crusader. In fact, it was a long, arduous journey from "Who am I?" to "Google me!" when it came to Disability identity and my eventual pride in the "D-word."

Like all stories of learning to take pride in one's identity, mine begins in the back of an Uber on my way to catch a Trance show and ends three years later in the back of an Uber on my way to *be* the show. The story began on a Friday. I was looking *cute* cute—heels, nails, fresh wig—in the back seat of an Uber Black (a baller move in 2018) on my way to da club. I was headed to catch Markus Schulz, a popular Trance DJ, spin our song "Far." As a working songwriter, I'd placed dozens of dance songs with major label imprints, but this was the first song worth any salt where I was the songwriter *and* the lead vocalist. This was a big deal. Like many DJ artists, Markus was known for pulling the vocalist onstage to join in hyping the crowd during the song. I was all the way ready!

As I sat back and ogled the song's Spotify stats, nose-to-phone—like we blindish do—I mouthed off to my accompanying friend about how we were about to be Trance gods, if only for the night. Then the Uber driver turned slightly toward us and asked, "You need glasses, sweetheart?"

The instant *pop* of my tenuous confidence balloon was nearly audible. I exhaled, sifted through my mental index cards, and went with, "I'm legally blind, and it's not correctable with glasses," in hopes the straightforwardness would quash any follow-ups. It didn't.

"Ah, so sorry to hear that, sweetheart. I got a brother-in-law with a handicapped—or, uhm . . . differently abled kid. Don't they got devices for you people?" and on and on (and on) with the concern-trolling, or as I like to call them, "Thank-You-Doctor-Isms."

We're gonna pause here. For fifty points and the lead in our game, what did the Uber driver do wrong? You guessed it! He started chatting with us, like this was Hollywood and he was working up to pitching us his rom-com script before dropping us off at the Chateau Marmont. Everyone in New York City knows that the invisible divider between the Uber driver dimension and the back-seat passenger dimension is real and sacred. We have an inalienable right to be back there gossiping about *Love Is Blind* scandals, lip waxing, and mailbox snooping without fear of being quoted on the cover of *New York* magazine.

But apart from that—and the cringeworthy use of "sweetheart"—wasn't he just trying to be friendly? He may have thought so, but all I heard at that moment was "Aw, you poor thing," and "Disabilities are for children." I'm sure his prodding was well intentioned. But good intentions don't excuse uncool behavior. Like historian Yuval Noah Harari said when asked about growing AI concerns, "When you give good people bad information, they make bad decisions." But it's okay to mess up, learn, and grow, so let's give Mr. Uber driver some good information to make small talk with.

Erasing Erasure

Euphemisms are indirect ways of expressing concepts considered shameful or unpleasant. Some euphemisms can be folksy—"Given the old heave-ho" to refer to being fired, for example. Others are downright comedic, like my favorite *poophemism* (i.e., a euphemism for pooping, and no, I did not make that word up): "Letting a dirty little secret slip through the crack." Still others can be patronizing, like saying "differently abled" to avoid using *disabled* or *disability*.

Katie Carr captures the issue of erasure in her 2023 Nora Project article, "The Harmful Reality of Disability Euphemisms." She writes that the U.S. has a long history of "institutions banning disabled folks from the public. In the past, this happened with the 'Ugly Laws' . . . leading to inhumane cruelty behind locked doors." She goes on to point out that today, people with disabilities still face societal pressures to remain hidden "despite being a part of the largest minority in the world." In 2025, the CDC revealed that 29 percent of U.S. adults (more than seventy million) reported having some form of disability—including nonapparent disabilities like asthma, lupus, sickle cell anemia, depression, and PTSD, but not yet including long COVID—but as a society we're still not talking about it.

Twenty-nine percent? And we're still not talking about it? That's like having four of those ten-foot-tall blue people from *Avatar* show up on the roster of an NBA team and their coach being all like, "What? We don't talk about this. Let's play ball!" According to the World Health Organization, 1.3 billion people globally (that's one in six) live with a disability. We collectively decided to stop saying "I don't see color"; it's time to stop "not seeing" disability.

Disability is *everywhere*. It's in your neighborhood, in your school, at your local store in the produce aisle, and sitting beside you at work using up the last of the cyan ink in the laser printer. Disability can be temporary (think SZA at the 2022 Grammys with a crutch) or due to aging like Joni Mitchell at the 2024 Grammys looking klutch! But we still cover it up like it's the Pentagon Papers. Worse, we encourage those with disabilities to do the same by erasing the very thing used to express the concept of disability, the word itself.

Such identity erasure can lead to deep isolation and identity-masking gymnastics. We get President Franklin D. Roosevelt keeping his wheelchair use a secret, Anthony Bourdain's secret struggle with depression, and Robin Williams's fear of his Lewy body dementia.

I get the fear of the word. A lot of folks associate the prefix *dis-* with rap battle exchanges, like the ones between Kendrick and Drake, or Nikki and Cardi, or 2Pac and the entire East Coast. In short, the prefix is assumed to be negative. But etymologically, *dis-* is the Latin prefix meaning "apart," and who wouldn't want traits that set them apart? If anyone's goal in life is to be a Basic Betty and not set themselves apart, then it's time to up them goals, queen!

Besides, there are plenty of great words that start with *dis-*. *Distinct*, like a Morgan Freeman voiceover. *Distinguished*, like Meryl Streep in anything. *Disruptor*, which every start-up with a CEO under forty aspires to be. It takes *discipline* to *discern* a *discovery*. And who doesn't love a good *discount*? Hello?

But being set apart means embracing difference, so "differently abled" should work, right? Well, first, everyone is differently abled. Some people can carry a tune. (Me.) Some can balance whatever a "checkbook" is. (Not me.) Some can walk; some are bilingual in English and American Sign Language. Singling out people with disabilities as "differently abled" implies that only disabled people's abilities are "different" and that nondisabled people are what? Normal-abled? Terms like *differently abled** rein-force stigma, deny reality, and make me wanna conjure up some Tank Davis energy.

Similarly, "special needs" gets a one-star rating from me. My daily needs aren't special needs, they're just my individual needs. The term often leads to educators having lower expectations of children with disabilities. A 2016 study out of the University of Wisconsin discovered that no one—not even you—likes the term *special needs*. Every human has their own unique needs, and ac-commodating them is the very definition of equity.

A lot of people really aren't rocking with *handicapped* anymore, either, mainly because it was assigned to us by people outside of the community. The term originally described the disadvantages of a horse in a horse race, and many have taken it to mean "poor" or "disadvantaged." But my disability is not a handicap or a disadvantage; it's a neutral difference. The Disability com-munity at large pans the word, so I'm thinking people outside the community should, too.

It's like someone saying "My name is Jessica," and I'm like, "I'll call you Becky." And she's like, "Please call me Jessica," and I'm like, "Okay, Becky." And she's like, "Don't call me Becky." and I'm like, "Okay, rude." The Disability community at large is like, "Don't call me handicapped." Instead of *handicapped*, con-sider describing accommodations by using terms like *accessible parking* and *accessible bathroom*.

The National Center on Disability and Journalism strongly

---

* Dysphemisms are replacement words that are more disparaging than the original word. It's like saying, "Sorry to hear your friend bit the big one and bought the farm, but at least she's six feet under pushing up daisies." Like, who is that for?

recommends avoiding euphemisms in its official Disability Language Style Guide. But it's the infantilizing "You can do it!" sentiment (yes, said like Rob Schneider in *The Waterboy*) behind the euphemisms that really gets under my skinsuit. For instance, referring to a disability as a superpower is giving wiggity wack. Last I checked, I don't wear my underwear outside my spandex. My blindness is not a supernatural power, it's a natural part of who I am, and when someone transitions into disability, their condition will become a natural part of who they are. While they won't gain Dua Lipa's ability to levitate, they will learn the new skills and tools needed to adapt to their life change.

While the term *disability* isn't universally defined, disability-affirming language is universally beneficial. Some folks reference the Americans with Disabilities Act definition. But you don't have to have a state-defined disability to recognize your Disability identity. We come in distinct and diverse body-minds that transition over time, and because of this, all human beings will eventually intersect with disability in their personal lives. This is the very not-so-scary truth of disability. Dodging the D-word just prolongs the inevitable need to accept it and reinforces the idea that, like Tom Cruise in *A Few Good Men*, you can't handle the truth.

But—and I say this from firsthand experience—you can.

Let's Paint a Picture

The task of opening people's perspectives to what they'd rather ignore often falls to artists. Notions of disability erasure, disability representation, and their impacts on dignity appear time and again throughout art and cultural history, in the works of American photographer Diane Arbus, German painter Otto Dix,

Kenyan painter Hezbon Owiti, and world-renowned Mexican artist Frida Kahlo, who boldly depicted her own physical disabilities throughout her works. But you can find examples as far back as fifteenth-century painter Hieronymus Bosch, who specialized in portraying humanity's greatest desires and fears. One of his most significant works, *Ship of Fools* (which hangs at the Louvre in Paris), depicts a densely packed boat full of people presumably with intellectual and mental health disabilities. The piece captures a common practice in medieval Europe: eradicating a town's mental health problems by gathering up the local disabled people and shipping them off to who knows where.

Mommy, Mommy! Look, I solved disability!

Early art is full of authentic portrayals of disability. Take the fourteenth century's *Luttrell Psalter*, an illustrated manuscript famous for its many depictions of everyday medieval life in rural England, which incorporates a number of illustrations of people with various disabilities going about their daily lives (it's now found in the British Library in London). Or take the seventeenth-century Diego Velázquez painting of Sebastián de Morra, a dwarf and jester at the court of Philip IV of Spain (it now hangs in the Prado in Madrid). Velázquez paints de Morra as stern, confident, and *fine*. After being exposed to this high-court, finer-things, "I may be a jester, but I ain't no punk" court jester, Velázquez started painting people with dwarfism in a warmer and more dignified light.

Another great example of art combating disability erasure is Marc Quinn's sculpture *Alison Lapper Pregnant*. Quinn depicts a pregnant Alison Lapper, a woman born without arms and with shortened legs, just chillin' in London's Trafalgar Square, like, "What? I'm a woman. I'm disabled. I'm in your face. Say something." Critics did say something—namely that Quinn was taking advantage of shock value, but others saw the work as a real-life homage to Venus de Milo . . . if Aphrodite got knocked up and was British. There was a beautiful dignity in Alison Lapper being right there, in central London, where people were forced to see, feel, and think.

∴ ∵ ∷

B ack in that Uber Black, the driver (who kept on talking, and talking . . . and talking) had really gotten me in my head like a Kid Cudi mixtape. Before long, I was questioning why I believed a blind girl like me thought she could hype up a crowd. By the time I came to, I was onstage at the club, and the DJ had his hands in the air, pantomiming that I should join in. I joined in, but I wasn't there to fully experience the milestone.

But why did a relatively innocuous exchange like the one with the Uberista do such a number on me? Because the D we all want is *dignity*. Even though I knew it wasn't intended as a microaggression, his words hit me right in my dignity-jugular. Back then, I wasn't fully comfortable with who I was. I hadn't yet found the suitable tools, hacks, and mantras with which to embrace my Disability identity. For my racial identity, I had my Black power fist. For my gender identity, I had my bra burning. For generational identity, I bore the dual "proud New Yorker but ready to board the next flight to my parents' home country if shit goes down" type of pride that all second-gens know about. But my Disability identity was wrapped in a handful of dignity-churning euphemisms and well-meaning people telling me I needed glasses.

Months after my Uber incident, I came across my first instance of disabled dignity, and it was transformative. And it came, of course, through pop culture. I caught an episode of Comedy Central's *Drunk History*, a show where historians would get hammered while recounting historical events. That episode highlighted a twenty-eight-day federal sit-in that eventually led to the passage of disability rights laws in the U.S. The trashed historian introduced me to the disabled activist Judy Heumann, the civil disobedience she helped lead alongside about one hundred disabled protesters, and the subsequent legislation. I put down my prosecco (because of course I was drinking along) and sat up straight, tears pooling at my lashline. How had I never heard of Judy Heumann, this badass disabled woman, who showed up with confidence, poise, and pride?

That's right. My life trajectory and understanding of Disability identity was forever changed by watching an episode of *Drunk History*.

Reclaiming "Crip"

EXTERIOR: A RUSTIC SUMMER CAMP SOMEWHERE IN UPSTATE NEW YORK IN THE EARLY 1970s.

It's morning. Not far from the '70s hippie haven of Woodstock, the camera pans across a picturesque wilderness dotted with cabins and fire rings. As the sun rises over the tranquil landscape, we witness a group of campers walking and wheeling their way toward the communal dining hall, their faces alight with anticipation. Yep, walking and *wheeling*. This is Camp Jened, a haven for teenagers with disabilities, offering a rare opportunity for camaraderie, self-discovery, empowerment, and belonging.

Against a backdrop of guitar circles, wheelchair races, and

late-night bonfires, we watch campers navigate daily challenges without the Lifetime TV movie saccharine sheen. The camp itself becomes a symbol of the growing disability rights movement.

That's the Oscar-nominated 2020 documentary *Crip Camp*, directed by James LeBrecht and Nicole Newnham, executive-produced by Barack and Michelle Obama, and featuring Judy Heumann. There's so much to dig into about this film, its message, and the people behind it, but I want to focus on the title. To be specific, one word. *Crip*.

Crip is shorthand for *cripple*, a generally derogatory term. Reclaimed words like *crip, queer, fat, mad,* and *bitch* were once used to disparage a group, but have since been claimed by and refined to empower that community, thus helping neutralize the marginalizing power they once held. A blog article on Crip Riot—a clothing store with shirt slogans like "F★★★ Stairs" and "No Spoons Only Knives"—put it best: "Words can be weapons, and for too long, disabled people held the blade instead of the handle." Reclamation puts the handle back in our hands.

Reclamation is spreading, too. Chicago-based store Rebirth Garments, which creates gender nonconforming wearables for queer and trans disabled folk, uses the term *QueerCrip* to describe its dress reform movement, combining two reclaimed terms. Rebirth's mission has been to help historically excluded people confidently express their individuality and identity and combat erasure. When I asked founder Sky Cubacub, a non-binary xenogender Filipinx, about their Disability identity, they proudly identified as mad, disabled, and neurodivergent (among others).

Reclaiming language gives you agency over your identity and your story and pride in your community. Today, words like *crip* are an integral part of the Disability Pride movement and identity discussions, with usages like #CripTheVote, Crip Theory . . . and *Crip Camp*.

Crip Camp filmmaker Jim LeBrecht was cool enough to get on a Zoom call with me to talk about the power of reclaiming the word. "Hollywood has been telling the same couple of old tropes," he said, lounging back in his wheelchair with his scruffy-bearded director smile. "Either 'I've become disabled, and even though I'm filthy rich and have a love interest, I want to go to Switzerland and die.' Or it's these super crips climbing Half Dome with their pinkies. They thought *we* were unable to tell stories . . . they didn't even think these stories existed, nor did they ask."

Jim went on. "Using the word *crip* . . . is an identifier. It's almost like a secret code within us that says, 'I politically or culturally identify with having a disability, and I'm going to use this radical term as a way to express my commitment, my identification, and my activist lean on this.' Not everybody likes the term. There are people who are offended by it."

I get it. I don't identify as or with *crip* but have used it to talk about accessible spaces as "crip friendly" or to refer to my Glam Cane as my "crip cane"* (which, yes, is immediately misinterpreted). Like with *queer* and other reclaimed terms, not all in the community are quick to embrace it, especially those with traumatic memories tied to the word.

Jim mentioned how he and Nicole Newnham ran into similar

---

* Crip vs. *crip*: While hip-hop star Christopher Wallace (a.k.a. Biggie) got mixed up in activity surrounding the Crips (a street gang) in his early life, he didn't officially become a *crip* (a person with a disability) until a car accident later in life left him using a wheelchair and eventually a cane.

apprehension when meeting with Netflix about bringing *Crip Camp* to streaming. "We're talking about the title," Jim said, "and they're like, 'People are going to think that the film is about a street gang.' In Netflix's defense, we are like an icebreaker. We are going into this company changing awareness. We are blowing away perceptions from marketing to content to just about anything. We are a community that some of these companies really had never dealt with on this level."

Crip Camp, from the film to the people behind it, shed a much-needed light on many facets of disability rights, as well as its human embodiment, Judy Heumann. She played a vital role in maintaining strong connections with other campers and eventually used that to propel the disability rights movement. The documentary follows her and other Camp Jened campers as they become activists. In my subsequent binge of Judy Heumann content, I found a Disabled World article claiming that Judy had led the charge to switch out the word *handicapped* for *disabled*, stating, "Others handicap us, but we are disabled people."

Say the Word

Less than a year after my fateful Uber ride, I got the message loud and clear. I was sitting in the audience at a 2019 Adweek presentation hosted by the Female Quotient, a women's equity production company. I didn't often watch presenters before my own set because they cut into my "hurry up and rehash my lines in a panic" me time, but that day I would be speaking and performing my song "Unafraid," and I figured I'd practice what I was about to preach. A man who sounded like actor Ray Romano sat in front of the audience and spoke unabashedly about Disability Pride. There was that D-word again. But then he said something else, and everything clicked right into place.

"Just say the word," he said. "Just say *disability*. I have cerebral palsy, and that's what we, the Disability community, want. Not all this tiptoeing and avoidance. What's the big deal? Just say the damn word. *Disability*." Instantly, I was a disciple of the word. In hindsight, it seems like I just needed permission.

Words are like money. They're just symbols, but they hold tremendous power. They yield an unspoken currency of understanding, of assigned value, and can establish or dismantle preconceived notions. Finally having the words to claim an elusive yet integral part of my identity allowed me to recognize my wholeness, my power, and to have healthy, curious, open discussions.

Saying the word also granted me the freedom to decide how I self-identify. As I write this, I prefer person-first language when referring to my big-umbrella Disability identity (i.e., "person/ artist with a disability," as opposed to "disabled person/artist"), but identity-first language when referring to my specific disability (i.e. "Blind woman" as opposed to "woman who is blind"). These preferences differ for everyone. Just ask* me what I prefer, and I'll tell you. I swear, it's that simple.

That Ray Romano voice belonged to Lawrence Carter-Long, director of engagement at the ReelAbilities film festival, renowned disability rights activist, and film history buff, who

---

* ATP (Ask the Person) is an acronym that encourages respectful communication with people about their identity and needs, and is preferred by the Disability community. It encourages asking someone their preferred language or if they need help before assuming, listening patiently, and communicating clearly.

launched the viral 2016 hashtag #SayTheWord in reference to disability. We're now good friends, so I called him up to ask what sparked the "Say the Word" campaign that grabbed me hook, line, and sinker back at that Adweek summit.

In 2016, Lawrence worked at the National Council on Disability, a federal agency with a mandate to recommend disability policy to the president, and they had been working with the White House to make President Obama's State of the Union Address as accessible as possible. "The night of the speech, we were all live-tweeting," he told me over Zoom. "We had our hashtags going, and it was just another one of those presidential speeches. But at the end of the night, the president was giving this laundry list of affinity groups. So he's talking about senior citizens, about people of color. And we thought, 'Man, we put in all this work. Maybe finally he'll recognize disability as one of those communities he should pay attention to.' He finished the speech and did not mention disability at all."

"So, in a hissy fit on Twitter," Lawrence continued, "I said, 'What's it going to take till we're recognized as a community, identity, culture . . . Look, it's really simple, folks. *Disability*. For God's sake, just say the word.' 'Say the word' was hashtagged. I downed a scotch, went to bed, and when I woke up the next morning, the thing had blown up globally—Wales, Australia, the UK. It became very clear to me that what had been a little hissy fit for me was something that many people were experiencing."

I asked Lawrence what the Disability community could do to assuage the anxiety of the nondisabled population, who are tired of being PC but fear that talking about disability in the wrong way could get them canceled.

"I'm borrowing this from Professor Loretta Ross," he said

without hesitation. "Call in before you call out. Befriend people, make it easier for them to feel a part of and be jazzed about what we do, not as an obligation, but because they friggin' dig it. We need to stop worrying about fitting in and be more forthright about being our wacky, wild, funky selves, and that'll make it easier for others to do the same. To say, 'Yeah, none of us have it figured out.' And to allow that kind of grace in ourselves and in others."

Amen. Preach! That call was invigorating. The #SayTheWord campaign struck a nerve for so many, reinforcing the need for the Disability community to own its language.

I'm Not Your "Poor Thing"

By the time 2022 pulled up, I'd released "Black Girl Cornrows," a song celebrating my self-description; founded RAMPD; and was on the other side of the world-wrenching pandemic. I was out in these New York streets like Julia Roberts after her *Pretty Woman* makeover, turning heads and taking names with a fresh sheen of confidence. By July, I was deep into my six-city "Disability Pride Tour," bringing my identity, community, and mission right out front.

My fourth tour stop was back in New York, and I was definitely feeling the high. Audiences were eating up my whole vibe. At each date I strutted onto the stage, glammed head to cane to heels in Black disabled sequin realness (imagine if Prince's iconic gold suit and Cardi B's 2024 Fendi fall-winter look had a baby with Selma Blair's 2019 Oscar couture), and instead of going to a lectern, I cued up my DJ or sat down at a grand piano like it was the Iron Throne and proceeded to blow the lid off the joint with song, dance, and NSFW jokes.

On my way to the Central Park Bandshell to perform, I stopped by the eye doctor for a quick checkup. Since I was going straight from the doc to the gig, I sat all decked out in the waiting room: "Pretty Girls Walk" heels, Met Gala–level evening gown, Glam Cane, jewelry, the works, standing out like Kim Kardashian when she showed up to KFC dressed head to toe in vintage Jean Paul Gaultier. Finally, I was called in and the doctor examined my eyes and looked at my chart. Then she looked at me and in actual, I-wish-I-was-lying seriousness, she said, "You poor thing."

What? That deserved a LeBron James press conference walkout. But this Lachi, 2022 Lachi, said, without missing a beat, "Check out my Instagram. I'm not poor." I didn't intend to be condescending, but I also intended to be *totally* condescending. The doc actually whipped out her phone and looked me up! Yes, I was cool with her after she smashed that follow button, but that's beside the point.

I rode in the backseat of an Uber Black to my Central Park concert, the one I was *giving* rather than attending, and this time I was all about that Disability Pride. I must say I crushed it at the Bandshell because I was feelin' not just *parts* of myself, but my whole self, including the parts Dr. "You Poor Thing" wasn't and still ain't ready for.

Here's a quick, megaphone-level PSA. (But again, I am just a Lachi, not a monolith.) Language is ever-changing, and preferred language is all about dignity and being seen, so when in doubt, just say the thing: deaf, blind, autism, little person, chronic pain, or developmental disability. Avoid terms that assume people are having a hard or unfulfilled life just because they're disabled, like "suffering from," "victim of," "stricken with," "confined to," or "wheelchair-bound." Because why automatically assume a wheelchair user is suffering or confined? The wheelchair is a tool of independence. A wheelchair user would be confined *without* it. Instead, consider using "living with," "has/is," "a person with," "wheelchair user" . . . or just ask the person what they prefer.

Take me, for instance. I'm not the biggest fan of "visually impaired." The Deaf community tossed *impaired* out eons ago. I prefer *blind* or *low vision*, because when I'm accommodated with zoom text, screen readers, my cane, or a companion, I'm still blind, but I'm not impaired. I can do everything I want to live my life and do my thang.

I'm also not here for *able-bodied*. You can be "able-bodied" and part of the disabled population. Me, I've run a nearly five-minute mile and give up my subway seat for pregnant people. I'm also blind. So am I able-bodied, disabled, or just bragging? (Hint: It's all three.) Also, the Invisible Disabilities Association reports that more than 70 percent of disabilities are non-apparent. Folks who are deaf, are neurodivergent, or have chronic or mental health conditions often identify as disabled, even though they are "able-bodied." And then there's the term *abled*. Is that the opposite of getting Cain'd? It's giving me "pwned" vibes, as in, *You just got abled!*

I prefer the term *nondisabled* since it centers disability. As Judy Heumann said to Trevor Noah in 2021, "I call you nondisabled because the likelihood of you acquiring a disability, whether temporarily or permanently, is statistically pretty high."

There's a lot of nuance when it comes to language, like there is for any marginalized community. For example, while saying "That's hysterical" to a woman after she tells a joke is okay (though we really should consider it to be iffy), saying "You're *being* hysterical" to your roommate after they calmly called you out for leaving the milk carton in the fridge—when you knew for damn sure there wasn't enough in there to satisfy a scavenger—is not okay. All I'm saying is there's nuance.

There are many commonly used phrases that might not seem inconsiderate at first, but I'd encourage you to toss 'em out. "I'm *sooo* OCD." (Nope, you're just meticulous.) "He's high-functioning." (That plays into ableist hierarchy.) "Did I stutter?" (It's okay if you did.) "You don't look disabled . . . Hey, I said you don't look disabled." (Sorry, I thought we were playing "be dismissive of each other's lived experience.")

If a disabled person corrects you for using an improper term, it's fine. Acknowledge it, ask them their preferred term, and then move on with your life more informed.

Referring to oneself as disabled or a person with a disability is not self-limiting. Avoiding the word keeps people in denial, preventing them from getting the help and community they need to thrive. Yes, Disability identity is about navigating a world not designed to accommodate all body-minds, and yes, we do play the game on "Hard" every day. But by acknowledging disability and calling us by our name, you are doing your part in breaking down age-old social stigmas, erasure, and systemic barriers. Bottom line, my disability is part of the totality of me. Don't focus on my "ability," my (dis)ability, or my disAbility. Focus on my whole, unapologetically glammed-up, decked-out self. My hair. My style. My humor. My skin. My community. My disability.

Say the word.

Chapter Three

Main Character Energy

On a warm winter's night—a little too warm for December 2023—PBS put a five-episode *American Masters* series-shaped ring on it, and I said, "Yes, yes, a thousand times yes." And it all started with me tumbling out of a plane from fourteen thousand feet. Okay, I jumped out voluntarily. Okay, hold up, here's the whole story.

My parents—and by extension my extended family—have no idea what I do for a living. If you asked my dad, he'd say, "She's a doctor at the uptown Mount Sinai," because I'm still maintaining the lie, like any good second-gen immigrant kid working in the arts. When I told my mom I was jumping out of a plane, she shouted, "Aye! Why on earth for?" I responded with "More like jumping *to* earth" and "For the internet." Her proverbial spit take was completely understandable. But I didn't feel the shock—I mean really *feel* it—until I was fourteen thousand feet in the air, my legs dangling from the mouth of a plane beside my tandem Piedmont Skydiving instructor, looking out over the earth *way* below me. By this time, August 2021, I'd lost a measurable amount of my vision, but not enough to not be scared shitless. I was looking down over clouds. Oh, and in case you were wondering, the earth *is* round.

But I dug deep, got right with Jesus, and said, "Let's *do* this!" And I did it. I jumped my ass out of a plane and flew like a Shondaland Peter Pan over the Mid-Carolina airfield to prove to YouTube that a blind girl could skydive. From the leap, to the flight, to my butt hitting the ground, the whole thing was exhilarating. Please, if you can do one thing in your life, skydive. People are like, "Aren't you sad you can't drive?" Bitch, I can fly! I have episode 14 of my 2021 YouTube series *Off Beat—Going Blind & Staying Fabulous in NYC* to prove it.

While that was the first (but not the last) time I would see my entire life flash before my eyes—and I mean *entire* life, from repressed memories to little white lies to all those perfect SAT words I could never remember when I needed them—I would happily do it, and the entire series, all over again. I was authentically representing my experience and doing it because I did not see enough of me, or people who looked like me or had my circumstance, represented in the media. That series was my tiny rebellion.

Film, TV, and online videos are the only contact many people have with the concept of disability—other than the whole parking spot thing—which means thoughtful disability stories that are authentically told and represented are incredibly important. Though one in four adults in the United States has some form of disability, only 3.1 percent of characters in TV and film portray disability, according to the 2021 Disability Data Report from Fordham University. Apply those same ratios to gender and only about 6 percent of characters in TV and movies would be female. *Friends* would only have Lisa Kudrow, with Jennifer Aniston and

Courteney Cox's characters swapped out for Danny DeVito and Arnold Schwarzenegger as quirky but lovable crime-solving twins. My point is, we would've missed out on the whole '90s Jennifer Aniston "women can be pretty *and* funny" renaissance.

Pop culture shapes how we all see, experience, and interact with disability and how disabled and neurodivergent people see themselves. With so few characters and such little authentic representation, distortions become easy. People watch one film, maybe an ad, and walk away like, *Oh, I completely get it now*, believing they understand something about the disability experience or what it might be like if they gained a disability.

Consider a film like *Million Dollar Baby*, in which a boxer begs to be euthanized after a spinal injury. Or *Gattaca*, in which Jude Law's character becomes a wheelchair user, gives up his career as an Olympic swimmer, and eventually ends his life. To illustrate, let's dissect the 2016 hit film *Me Before You*. Will Traynor, a wealthy young man, becomes a quadriplegic after an accident and his family hires a beautiful woman to be his caregiver. Despite having all the money in the world, a loving family, and this British hottie falling for him, Will chooses assisted suicide over burdening his caregiver. (Oops, I forgot to say "Spoiler alert.")

These films were very popular or won awards, and they all told their audiences, "Disabled people would rather die than live disabled, and if you became disabled, you'd rather die, too, even if you have a zillion dollars and Emilia Clarke as your love interest."

These films turn the termination of a disabled life into a happy ending. *Really?* Because the second I got the diagnosis that I would completely lose my vision one day, my first thought was literally, "Okay. Time to finally *live!*" These one-dimensional narratives stem from the lack of disabled professionals sitting in the writers' rooms and directors' chairs, not to mention the lack of on-screen representation of real-life disabled performers. Can you spot any of the following in some of the recent blockbusters or viral content you've consumed? Yes, it's time for our game, "Fun with Disability Tropes!"

* **The Victim Edit:** A character with a disability is portrayed as suffering, pitiful, or tragic, often believing death, institutionalization, or a life of inspiring tragedy is their happy (or inevitable) ending. This group includes the aforementioned *Me Before You, Million Dollar Baby,* and *Gattaca,* along with Tiny Tim of Charles Dickens's *A Christmas Carol* and dramatizations of historical figures like Joseph Merrick, a.k.a. the "Elephant Man."

* **Tragical but Magical:** A character with a disability is portrayed as a mythical freak of nature possessing ethereal powers, such as the blind oracle (which is obviously untrue because I'd have put the New York lotto system out of business by now) or the fairy-tale little person: Oompa-Loompas, Munchkins, leprechauns. This has led to people asking me to read their palms—yes, really. (I want to tell them, "I see you boycotting movies and TV shows that don't represent disability authentically.") This also means people with dwarfism are often relegated to stereotypical or sight gag roles to make ends meet in Hollywood.

* **The Super Crip:** No, this is not Snoop Dogg's 2016 rap-meets-comic-book-hero renaissance. It's when a character

possesses supernatural skills due to their disability, like *Daredevil*'s superhuman senses, or the autistic savant (a.k.a. "Hollywood Autism") like Dustin Hoffman's character in *Rain Man* and Sheldon in *The Big Bang Theory*. This goes back to that inane "Your disability is your superpower!" idea. No, my ability to pay post-COVID Manhattan rent is my superpower.

- **The Villain Edit:** Characters with disabilities, disfigurements, or mental health conditions are painted as evil or depraved, often as a result of their condition. Sheesh, there are too many to list. How about nearly every Batman villain? Nearly every James Bond villain? Freddy Krueger, Captain Hook, Scar, Darth Vader. Children see disability vilified and grow into adults who instinctively associate negativity and wrongness with Disability identity. This leads to people avoiding or even yelling obscenities at folks with deformities and skin differences and leads children with these conditions to struggle with their self-worth. Films like *Split*, which villainizes people with dissociative identity disorder (formerly multiple personality disorder), can keep people with this condition isolated and feeling undeserving of friends and relationships.

- **Inspiration Porn:** This is today's most common everyday portrayal of people with disabilities and the only porn you'll find with Sarah McLachlan's "Angel" as the backing track. Inspiration porn is the exploitation of people with disabilities as inspirational props for the feel-good benefit or gratification of onlookers, and it's *everywhere*. For example, a video of a child with one arm putting on a shirt with the caption "This amazing little guy never gave up, so what's your excuse?" We see this in films like *Radio* and *The Soloist*, where a character with intellectual disabilities helps a town or team realize they can be better people, but meanwhile, homey still has no rights. Ever see a disabled person and think, *Wow, how inspiring that they're out of the house on their own?* It's why the late disability activist Stella Young said "I'm not your inspiration" in her 2014 TED Talk.

Mimicry: The Good, the Bad, and the Ugh

Day Al-Mohamed, a policy adviser, writer, and documentary film director, was living her own main-character blind-girl back-story when she stumbled across my quirky little YouTube series with its five thousand subscribers. And voilà! She'd found the unicorn she'd been hunting for, an experienced but hungry, up-and-coming, authentically disabled woman-of-color series host. Day was working on a PBS pilot for a digital series exploring disabled historical figures, and she was determined to have an authentically disabled host. And *that*, friends and neighbors, is why we need disabled people on creative teams, on the crew, in the writers' room, on the party planning committee, above the line, below the line, brokering the deals, and signing the checks. A Day Al-Mohamed behind the curtain begets a Lachi in front of it.

When I was younger (silly me), I thought that when I saw a disabled character on TV, that actor actually had a disability. Artie the wheelchair user from *Glee* got me. Abed the autistic student from *Community* got me. I'm sure Murphy, the blind girl from

In the Dark, got a lot of folks. There are a lot of people *cripping up* in Hollywood, that is, mimicking the lived experience of disability for the camera. (JFYI, *mimicry* is the acceptable term for when a nondisabled actor portrays a disabled character. Using terms like *cripface* or comparing disabled mimicry to blackface are considered cultural appropriation.) Mimicry happens when our deep, rich stories are written, cast, and told from an outsider perspective.

For y'all in the back, the textbook example of disability mimicry is pretending to need a wheelchair for an audition, confidently whispering "You got this" to the actual wheelchair-using auditioners waiting in line, then side-eyeing them as they watch you ditch your Amazon-bought prop chair at the top of the staircase. Jacob Stolworthy's article in *The Independent* titled *"Run* Director Says Some Actors Faked Disability to Audition for Wheelchair User in New Film" highlights how not unusual this sort of thing is.

From Eddie Redmayne mimicking Stephen Hawking in *The Theory of Everything* to Daniel Day-Lewis mimicking cerebral palsy in *My Left Foot* to Colton Dunn mimicking wheelchair use in *Superstore*, pop culture is filled with inauthentic mimicry of the Disability identity and lived experience.

A 2018 study conducted by the Ruderman Family Foundation found that on network and streaming TV programs, nondisabled performers play four in five characters with a disability. To turn that around, this means that professionally trained disabled and neurodivergent actors are denied about 80 percent of disabled and neurodivergent role opportunities. So riddle me this: Why is faking a disability wrong off-screen, but mimicking a disability for Hollywood is okay?

Now some of y'all might be thinking, *But Lachi, it's not mimicry. They're acting.* You say tomato, I say "appropriating lived experience and misrepresenting a historically oppressed identity for the sake of entertainment."

But Lachi, what disabled actor in their right mind would want to play the William Traynor character in Me Before You *where he would rather die than live disabled?* Now you're getting it! None that I can think of. Not with that ending. But I can't blame any disabled actors out here for taking the roles they *can* get, even if they aren't the best look.

However, bring in a couple of screenwriters with disabilities, maybe a disabled director, and toss in a diverse cast and crew behind an authentically cast William Traynor, and maybe you'll end up with a guy who realizes how lucky he is, who says, "Fuck it, I'm rich, biotch!," buys a yacht and a three-story Brioni-only closet he never uses, who starts a family on either coast, and they don't care 'cause every single one of them flies for free, and who maybe even starts a bucket list that includes a skydive from fourteen thousand feet.

Bet on Us

Does authentic casting seem far-fetched? Not really. Films with a crew hell-bent on telling our untold stories from a place of authenticity have been making indelible marks in history.

The 1932 horror film *Freaks,* directed by Tod Browning, was a groundbreaking piece of authentic disability representation. The cult classic is a thesis on how the most beautiful people can be the most monstrous, and follows a sideshow troupe of authentically cast working-class performers with different disabilities as they come together to combat ableist injustice. Lines like "They don't realize I'm a man with the same feelings they have," expressed by the lead actor and little person Harry Earles, enabled audiences to empathize with the disabled characters rather than the nondisabled villains.

"Gooble gobble, gooble gobble, one of us" was an expression of acceptance and disability solidarity used in the film when the group of disabled friends celebrated the possible addition of a nondisabled woman to their group once she'd gotten engaged to Harry Earles's character. Mat Fraser—actor and writer on *Code of the Freaks*, a documentary analyzing Hollywood's take on disability—said of *Freaks*, "I can't think of a Hollywood film that [better] captures that camaraderie and edgy outsider necessity of collective difference." I love that term "collective difference." It's such an affirmation of Disability community as opposed to the general disabled population. *Freaks* was recognized by the National Film Preservation Board for being culturally and historically significant as a canonical work of Hollywood's pre-Code period.

(Fun fact: Did you know that disability was front and center in the country's earliest feature film? Yep. *Richard III*, about Shakespeare's king with multiple disabilities, is the oldest surviving American feature-length film, released in 1912, and the first feature-length Shakespearean adaptation ever made.)

For another great example of history-making, intentional representation, let's cue up the film *The Best Years of Our Lives*. The postwar epic follows three World War II vets as they struggle to reacclimate to civilian life. One of the characters, Homer, who lost both hands in combat, finds his life is now limited and questions why his fiancé doesn't just abandon him.

Harold Russell, who played Homer, was an actual double-amputee who lost his hands to a defective explosive during the war. After director William Wyler saw him in a 1945 Department of War documentary, he approached Russell to cast him for the film. Russell turned down Wyler on numerous occasions, because of his lack of acting experience. I'm picturing Wyler popping out of bushes or turning up as a waiter in Groucho glasses while Russell's trying to order, hitting the veteran with a cheerful "How 'bout now?" Wyler was determined to tell this postwar story as authentically as possible and kept at Russell until he eventually won him over.

Released in 1946, just a year after the end of the war, *The Best Years of Our Lives* was the highest-grossing film of the year and cleaned up at the Oscars. But more important, Harold Russell, who kicked off the film by signing a document and lighting a round of cigarettes with his hooks, won two Academy Awards for the same role, something never done before or since. He took home Best Supporting Actor and an Honorary Achievement Award, as well as a Golden Globe. He also received a star on the Walk of Fame. (According to writer Jill Blake, Academy voters were "convinced he wasn't going to win," so they created an Honorary Award to thank him for his service as a veteran— essentially a PR stunt. Then, oops, he also won Best Supporting Actor. He took home those two Oscar trophies, only to drink champagne out of them with Jay-Z in my fanfic.)

Russell's authentic portrayal of Homer made the film four-dimensional, real and raw, earning the film a well-deserved seat in Oscar-accolade history. MovieWeb contributor Patrick Hayes described Russell's impact on Hollywood as "a catalyst for greater awareness and acceptance of disability in the United States. Russell challenged the stigma around disability in Hollywood." But we can't highlight the Russell story without fist-bumping Wyler for his artistic intentionality for authentic representation. Wyler didn't take a risk; he chased the sure bet, knowing full well it would pay off. And he was right.

It's important to mention that the directors of both aforementioned films were nondisabled. While there *are* disabled and neurodivergent writers and directors in the rooms, their disabilities are generally undisclosed due to the stigmas of the very shows and films they write on.

Despite this, performers who openly identify with their disabilities have landed some pretty cool roles, like Linda Bove, a Deaf actress who played herself on *Sesame Street*; Chris Burke, who authentically represented Corky, a man with Down syndrome, on ABC's hit series *Life Goes On*; and Joe Dougherty, who originally voiced Porky Pig and shared his stutter. Kenny Baker, who played R2-D2 in the *Star Wars* films, Felix Silla, known for his role as Cousin Itt on *The Addams Family*, and Pat Bilon, who played the alien in *E.T.*, were all little people.

We've also got some award wins. Marlee Matlin, Troy Kotsur, and Helen Keller all won Oscars. *Rising Phoenix* won an Emmy. Ali Stroker took home a Tony. Black Coffee, Questlove, and Stevie Wonder (along with several other blind musicians) have grabbed Grammys. However, the disabled population as a whole barely has an EGOT to its name. Wins are important. They create role models. Seeing the possibility of your future baller self accepting a baller award and catwalking across a big baller stage is crucial.

When you're a kid, everything's possible. Role models and heroes help us channel that big-dream energy and give us permission to pursue those dreams. Jillian Mercado, a model and actress on Showtime's *The L Word: Generation Q*, always appreciated fashion as a kid. She's a wheelchair user, and her interest in fashion as a career peaked after witnessing Aimee Mullins, a below-the-knee double-amputee, walk in Alexander McQueen's 1999 runway show. McQueen celebrated Mullins with high-fashion knee-high boot-shaped prosthetics.

"I don't think people realize how monumental that moment really was, and I wish it was celebrated more, because she would have been as big as Naomi Campbell," Jillian told me on a call. I'd caught up with her to ask about fashion wins, and I couldn't help but relate, as I, too, had my holy shit moment after witnessing a woman proudly rock a different disability than mine. "I've seen so many wins, like the girls doing the Victoria's Secret shows. I go through their social media and see what else they are doing that I can celebrate or be in service of to help further the conversation or moment in time."

The Victoria's Secret adaptive wear debut at the Runway of Dreams 2023 New York Fashion Week show offered a groundbreaking display of intimates for women with disabilities. Like Jillian, I wanted to know more about the women involved and if they, too, felt it was a win. Runway model Bri Scalesse was a highlight of that Victoria's Secret debut. I asked Bri how the whole thing made her feel.

"I felt sexy and strong in front of the camera as a disabled woman," she said. "I think constant representation has a quiet way of changing minds over a long period of time, so as long as we continue to see major brands like Victoria's Secret employing disabled models . . . then it will have an impact on societal perceptions."

I've walked that same Runway of Dreams, strutting across the platform in a yellow sweater, black heels, and matching yellow-

and-black Glam Cane, whipping my braids like a lasso for my pose-and-twirl. In that moment, with all eyes on me, my cane, my statement, I felt on top of the world.

"On that runway you feel really fucking powerful," Jillian said on our call. "It's a really powerful moment and a huge responsibility that you have now. On that runway you feel royal."

Seeing disabled icons do dope things is literally world-changing. In 2016, the Olympics and Paralympics took place in Rio de Janeiro, and those Paralympics were the biggest and most-watched in history up to that point. But the cool thing about it was that just two years later, the percentage of people in Brazil who self-identified as having a disability went up by *49 percent*. After watching all those fine-ass triathletes, cyclists, and swimmers with disabilities train, compete, achieve, and win, Brazilians saw disabled people as doers, winners, and champions. It may take a second, but then it's like, "Wait, I'm part of that identity. I'm part of that winning community."

We Get the Job Done

Remember the movie *Run* that I mentioned, where actresses faked being wheelchair users to try to land the lead role? I caught up with the authentic wheelchair user who snagged the part, Kiera Allen, an actress now acclaimed for her intense performance in the 2020 Hulu original thriller. Kiera plays Chloe, a fiery young disabled woman terrorized by her unstable mother, played by Sarah Paulson. Kiera met up with me in Manhattan and shared how thrilled she was to know that the writers and directors insisted on authentically casting the film.

"I knew this was unlike anything I had seen or read before for a disabled actor," she said. "I knew immediately I would do anything for this role. The stakes felt really high, because I had never seen anything like this starring a wheelchair user, especially where the wheelchair user was an action hero."

Run gave Kiera her Sigourney Weaver moment. Horror buffs, y'all remember *Alien*? Back in 1979, women were *not* action heroes. Best-case scenario, we played a damsel in distress à la Olive Oyl. All of a sudden, here comes Sigourney's Ellen Ripley, who's tougher, smarter, and more resourceful than all the men in the film. She changed the game for women in action movies. Without her, there's no Sarah Connor in *The Terminator*, no Gal Gadot as *Wonder Woman*, no Shuri kicking ass in *Black Panther*.

Now here comes Kiera, changing the game again by playing a tenacious woman in a wheelchair. "I'm so lucky that I got to be part of this step forward in that kind of representation," she said. "At the same time, it was quite a bit of pressure. Why am I the first? There should have been so many more before me. We're in uncharted territory here, and maybe this will clear a path for more people to follow . . . But there is, for me, a little bit of grief, too. Why is this seventy years too late?"

Kiera and I also talked about the notable absence of actors and performers with disabilities. "I read a lot of opinions saying 'You can't cast disabled people in lead roles because there are no known disabled people,'" she said. "[They] have to be cast at all levels in the industry so they can work their way up the way their nondisabled peers do. By the time they get to the point of playing lead roles, they will be better prepared.

"Disabled people, we get it done," she continued. "We make it happen. You just haven't seen the depth of talent that's out there in this community because there are so many obstacles to us being included in those stories or being able to tell our own stories—sometimes, even something like not being able to get into the building for the audition. It creates a vicious cycle where people believe that talented disabled people don't exist. But we really, really do."

Being Seen Matters

There is power in being seen, in being heard. People with disabilities deserve to be acknowledged and deserve the power that comes with that acknowledgment. Some time in late 2023, I was strutting down a Manhattan avenue in flats and a tee—I had my Glam Cane and my braids were fresh, so I was still out there serving—when a preteen in a wheelchair and her mom approached. The girl in the wheelchair held a pen and notepad in her lap. "Hey! You're . . . Lachi, right?" the mom called eagerly, and I nod-smiled through that unique blend of panic and flattery one feels when recognized.

I recovered my poise and said to the preteen, "Yes! And what's your name?" Before she could speak, Mom swooped in with her name—let's say Susie—and said, "Her name is Susie and she's such a huge fan!"

"Oh really?" I said, addressing the girl.

"Yep." Mom again. I was waiting for an "Isn't that right, sweetie?" or some acknowledgment that her daughter was *right there.* But nope. "She absolutely adores your music!"

At this, I wedged myself between mom and Susie, knelt beside the girl, and said, "You must have caught the 'Lift Me Up' music video," assuming she'd learned of me through our alternative-pop track that was charting at the time. I figured the girl might be non-speaking, so I squinted down at the pad in case she was planning to write. Instead, she handed me the pen.

"Yeah, 'Lift Me Up' is my favorite!" she gushed. "But actually I first saw you on that PBS thing about Kitty O'Neil! By the way, can I get your autograph in my notebook?"

I chose to glaze over Helicopter Mom's handler complex. *Handler complex* is a term I use to describe the need (usually by a parent, guardian, or caregiver) to speak or accomplish tasks for a person with a disability before they have the opportunity to do so, because it is assumed they do not have the capacity. It also refers to the tendency of others to speak to the "handler" instead of the disabled person. It results in the loss of power, dignity, and skill building for that person.

I don't know a lot about being a parent, but I *do* know a lot about being a seen-but-not-heard disabled kid. I do know what it's like to not see myself as deserving of power. I do know what it's like to *need* disabled-led content, disabled-centered community, and powerful disabled icons . . . and to not have them. I do know that any opportunity I have to break that cycle for future generations, I will take.

In fact, I already had. Susie was referring to the PBS pilot I'd filmed with Day and a majority disabled-girl-power team celebrating unsung legends like deaf race car driver Kitty O'Neil. The public received the pilot with such enthusiasm that PBS decided to turn it into a five-episode *American Masters* series called *Renegades*, highlighting the renegades and revolutionaries with disabilities who helped shape America, with yours truly as series host. Boom!

I signed Susie's notebook. She thanked me, and I thanked her right back.

Not only did Susie see me as a role model and a hero (an idea that still humbles me), but Susie's mother got to see the hero her daughter could become once she finally allows her to soar. Cultures need heroes, and Disability Culture is no different. One of my disabled-girl-realness heroes was Judy Heumann. You know that saying "Never meet your heroes"? In Judy's case, I'm gonna have to disagree.

About a year and a half after learning about her on *Drunk History*, I got a DM on Twitter from Judy's assistant. (For all you young folk, Twitter was a social media platform the world once used to discuss public events, but we broke up with it, so now it's an "X.") Apparently Judy loved my music and wanted to use my song "Dragon" to open a podcast series she was putting together. My first thought was *Wait, Judy from the TV?*

Learning of her story single-handedly catapulted my trajectory toward disability advocacy. Furthermore, her work made possible some of the privileges I now enjoy as a person open about my Disability identity. This woman took on the New York City Board of Education—in the first disabled rights case ever brought to federal court—and won! In doing so, she became New York City's first-ever wheelchair-using teacher. She also played a role in implementing the Americans with Disabilities Act, starting with that sit-in I referenced a while back. And she wanted to talk to *me*?

When we finally did meet, it was over. We were fellow Bad Bitches in Chief for life. We laughed, we argued, we laughed some more. I also made the mistake of giving Judy my phone number. She'd call me at any hour of the day or night, and we would gab and gab until one of us got another call. But most important, she taught me that learning and growing never stop and that community is power. Judy was the mentor I'd been looking for. She was always quick to give me my flowers, offered seeds of encouragement, and generously connected me with people she thought would be great for me to collaborate with, including Jim LeBrecht and Day Al-Mohamed.

Jumping out of a plane is pretty damn gutsy, but Judy encouraged my most courageous act: building and cultivating my own community, RAMPD. Today, RAMPD is the only major platform amplifying Disability Culture within the music industry. I'll get more into how RAMPD grew to be the powerhouse it is today, but for now I'll just say that it was born of necessity. I'm not an executive director or community organizer. I'm an entertainer. I like to sing, play the keys, and crack a few jokes. But like the disabled change-makers before me, I work to amplify Disability Culture, pride, and identity because somebody has to.

But what exactly *is* Disability Culture? Disability Culture is the unique art, music, stories, and worldviews that come from our different body-minds. It is the shared identity, self-worth, and evolving language born of social oppression, erasure, and being chronically underestimated. It's rooted in the adaptability, innovative thinking, and visionary attributes that come with working to navigate autonomously in a world not built with one's autonomy in mind. It's unapologetic visibility, and through it we create paradigm shifts.

Music—the soul's truest form of storytelling—is humanity's greatest channel for communicating culture. As hip-hop has elevated Black culture and country music has elevated rural culture, RAMPD works to elevate Disability Culture by amplifying authentic disability narratives within the music industry, from the green room to the mail room to the boardroom.

While most people might have thousands of popular music artists who represent each of their intersectional identities, disabled music listeners barely have a handful, and a sizable fraction of those do not advocate for that part of their identity out of an understandable need for self-preservation. I spent most of my young-disabled-girl life hoping someone would give me the opportunity to compete in the fast-paced music industry. Then I realized that blue sky won't come until someone stands up to champion change.

So here we are at RAMPD—my friends, my passionate colleagues, and myself—standing up. Thanks to the first of my many disabled heroes, Judy Heumann. Judy built community around disability rights. We at RAMPD are taking disability to a whole other level, building community around Disability Culture.

We Are Main Characters

But heroes aren't just people in the limelight. A hero is anyone who seizes an opportunity and uses it to lead and pave the way for people who otherwise wouldn't enjoy the same opportunity. A director working quietly and consistently to hire disabled actors in paid and visible positions is a hero. A writer looking to tell bold authentic stories, or a producer looking to go the distance on various accommodation needs, is a hero. A disabled hero doesn't succeed despite their disability; they succeed despite ableism.*

---

* Ableism: Most people define *ableism* as discrimination against people with disabilities. I go further to say it's the general act of being a jerk—believing one race, gender, body type, etc., is more "able" or worthy than another—whether intentional

In October 2023, in honor of National Disability Employment Awareness Month, PBS announced a commitment to increase documentary programming by, for, and about Disability communities, starting with the digital series *Renegades* that I mentioned earlier. With input from the community and accessibility experts, the five-episode incubator saw five teams of disabled filmmakers produce, direct, and write episodes highlighting five different historical figures, truly promoting disability representation in front of the camera, behind the camera, and through authentic storytelling. The series premiered at the Kennedy Center in the fall of 2024, enjoyed hundreds of thousands of views online within weeks, aired on network television in the spring of 2025, and took home a Webby Award.

All because fierce disabled people like Day Al-Mohamed got in the room and said, "Let's *do* this!" That's a hero.

But the funny thing about heroism is that most of the time, the real heroes don't know they're heroes. There's no set of qualifications. No one shows up at your house to hand you a sash that says "HERO!" in obnoxious script lettering (though that really should be a thing). You're just showing up, walking your talk, and being true to who you say you are. You probably have no idea who you're inspiring.

Exhibit A: Mandy Harvey. Mandy is a singer-songwriter who became deaf at age eighteen and went on to gain widespread acclaim after participating in *America's Got Talent* in 2017. She's

---

or not. For instance, I gave my friend, who is blind, a cello twice her size to fly back to her home with. "Who's gonna help you with the cello at the airport?" I asked. "I can get around all by myself, thank you," she said. Immediately realizing the issue, I said, "Oh snap! I wasn't being *ableist*, I was actually being *sexist*, my bad."

gone on to release several albums, write a memoir, and start a family. But when I interviewed Mandy, she told me a story that drove home the idea that heroes can be anyone.

"I did the *Today* show, and Morgan Freeman was supposed to be the long segment at the top, and I was supposed to follow his segment with a shorter segment," she said on our captioned Zoom call. "But Morgan got stuck in traffic and was late, so they gave me the long segment where they asked me a bunch of questions, and then I performed. Because I was doing that segment, Morgan was in the hallway watching my song before he went on. When I finished, I passed him in the hallway, and I was like, 'I just wanted to let you know you're one of the voices I remember'— because I heard him growing up—'and I wanted to say thank you.'

"Well, Morgan was just like, 'That's silly. I'm the one who's supposed to be saying thank you to you,'" Mandy continued. "'I think you're amazing, and I hope that you continue to do what you're doing because it's important.' Then he shook my hand, and somebody took a picture. I got a high five, basically, from God. That was pretty cool."

Being a hero means acknowledging those who've come before while paving the way for those who come after. I don't want any other disabled kid to grow up questioning their self-worth, their beauty, and whether they deserve power, happiness, or dignity simply because they don't see a happy, dignified, powerful version of themselves reflected in the media. That's why representation matters.

If we're going to change the narrative and make the world better for those who are—or will one day transition into—living with disability, neurodivergence, and other conditions, we've got to start with busting stigma and amplifying cool shit à la Disability identity. We've got to fill up popular culture with our stories, art, perspectives, and badassery, all from a place of power and dignity. This will encourage those in decision-making positions to not only acknowledge and perhaps even celebrate their own Disability identity, but to bet on it.

Christopher Reeve's iconic speech at the 1996 Academy Awards—his first public appearance since the 1995 riding accident that left him a quadriplegic—was a powerful moment. But challenging tropes and replacing false narratives with authentic stories should not just be a moment, it should be a pervasive *movement*. I want to see characters who look like me tell stories about being imperfect, joyful, and messy, then ride off into the sunset with the love interest in the end. My story is the disability story, and like everything in life, disability can be hard at times. But it can be beautiful and powerful, and it can even make you friends with the man who voiced God.

So when will all of me, my story, and the disability story be good enough for pop culture? I'll tell you when.

Now.

Chapter Four

Am I Them? Are You Us? The Identity Question

W as that yours or mine?" my friend Precious asked after knocking back a generously large "sip" of my meticulously measured tequila screwdriver.

"Well, it's yours now." I chuckled, sliding the near-empty glass back toward her hand.

Where: A Lower East Side rooftop bar.

When: The weekend.

Who: Myself and five girlfriends.

It was a girls' night, after all. The goal was to get drunk and rowdy, and it didn't really matter who drank what to get us there. We were hamming up some blind-and-successful-girl realness with neat tequilas and orange juice we'd snuck in ourselves because everybody knows pulp is better.

There was me, the touring entertainer "high partial" (meaning I have some usable vision, e.g., I can't tell if he's cute from across the room, but I can pull an emergency "It's not you, it's me" and pull the ripcord right before we make out). There was Khadija, a low-partial (i.e., very limited usable vision) boss by day / restaurateur by night who opened a Pakistani American fusion spot during COVID because a huge *yes* to brown girls buying property and starting businesses while the rest of y'all were out here struggling to install Zoom. We had Jennifer, a beauty influencer with albinism (many people with albinism are legally blind due to a lack of melanin in the retina) whose line of beauty products for albino women went viral several times over. There were Precious, our resident drink thief and Boricua vocalist; and Nefertiti, an audio description narrator for film and TV, among other things, both totally blind. And there was everyone's favorite boss-ass film director, Day Al-Mohamed, who generally uses a guide dog to navigate.

Different shades of brown, different shades of woman, different shades of blind, and different shades of tipsy, all having a great time comparing makeup tips, sharing dirt on garbage reality TV series, and trashing men. All bad and bougie.

Precious and Neff joked about how they can still read their Braille books after lights out. Jennifer and I lamented the *American Ninja Warrior*–esque obstacle course that is navigating a buffet among Sighties. Khadija and Day jokingly griped about married life. Many assume blindness is a man with dark glasses, a dog, and a piano, who sees only black, but blindness is also six very different, very confident women *owning* a rooftop bar while swilling very spiked, very smuggled-in orange juice.

A Spectrum Is Not Binary

On that particular evening, our sexy sextet was a microcosm of the complex, slightly messy, often confusing spectrum of disability. Disability is *not* binary. There is no on-off, disabled-or-nondisabled light switch. Disability identity is more like the Photoshop ROYGBIV color palette slider. We all slide along an infinitely nuanced and intersectional spectrum of varied disability experiences and realities. Some have more than one disability, while others have disabilities that evolve over time, like your girl here.

Take blindness, for example. Someone could be totally blind, high partial, low partial, deafblind, legally or registered blind (a threshold by which one is considered irreparably blind for legal and benefits purposes), have night blindness, light sensitivity, and so much in between. Some people have 20/20 central vision while being blind in their peripheral vision, so they can legally drive while being legally blind. Millions, from Brittany Howard (who is blind in one eye) to Dame Judi Dench (who has macular degeneration) to Kristen Bell (who has strabismus—a condition where the eyes are not aligned) and Joseph Pulitzer (who had a grab bag of retinal conditions), are on the vision loss spectrum. In fact, according to the American Foundation for the Blind, fewer than 15 percent of blind folks are totally blind. That means most blind people out here can see, just like my blind girl crew and me, as we break it down on the dance floor, showing up all the wallflowers, 'cause turn down for what? Fewer than 8 percent of blind folks use a cane and only around 2 percent use a guide dog. Most blind folk are out here free-balling it with no accommodations because of fear of social stigma. Turns out blindness defies convenient stereotyping.

What about deafness? People can be hard of hearing; mildly, moderately, severely, or profoundly deaf; unilaterally deaf; deafblind (again); identify as culturally Deaf; be born with hearing loss or acquire it later in life because of aging, tinnitus, or injury;

can communicate with their own voice or through an interpreter; can prefer sign language, lip reading, or text. Lou Ferrigno, *A Quiet Place*'s Millicent Simmonds, Marlee Matlin, and Chris Martin along with a ton of other musicians with severe tinnitus reside somewhere on the d/Deaf* and hard-of-hearing spectrums. And that's just the tip of the iceberg. Some wheelchair users, like Broadway actress Jenna Bainbridge, are ambulatory, meaning they don't need the chair all the time and can get up and walk around when they've got the energy or capacity. Some people with arthritis, fibromyalgia, or lupus can have high-activity days or high-chronic-pain days. We've got extroverted folks with general anxiety and folks with major depression cheering people up. And don't even get me started on neurodivergence and developmental disabilities, which both exist along broad spectrums encompassing a premium blend of complex, often misunderstood experiences.

Disability doesn't fit neatly in a box—or a checkbox. Journalist and historian David M. Perry hit a sweet spot in his blog *Disabilities and Identity* when he wrote, "People are not either perfectly disabled or perfectly [nondisabled]. Rather, we are all at the most temporarily nondisabled, moving in and sometimes out of states of disability throughout our lives, or even just in a single day as we expend whatever strength we have." For example, my left arm is currently out to lunch because of a recent muscle spasm, so I'm chicken-pecking through this paragraph as we speak, weaving

---

* *d/Deaf* is a term used to refer to both people who *are* deaf and people who *identify as* Deaf. Generally, when referring to someone who is deaf, a lowercase *d* is used, and when referring to someone who identifies with Deaf Culture, an uppercase *D* is used. I once asked a deaf person if she preferred big *D* or little *d*, and she said, "Size shouldn't matter." *Rim shot.*

through the spectrum of my temporary, long-standing, visible, non-apparent, and eventual disabilities just like everyone else is . . . just like you are.

Nevertheless, it's difficult to climb out of that all-or-nothing mindset. Let's Wayback Machine it to 2019, that medieval period between "coming out" about my blindness and when I began using a cane. During this time, I was going through my "Ooh, damn, I'm *fine*" phase and decided to toss modeling into my smorgasbord of ambitions. That meant getting a talent agent. Easy, right?

"Nope," said every model I knew from New York to Hollywood to Tokyo, but I wasn't hearing it. I had a handful of cute professional shoots under my belt, so I licked some stamps, sent my portfolio to all the big-boy-pants agencies, and waited by the mailbox for the offers to pour in.

Cue the time-lapse cinematography—the sun rising and setting, leaves changing, and so on. *Nada.* I came to find that the big agents weren't feeling my different "look." Okay, all good. Plan B. I turned my attention to agencies that specialized in clients with disabilities, figuring they would be more amenable to my "look." A few were popping up around that time, and a friend who was part of the largest one, KMR Talent Agency, hooked me up with one of their head agents. Excited and confident that I was on my way to becoming Naomi Campbell 2.0, I met with the agent and we had a great conversation. And . . .

Cue the crickets.

Eventually, I reached out and asked the agent, "Where you at, dawg? Was KMR going to sign me or . . . ?" She said, "I'm sorry, I can't help you because you don't look disabled."

Wait, what? I took a deep breath and politely said, "But I'm legally blind. I give talks and do social media posts about blindness." But in my head I was thinking, *Girl, I'm Blind with a capital B, I'm bligitty blind, I'm so blind, I'm window blinds, I'm the Blind Boys of Alabama!*

She said, "We only really pitch for stuff that is about disability, and you really don't 'look' blind. I'm sorry."

Wow. I was too disabled for the mainstream agencies and apparently not disabled enough for the agencies that represented talent with disabilities. Was I really not disabled enough to be disabled? That encounter sent me on a deep dive into understanding, claiming, and shaping my public identity.

Defining Disability

Before I'd gone to the club that night to meet with my girls, I'd stopped by the eye clinic. I had on heels and a matching Glam Cane,* and I entered the elevator behind a young gentleman who did not have a cane. He asked me what floor I wanted, then stepped nose-level-close to the elevator buttons, finding the correct button after several seconds of scanning. Once the elevator doors opened, he walked forward only to bump into a nearby garbage bin and trip on an empty wheelchair. He smiled back over at me as I maneuvered around his missteps, and he said, "You sure know how to handle that cane." *Ugh, men.* I think the refusal to use a cane and the refusal to ask for directions must both be coded into the Y chromosome.

---

* Do you always get dressed up for doctor visits? When I can, I do get evening wear–level dressed up for doctor visits. It's one of the many ways I work to minimize medical gaslighting.

It was surreal to be a blindish person *with* a cane watching a blindish person *need* a cane. Both of us were functionally blind, and neither of us fit into society's prevailing "You are blind" checkbox. But someone watching us without knowing more could accuse me of not needing a cane while chiding him for not using his. Apparently, he would rather do what he can to appear nondisabled so's to minimize the stares and load of societal BS coming his way, whereas I choose to accept the gawks and instances of "Are you really blind?" while opening myself up to accommodation and interdependence. Neither approach is right or wrong. We're both just doing our best to handle the wear and tear of navigating a world not quite built with our autonomy in mind.

The term *disability* is complex and constantly evolving. Some feel empowered by it, while it makes others uneasy. Some view it only within the context of medical conditions or the protection of public benefits and accommodations, while others view it as a social construct. The Americans with Disabilities Act (ADA) defines disability as a physical or mental impairment that substantially limits major life activities. While this is often used as a catchall definition, the ADA establishes a legal definition that can change with the stroke of a pen and is often reduced to its workplace legal implications. For this reason, some people feel they can't claim or even acknowledge their Disability identity if it doesn't neatly fit into the legal or medical definition or doesn't revolve around benefits. However, health policy nonprofit KFF reported in 2024 that most working-age Americans with disabilities don't receive benefits.

Merriam-Webster—a source that's a whole lot more reactive to language usage—defines disability as "A physical, mental, cognitive, or developmental condition that impairs, interferes with, or limits a person's ability to engage in certain tasks or participate in typical daily activities and interactions." Not terrible, but it also revolves around the idea that one's condition is solely what impairs or limits their ability—as opposed to, say, a limiting physical barrier or debilitating social stigma that would affect anyone, regardless of their physical or mental capacity.

Again, for the people who came in late, my blindness doesn't impair me; it's just a trait. Just like retired reality stars, it can't really *do* anything on its own. Give me my tools, my cane, and some non-judgy company, and while I'm still blind, I'm no longer impaired. After hanging out with and learning from friends and leaders who I deeply respect within the Disability community, I've come to define disability as a condition of the body or mind, or the way one processes emotion, that increases the level of difficulty one has in navigating a social construct or barrier unaided.

Sarah Horton and Whitney Quesenbery capture this concept elegantly in their book, *A Web for Everyone*, in which they define disability as follows: "Ability + Barrier = Disability." In this equation, Ability is someone's functional capability. A Barrier can be anything from a physical obstacle or a communication breakdown to a lack of transportation or a social barrier like stigma, stereotyping, and prejudice. Disability is a conflict between the person's ability and the barrier. But it's the *barrier* that's the cause of the friction and difficulty, not the individual or their condition.

Steve Barnett and Nicola du Toit, two UX (user experience) designers, take this a step further in their article "Disability Is a Spectrum, Not a Binary," in the blog *24 Accessibility*, creating a sample chart that breaks down this equation with even more precision:

Someone's functional capability could be affected by:

TYPES OF DISABILITY		
COGNITIVE	**PHYSICAL**	**VISUAL**
having autism, dyslexia, or a learning disability	having a condition like arthritis, cerebral palsy, fibromyalgia, or lupus	being blind
being tired, stressed, or depressed	having an injury	being color blind (color vision deficiency)
reading something that's not in their first language	having decreased and less-precise motor control (perhaps from old age)	having low vision or poor eyesight (perhaps from old age)
being distracted or in a rush	being in a moving vehicle like a bus or train	being outside on a sunny day with a backlit LCD screen

Barnett and du Toit ask if we know a friend, colleague, or family member who matches one or a few of the descriptions in the chart, or if we match them ourselves. They state, "This is what the world is like. Maybe . . . on/off switches aren't quite the right way of looking at it."

So is there a *right* way to look at disability? Should we look at it as a medical condition or a societal barrier? Well, there are several frameworks for how people think and feel about disability, called *models of disability.* These are the major ones:

- **The Medical Model:** This model assumes impairment is the sole result of one's biology rather than social and physical barriers. In this view, Disability identity is pathologized; it's a disease to be cured, and something to be regarded with dread. The onus is on the disabled individual to get fixed or they'll get kicked off the Island. Basically any difficulties I have navigating society are the fault of whatever slow jams my parents were listening to when I was conceived rather than societal barriers. Point is, this model centers the cure, and it's up to my parents, my doctors, and/or me to figure out how to make me "normal."

- **The Charity Model:** Under this model, disabled people are victims or objects of pity who must rely on the goodwill of generous benefactors. This one makes me want to regurgitate my breakfast *Exorcist*-style. It rewards the benefactor by casting them as the admirable protagonist helping the poor lil' blind girl. This model fails to recognize the role society plays in restricting access and undermining autonomy. Essentially, it's disability as an opportunity to engage in virtue signaling. Bish, please . . .

- **The Grievance Model:** This happens when someone views a person with a certain disability as a potential problem who will file a grievance at some point. For example, a restaurant owner sees a person on a scooter approaching her restaurant and thinks, *Oh no, if I let him in, he's going to* *complain about something not being accessible,* while praying he zooms past. This might not be an official model (yet), but I've coined the term because it is a very real lens through which many view disability. Grievance is one tiny slice of a disabled person's full, lived experience, but because of consistent denial of accommodations, people with disabilities often have cause to raise their voices and lodge a complaint. But we'd rather just be treated with dignity and respect than depend on someone's fear of a lawsuit in order to receive equitable treatment.

- **The Social Model:** This model posits that impairment is a result of physical and systemic barriers that society could fix if it felt like it. Instead of John the wheelchair user having to wait all his life for a cure, or praying that a Mother Teresa with massive biceps will come along to carry him so he can finally get up the staircase to grab a beer at the local bar, the bar could just order a portable ramp off Amazon for . . . Really? Less than two hundred bucks? Okay, adding to cart. The social model is about the societal barriers that make life difficult, and it focuses on everyone's responsibility to remove those barriers. If society were accessible and inclusive enough for everyone to thrive, then no one would experience impairment. So, if accommodating bar patrons with disabilities were top of mind, not an afterthought, my mom's prenatal slow jams mixtape would have nothing to do with my ability to grab a beer.

- **The Cultural Model:** Finally, this model recognizes and celebrates the shared experiences, perspectives, and cultures of individuals with disabilities. This model, of which I am a disciple, promotes a sense of belonging and social identity among the different Disability communities. Under this model, we recognize mobility devices as tools of independence, recognize sign language as a language, recognize that you can be disabled and perfectly healthy, and recognize that one can be medically blind, legally blind, and identify as Blind all at the same time.

You'll notice that while some of these models are empowering and inclusive, others are belittling. But it's not all black and white. For example, the medical model champions research that can lead to things like temporary solutions to chronic pain or therapies and technologies that can improve the lives and well-being of people across the disability spectrum, and that's not a bad thing. However, when a core dimension of someone's identity becomes a pathologized problem for doctors to solve, the shame and embarrassment can be debilitating.

As for the charity model, home of your saviors, noblemen, and tax havens (oops, did I say that out loud?), I get that we could all get by with a little help from our friends, but it should never be at the expense of the dignity of the person with the disability. In fact, my track "Diseducation"—about how folks who want to underestimate me because of my needs should be diseducated of that notation and reeducated on disability—combats ableism with joy and power and was written in response to the charity model. Because, let's face it, ableism only gets in the way of what's already perfect. Are y'all with me? If not, buckle up, buttercup. Because we're about to dial the good kind of uncomfortable all the way, as *This Is Spinal Tap*'s Nigel Tufnel said, to eleven.

The Great Transition

My great-uncle on my mom's side, Vincent, is well over one hundred and some-teen years old. Living in Nigeria and sporting a second (much younger) wife and about a zillion offspring, he, to this day, tends a fruitful farm and enjoys his daily walks. The last time I saw him was about eight years ago, and he was running up and down stairs, hopping in and out of the kitchen, and telling first-person stories corroborating the events in Chinua Achebe's novel *Things Fall Apart*, which, in case you've never read it or don't remember it from English class, is set in the late 1800s. I get that Black don't crack, but *damn*.

Now, not everyone's going to age like Great-Uncle Vincent. The reality is that most of us who are fortunate enough to still be twerking at this banquet called life by seventy-five will have transitioned or be transitioning into some form of age-related disability, whether it's due to macular degeneration or osteoarthritis. So, "Gooble gobble, gooble gobble, one of us!" But many people who age into disability are reluctant to embrace any sense of Disability identity, and they claim very little real estate within the disability rights and justice movements, which have been predominantly characterized by young to middle-aged adults.

A 2021 Mount Saint Mary College thesis examined the physical, environmental, and social changes of aging into disability as a distinct challenge, especially for America's nearly eighty million baby boomers. The research found that when older adults acquire age-related disabilities, they don't think of themselves as aging into disability, but just aging. The thinking goes something like "I don't use a walker because I have a disability, I use a walker because I'm old." It's not denial, exactly, but more the false belief that disabled equals no longer productive, and the fear that self-identifying as disabled would be self-limiting.

Disability avoidance enables older folks to guard their self-esteem—and maybe even engage in a little "this too shall pass" magical thinking—while navigating a social landscape not built with their continued development in mind. It also hinders them from insisting on accommodations, forming bonds with other folks who are aging into disability, and being comfortably inter-dependent. Disability avoidance may offer a temporary salve of self-preservation, but anyone who denies their Disability identity is not at peace.

The truth is, a disability can be acquired at any stage in life because of the development of a condition (anything from ALS to menopausal joint pain to severe allergies), external circumstances like injuries, natural or environmental changes, or the result of military service. Viewed through the right lens, the transition can not only be seamless, but empowering and life-affirming. Henri Matisse is a great example of "I'm dope when I'm nondisabled" and "I'm dope when I am disabled." One of the most recognized figures in modern art, the French artist enjoyed a great deal of success with renowned paintings like *Woman with a Hat* and *The Green Stripe*, redefining the use of color. Around age seventy, he underwent major surgery to remove a tumor, which transitioned him into becoming a wheelchair user.

Matisse referred to this stage of his life as "une seconde vie," a second life. He was filled with a new and unexpected energy. His newfound situation opened him to exploring new ways to create art—namely, what he called "drawing with scissors." Matisse's paper cutout pieces are some of the most influential works of his career, including *Blue Nude*, the hippie wall art that hangs in every college dorm room. American artist Georgia O'Keeffe also pivoted during her illustrious career—from painting to sculpting—as a result of age-related macular degeneration. Then there was Chuck Close, who continued his painting career after what he called "The Event"—a collapse of a spinal artery that led to paralysis—and created some of his most important and striking works. Matisse, O'Keeffe, and Close illustrate that transitioning from nondisability into the world of disability is really just a change in the way we navigate and perceive our bodies, our minds, and the world around us.

That's So Neurotypical

"My name is Medusa. My pronouns are they/them. I am wearing a green blazer; I am wearing black pants; and I am wearing a look of fear as well." The second I heard that self-description uttered from the Wavy Awards stage, I was obsessed.

Backtrack. In late 2021, I was up for a Wavy along with Mezzo, an a cappella group I'd founded in New York, for our collaborative performance of LSD and Lil Wayne's "Genius Remix"—one of my most meticulous arrangements. The Wavy Awards recognize artistic works from historically marginalized talent, so of course I came through with Khadija, Jennifer, and the rest of the blind baddies crew, leaving trails of sequins in our wake. Beyond sign language, I'd requested the organizers encourage all presenters and performers to self-describe, and *wow* did this make for the most feel-good night of 2021.

Medusa's self-description took the cake for me, but we had everything from "I'm an extremely attractive Afro-Latino man" to "My hair is giving Kurt Cobain meets David Byrne vibes" to

"I'm wearing a black-and-silver robe that I had custom made in Shanghai 'cause I wanted to look more like Jet Li in a kung fu movie."

These requests for self-descriptions have been paying off. More and more high-visibility events are seamlessly incorporating them. The 2024 Adcolor conference—a prestigious three-day annual event celebrating inclusion in creative industries—saw everyone from Queen Latifah to Shaboozey self-describing on the main stage. Quick aside about Adcolor 2024: During a panel hosted by *The Shop*, I sat in and watched as the celebrity speakers described themselves—all but Jon Batiste, because we all know Jon Batiste is just too smooth for all that. But y'all know that's not how this anecdote ends. After the panel, Jon, his team, and about a million bodyguards scurried down the hall.

"Jon," I called casually while holding a Glam Cane and wearing a T-shirt with "Eating Barriers for Breakfast" printed on it. "You didn't do your self-description." At this, Jon and the entourage came to a stop. "I'm a Black man wearing black pants and a green shirt with a black rose kind of thing on it," he said, smiling.

"That's a cool shirt," I said.

"Hey, your shirt's cool, too," he said. Smooth. And there you have it, folks. My first conversation with Jon Batiste was the result of a self-description.

With integrated self-description, stage action is accessible not only to us blind folks—the space being created with us in mind—but also to neurodivergent folks, who feel far more connected to and comfortable with the presenters as a result. Self-descriptions are great for helping with processing, remembering, and understanding information about someone, their vibe, and how they are feeling about themselves and their current situation.

Neurodiversity, just like the cable TV/phone/internet three-in-one bundling service, has claimed the term *spectrum*. Like gender and racial diversity, we're all neurodiverse—that is, we all have a unique way we behave and process information. Neurodivergence is a colloquial (i.e., nonmedical) term used to describe the experience of not being neurotypical. And neurotypical is . . . Have you ever thought, there's no way anyone can be *that* well-adjusted? Well, that guy's neurotypical. It's the assumed default factory setting.

Neurodivergence generally includes autism, ADHD, OCD, dyslexia, Tourette's, and other similar sensory, cognitive, and processing disorders. Some use the term *neurospicy* to add a touch of playfulness and flavor, though that term does skirt the euphemism line. But does neurodivergence really fall under the disability big umbrella? As someone who identifies as neurodivergent myself, I see neurodivergence as a function of a world not built with all types of mental and behavioral processing in mind. I place it within the disability big umbrella because I find the D-word empowering. It gives me the sense that I'm crushing the game at its highest level while others are still consulting the manual.

Some within the neurodivergent communities view neurodiversity and disability as separate but intersecting spectrums, depending on what kind of barriers they're facing and how effectively they're able to overcome them. So I tend to give it its own space on the color wheel out of respect to those in our community who are not quite there.

To that end, I sometimes hear this argument: "My autism/synesthesia/hyperlexia gives me an advantage over others, not a 'dis'advantage, so I'm not 'dis'abled."

Permit me to riposte, *mon ami*. My blindness absolutely gives me advantages, such as crossing the street whenever I dang well please and bringing traffic to a tire-screeching, rubber-laying halt (though I *really* should quit doing that). That still doesn't mean the system was built with my independence in mind. Autism, ADHD, dyslexia—these are all covered under the ADA, just like blindness. So legally, we're all in the same boat, even if we're hanging out on different decks.

That said, I will be the first to admit that accommodating my Blind identity has been far less of a struggle than accommodating my neurodivergence.

Once upon a time, I ditched my anxiety meds for a journal and meditation. Toss in a calendaring app and a boobs-forward gait and I could almost pass for neurotypical. *Almost.* Your neurotype is not about how you present on the outside, but how you process on the inside. So while I can manage my general anxiety disorder sans meds, can zhuzh up my blindness, and downright love my ADHD, recognizing when I've gone deep into OCD territory is challenging. But as I continue finding my way, my go-to remedy will forever be self-compassion and community.

Tapping in with my community, I spoke with captivating Wavy Awards self-describer, visual artist, trans and autistic lyricist, and now my great friend Medusa, who fosters a platform for fans to celebrate neurodivergence and advocate for trans rights. "I think that oftentimes, people say *neurodivergent* because they aren't necessarily sure what it is they're going through . . . but people also say it because they are afraid to say the word *autistic* or what it actually is," they said over our Zoom chat. "There is power in identifying completely and publicly with your identity, but there's also risk . . . you need to be willing and able and privileged enough to take on the responsibility of being known to be that thing. The medical model of disability scares people because it's frightening to have your identity be medicalized, be pathologized."

Medusa continued, "I think in order to reach cultural acceptance, some people reject the application of disability to neurodivergence. For me . . . when I am feeling I have to prove that this is not disabling for me, in order to legitimize that I am capable and a functioning member of society, it's really important for me to be realistic about the aspects of my life in which I am walking through a world that was not made for me, that does not accommodate me."

I asked them about medical diagnosis versus identity when it comes to neurodivergence.

"The reliance on medical diagnostic criteria can pose a variety of problems," Medusa said. "There is a strong financial barrier for a lot of people to receive medical diagnoses. But also, people of color and people raised as female often are diagnosed with very different conditions than those who are not. When I was a child, I was diagnosed as just being super productive and smart . . . I finally received testing for ADHD as an adult. Before that, I was given no support for my challenges."

That all tracks: The journal *Autism Research* reports that one in four autistic children grow up undiagnosed, and the Learning Disabilities Association of America estimates that more than 60 percent of adults with literacy problems have undetected learning disabilities.

I asked Medusa if their neurodivergence informs their trans identity.

"I believe that I would have known much earlier in life that what I was experiencing was dysphoria if I had the tools and knowledge on how to better interact with my body and feelings," they said, "because alexithymia—challenges with feeling emotions—amongst autistic people is very prevalent. If I had seen just a single trans person in my youth, I think that would have brought me such understanding so much earlier in my life."

That part. I felt that deep in my bones. I asked Medusa if they felt a desire to be that beacon for the next generation and if that informed their career path.

"When you're a musician whose audience is primarily autistic, they've really got to want to come," they said. "I try to cultivate a space that says, 'You're not an afterthought. You get to be here because you are the person who we want here. It's not like you have to change some part of yourself to fit into this space. No, this is actually for you.' But it's very difficult for me as an autistic person myself to go out and do the highly social, highly public act of, for instance, going on tour. There is the management of time, which is difficult for my ADHD. There are the constant interactions onstage and backstage. But that is always made worth it when there is someone who, after the show, comes up and tells me that I am the first person who they've ever talked to who's like them."

I'm pretty sure I was that someone when I heard their self-description.

Camouflaging

"Do you think the Endies will get the airport joke?" I asked Arthur.

"Uh . . . what are Endies?"

"The nondisabled. N.D. But also Endies because disabled people have to constantly navigate new beginnings due to barriers set by Endies."

"Ah, so Endies is an underhanded pejorative?" Arthur asked.

"No, that would be *Undies.*"

Rim shot. I'll be here all week.

Generally, when I think about a nondisabled, neurotypical person with no other chronic or physical differences, I think, *Yawn, let's get you some adversity.* But more often than not, I'm finding that after kicking back with a seemingly nondisabled and neurotypical person, preaching my Big Dis Energy and brandishing a rhinestone cane between sips of champagne, folks start revealing all sorts of disabilities and neurodivergences they've never claimed openly . . . or realized they *can* claim. And they do so all while joking about the goofy accessibility issues they've had to navigate.

Bam! Community.

Masking. Code-switching. Camouflaging. All terms to describe the maneuvers people use in trying to pass as "normal," typical, or socially acceptable. We see this often in racial and gender contexts, like when a Black man transforms from Tyga to Tiger Woods upon entering his very non-Black workplace, or when an overwhelmed mother of three transforms to career-first power suit–wearing badass whose hair always wafts suggestively behind her—wind or no wind—for her pitch session to an all-male panel of VCs.

The same applies to folks with non-apparent or undiagnosed disabilities who do what they can to conceal their condition to "fit in" with the Endies. Also remember that more than 70 percent of disabilities are non-apparent. This can include folks with mental health conditions* like general anxiety, major depression, PTSD, or personality disorders; chronic conditions like diabetes, Crohn's, chronic migraines, or cystic fibrosis; sensory loss like hearing or vision loss; neurodivergence, narcolepsy, bipolar, long COVID, and the list goes on. People with non-apparent disabilities often find themselves in a challenging limbo where we hide our disabilities to potentially get ahead, but we are doubted and denied the accommodations we need to keep us ahead. Non-apparent disabilities are sometimes referred to as invisible or non-visible disabilities; however, *non-apparent* is a more inclusive term because some conditions can waft in and out of being detectable.

For instance, I have undiagnosed PTSD. Like many, I don't talk about it much, mainly out of self-preservation. But when I was toddler-young, something very not good was done to me by someone who was trusted in our community. Young people with disabilities tend to acquire comorbid mental health conditions due to being the target of meanies and due to the pressures of navigating a big, scary, inaccessible world. Most of these mental health conditions remain undiagnosed because of the crap nature of the mental healthcare system and the vigilante-level distrust built up by folks living in the mental health shadows.

Twenty-nine percent of Americans might report having some form of disability, but by now everybody and their mama knows

---

* *Mental health condition* vs. *mental illness/disorder*: I always wondered if there was a meaningful difference in these terms. I found that some organizations, like the National Institute of Mental Health and the National Alliance of Mental Illness, use the terms interchangeably. Others feel the term *mental health condition* is more inclusive, as it can encompass everything from mild to severe mood, behavioral, and psychosocial disorders.

it's much higher. In fact, everyone and their mama has some form of Disability identity, whether or not they acknowledge or even realize it. So then why is the official percentage so low? For some, it's fear of confronting disability. For others, it's the shame heaped on people who ask for accommodation. Maybe it's the fear of being seen through a grievance model lens, which could jeopardize a job or a relationship. That's why so many people pretzel-twist themselves trying to conceal their disability from others—and sometimes, from themselves. But ironically, by camouflaging, they're just denying themselves the accommodation they need and deserve, a community to kick back with, and most important, a sense of wholeness.

For a long time, I did exactly that. One night early in my career, pre-cane, I found myself wallflowering at a dimly lit, very "who's who" Manhattan cocktail hour. I felt anxious, unable to see because of how dark the room was, and I was so self-conscious that I ended up leaving, having spoken to no one. Only later did I learn that the music executive whose assistant had invited me to the event had waved me over to his table . . . and felt snubbed when I didn't wave back. He had no idea I couldn't see him. That was one of my roughest wake-up calls to stop masking my vision loss.

Concealing my neurodivergences has also led me to some dark internal chambers, leaving me wondering if I was two different people or thinking there was no one else on the planet who could ever relate to my situation. I didn't know how to show up authentically or why social situations always felt off. I hadn't realized yet that embracing my Disability identity would make me whole.

In late 2019 my then-manager, Gary Salzman, said he would

accompany me to a New York Chapter Recording Academy mixer, and I jumped at the opportunity. I got all gussied up, nails did, hair did, makeup did. On a whim, I decided, *I'm gonna test out bringing my cane. Gary's there if I feel awkward about it, so let's do this!* It would be my first time using my cane in my public career. This was a *big* deal. It was one thing to come out about my vision loss, quite another to show up at a networking event with a cane. Then, as the Uber pulled up, Gary called and canceled with a "Just go ahead without me, you'll do great, kid!" Plot twist!

Mortified but resolute, I got into the Uber. When I walked through the doors of the swanky Midtown dining hall, a woman I could hardly make out immediately approached me, looked me up and down, and said, "Hey Lachi, it's Lucy! How are you?" For the rest of the night, everyone came up to *me* and said hello. I've never missed another wave.

In 2021, actress Christina Applegate came out about her MS on Twitter, then went on *The Kelly Clarkson Show* to say that she used humor to "make people not scared to be around me." In 2023, *It's Always Sunny in Philadelphia* actor Rob McElhenney revealed that he'd been diagnosed with "a host of neurodevelopmental disorders and learning disabilities" as a way of letting others in similar situations know they weren't alone. Selena Gomez's "F★★★ off!" statement at a Women in Film dinner, asserting that it's not shameful for her to disclose her bipolar and other mental health conditions, was definitely a moment.

But it's not all about celebrity reveals. Craig Cincotta, head of Cloud Communications at Microsoft, opened up to his colleagues about his OCD and anxiety attacks and found that his honesty encouraged others to disclose, bringing in more team-wide compassion and diverse perspectives. "It was the toughest decision of my life. It was also the best decision I ever made," he wrote in *Entrepreneur*, adding, "I know that when people put themselves out there so they can truly be their best, that is what they find in the end."

That's the thing about camouflage: When you wear it, you end up sitting in the backseat of your own life. It denies you the freedom to define yourself and live your best life. When you come into the light, blinking and nervous, more often than not you find there's a whole world of people who *do* understand and are waiting to say, "Welcome!"

Malingering

But remember what Sir Isaac Newton said: For every person with a legit disability concealing it out of fear, there's an equal and opposite asshat alleging to have a disability they don't have. I'll illustrate. For an episode of the *OffBeat* YouTube series, my friend Jennifer and I headed downtown to catch my friend DJ Lolo Mayhew's set at a swanky rooftop bar (and to see if she'd let me stumble through a disastrous ones-and-twos session in front of all of her friends, fans, and family). Jenn and I were a couple of tens, dressed to the nines, and definitely ate: skirts, Glam Canes, heels, you know the drill. But as soon as we settled at the bar to order drinks, some guy approached us and said, "Y'all too cute to be blind."

Nineties prom record scratch. The camera whirls to a hard focus on this guy and me as a spotlight pins us to the floor. *Excuse me?* First, saying I'm "too cute to be blind" is like saying I'm "too good at math to be female" or "too non-threatening to be Black." UK personality Lucy Edwards once told me she calls these "non-plements." Worse, it's actually a passive-aggressive accusation of *malingering*—pretending to have a disability you do not have. People like me (blind but not totally blind) are often accused of malingering by folks who don't understand that blindness encompasses a full spectrum of visual acuity. This, in turn, perpetuates the desire to camouflage. Honestly, I think it's hilarious that some people accuse me of pretending I'm blind while I've spent most of my life pretending I can see.

But malingering is really, really, I mean *really* not good. Just as "stolen valor" (wearing medals you didn't earn) horrifies military folk, there might be no greater sin against the disabled population than *malingering*. The word was originally used to describe soldiers who feigned illness to get out of military service. But today, people feign having a disability or health condition for all sorts of reasons: to get out of school or work, for sympathy and attention, to get public benefits, to win a legal judgment, or to get pain meds. Hell, cripping up to snag an audition qualifies, as does faking it to earn the almighty "click, like, and subscribe" on the social medias.

One of the earliest examples of online malingering came to light in 2014, after the viral Australian wellness guru Belle Gibson claimed to have beaten cancer multiple times just by eating healthy and working out (yes, as a chronic condition, cancer fits under big-umbrella disability). She ended up having a popular wellness app, a lucrative book deal, and lots of prime-time media exposure, but one thing she never had was *cancer.* It was all one big con. She got found out, and the Australian government sued her, raided her home, and seized her properties, but I'm 100 percent certain her saddest moment came when the BBC dubbed her a *bad influencer.*

But Ms. Gibson was only the tip of the iceberg of illicit illnesses, patient pretenders, and cancer cons. The COVID quarantine saw a full-blown renaissance of malingering on TikTok. Tourette's syndrome, autism, and dissociative identity disorder became some of the most prevalent of what WebMD calls "TikTok Tics:" fictitious disabilities for clicks. After all, appropriating an identity for clout is a tale as old as Black America (see Dolezal, Rachel).

"But what's the real harm? Aren't they just performing to grow their channels?" you ask. Answer: Malingerers steal resources, awareness, and authentic community away from genuinely disabled and neurodivergent people. The prevalence of online malingering has even led to hashtags like #ActuallyAutistic, which started back in 2011 and has spread across all social media platforms.

The trend has also led to an increase in false accusations of malingering against people with legitimate disabilities. From keying cars parked in accessible spots to physical and verbal assaults to full-on denial of treatment, people constantly harass folks who don't fit neatly into their misguided, Hollywood notion of disability. A nondisabled person—it's there in the word—is not the expert on a disability experience that is not their own. This leads to disabled people—myself included—sometimes feeling we need to lean into the stereotypical assumptions of our disabilities for the sake of our safety and privacy. I use a white cane primarily as an indicator to others that I'm legally blind. Mobility is actually my secondary concern—and, surprisingly, blinged-out blind glam realness comes in third.

I have a wild idea. Instead of trying to "do your part" by accusing people with legitimate disabilities of faking it, howze about you advocate for the dignity and rights of people who need and deserve them? To those malingering on TikTok for clout, be the first to start the "Salvaged Savage: The Redemption of a Recovered Malingerer" TikTok page. When that idea goes viral, I *will* be there for my 15 percent.

Sliding into the DM (Disability Movement)

You may be thinking, "Well, you say everyone has a Disability identity, but does that include me? I'm not like *them*."

I believe less in "disabled versus nondisabled" and more in a sliding-acceptance-level scale of one's Disability identity. You can acknowledge your Disability identity even if you wouldn't consider calling yourself disabled. You may have a mental health condition, chronic pain, or a physical, sensory, or learning difference, but you still might not fully identify as disabled. The key is to accept and embrace the parts of yourself society suggests are limiting, and to build strength, community, and power around that.

For me, it's all about community. Two months before our 2022 Disability Pride tour, I invited Precious and Khadija out for drinks and dancing at a dive bar in Brooklyn so they could be part of the "people drinking and dancing at a dive bar in Brooklyn" scene for a music video.

But the cast for this club scene was not your run-of-the-mill stock spring break scene cast. The dance floor was packed with Deaf folks, blind folks, deafblind, and neurodivergent folks using sign language, tactile sign language, canes, Glam Canes, and fidget spinners—all of us grown and sexy, rocking out to my heavy-bass electronic dance song "Bad Choices" and getting trashed. Kevin Newbury and Brandon Kazen-Maddox, the founders of Up Until Now Productions, had helped me curate this beautifully queer-safe crip space of deep connection. From minute one to minute done, the love energy was palpable.

At the start of the shoot, like with all Team Lachi shoots, we conducted an access check-in, something we learned from Production Accessibility Coordinator Kiah Amara. Everyone on set states their name, does a brief self-description, and states any access needs they may have. This is obviously helpful for blind folks, is a game changer for neurodivergent comfort, and normalizes access and communication needs on the set. But most important, it gets the Endies feeling more connected to the community and to themselves. Example: "I'm Thom, a white guy with red glasses. New dad, ergo not much sleep, so I may move a little slower than usual today and you may catch me on a quick FaceTime with the other half." There you have it. Thom, our new dad Endie, is also heard and seen, and his access needs are recognized. The love works both ways.

As the night progressed, the room became a haven of deep communication, with hand signs and cane sparkles amplified by flashing lights, arms linking, and glasses clinking amid the thumping beat. The intention was clear: to express happiness, togetherness, unbreakable spirit, and gratitude for the opportunity to get away from the stares, stigma, and masking, and just get drunk with friends who get it and accept you as is.

That magical night, that safe space, with its harmonious overlays of myriad forms of communication, felt novel. But it shouldn't have. A shared space where everyone can feel safe, seen, independent, and understood, with their access needs met, should be the starting point for *any* community.

Disability Culture celebrates the diversity of Disability identity and is born from a hunger for collective liberation. It is a vibrant resistance to the stigma and exclusion that too many have experienced. Some people have non-apparent disabilities, some are masking from others and themselves, and some are transitioning into disability yet not quite ready to accept that reality. But it's not about us versus them. It's about *we*. Each of us sits at our own point on the spectrum of Disability identity.

So . . . where do you sit?

Chapter Five

Vice, Spice, and Everything Nice

I like big Struts and I cannot lie.

If you've ever had a video go viral and found yourself giving up tiny pieces of your humanity in attempts to re-create that elusive magic, you have encountered a real, live, fire-breathing dragon. That dragon's name is Algorithm. When I hear her stomach growl, I know it's time to go out onto the streets of New York, speak softly, and carry my big stick, a.k.a. do some Struts.

Struts are short video vignettes of me taking to a busy city street and catwalking down the avenue serving up chic and expensive, wearing a dope fit and sarcastically tall heels, braids bouncing to and fro, Glam Cane glinting in the sunlight, sporting the fierce "go ahead and try me" look of a true Aries powder keg.

Arthur captures this extravagant display, my brand manager, Kylie, edits it down, and we toss it up on social channels. It's all very John Travolta in the opening scene of *Saturday Night Fever*, except instead of the Bee Gees, we'll add in more of a GloRilla or Ice Spice musical undercurrent from the Sounds menu. I've done full-on Strut videos across the globe, roping in local mayors, international ambassadors, and world leaders like Hillary Clinton, and I've posed for the grid in full Strut regalia with innovators like LeVar Burton, Billie Eilish, and Bill Gates.

Most folks in the comments section of these Struts love the brazen confidence, but there's also that consistent trickle of skeptical comments like:

"She can't dress like that and be blind."

"Come on, a blind person can't actually walk that well."

"Why would she care what she looks like if she's blind?"

It's that last one that grinds my gear lever. A cynic might argue I only want to look fly for the likes and follows, and yes, we've established I do the Struts in ritualistic tribute to the great god Algorithm. But beyond social media, the real reason I doll up in Alexander McQueen ball gowns and Saks Fifth Avenue heels is because I love knowing that I look *good* when I go out. And when the day comes (and it will) that I lose my vision completely, I will still be hitting the town in luscious fabrics cut high on the thigh, with jewel-studded nails and stilettos that show off these here runner's calves.

Because I live in a world that wasn't built for such Blind Queen Energy, there are too many days when just existing requires being an advocate, seeking change, being unapologetic, and blowing the horn on ableism like the White Walkers were coming. Still, there are some days when I'd rather fight oppression with joy, erasure with glam, the grievance model with charm, and exclusion with celebration. Contrary to mainstream beliefs, we've got bougies in the Disability community who relish the finer things in life, from gourmet food to fine wine to luxe threads.

Many folks assume that disabled passersby are virtuous ascetics with few desires beyond survival, or saints indifferent to creature comforts. But this trope just denies us one of the most fundamental aspects of the human experience: gratifying self-indulgence. Whether it's as elevated as *Tosca* at the Met and dinner at a Michelin three-star or as trashy as a six-pack of White Claw and binge-watching Tubi, we're here for it! I've been known to say, "If you don't think disabled people *get down*, you must not know Lachi." Odds are the people yelling beside you at the bar with Fireball breath, moshing with you on the front lines of a thrash metal concert, or not calling you back after a weird date have non-apparent conditions. Statistically speaking, that person is you, and you like cool luxury shit sometimes, right?

Disability loves decadence, consumption, glamour, and impiety just like any other culture. But I'm not gonna make my case by talking about sex, drugs, or rock 'n' roll—at least, not yet. Right now, I want to talk about Glam Canes.

Going Glam

In 1971, American model Joanne Dusseau uttered the phrase "Because I'm worth it" in a commercial for L'Oreal Paris hair dye, and the slogan exploded, helping to elevate the women's rights movement of the time and empower the female consumer. In 2017, Rihanna paved the way when she debuted her Fenty line of beauty products centering on the Black consumer community, telling Black women, "It's worth spending a little extra on makeup made for *you,* for your skin."

My Glam Cane lines are my contribution to that Yaaas Queen Energy legacy. They tell the blind and cane-using communities, "You are worth being seen and feeling sophisticated and high-key elegant." Our slogan is "We don't sell canes, we promote confidence." Facts. But that's not something we're used to hearing. My canes are also physical, bedazzled, posh reminders that having a disability and relishing the finer things in life can, and do, most definitely coexist.

My younger self spent years rejecting the idea of using a mobility cane, and as a result, I ran face-first into my share of glass doors, thorny bushes, and exes I'd been ghosting. This lack of situational control often triggered my OCD, but in my mind, not using a cane was a small price to pay for being able to camouflage and pass as a Sightling, as many people with vision loss do. Finally, during the pandemic, something woke me up regarding how I presented to the world, and it would alter my life's trajectory forever.

My talent and tenacity were getting me invited into bigger, more important music industry spaces, and I began to feel more confident, beautiful, and deserving of those opportunities. After attending a few exclusive events and missing those deal-making hand waves, or being told I appeared standoffish—in both cases, because I simply couldn't see—I decided to begin carrying my collapsible white cane around in my purse. An aha moment came in May 2021, when Day Al-Mohamed and I were on set for the PBS *Renegades* pilot. Day, a guide dog user with partial vision herself, clocked me pretty quickly, and politely asked why I wasn't using my cane.

"I don't need it during the daytime," I said, lying to her, God, and everyone present. Later that evening, I said to myself, *Bitch, you're going blind, and you* do *need a cane. Just use the damned thing.*

I started out using the plain-Jane white cane, and it definitely helped me get around, detect walls, steps, and edges, and stop mistaking topiaries, cardboard cutouts, and inflatable arm-flailing tube men for old friends. It also communicated to everyone that I was legally blind without me having to waste precious moneymaking time explaining anything. But as I became more visible and upped my game, pedigree, and wardrobe accordingly, I said to myself, "This whole cane thing could be a vibe." Since COVID, Arthur had already become my all-purpose styling and makeup stand-in. Now I went to him with yet another fashion proposition: Help me up my cane game.

But exactly how do you make a cane look . . . chic? We started off painting them, but they came off too high school craft class for the evening looks we were lining up. The cane was becoming a permanent extension of me, so it would have to become an extension of my personal style, too. I was developing a classy yet authentic, passionate yet cheeky personal brand, and I needed a cane to match. So we started covering the canes with glitter, an arduous four-day process of glazing and glittering that left Arthur and me picking sparkly bits out of our braces, faces, and hard-to-reach places. Someday, I'll have a very festive colonoscopy!

It was worth all the hassle. I started using what I called "glitter canes" everywhere I went, receiving endless positive "I see yous" and "You betta works" and starting fun, comfortable conversations about blindness and Disability Culture. I rocked a sparkly red cane to go with a red sequined Alex Perry, a sparkly pink cane to go with a pink flowy Mac Duggal, and a black glittery stunner to match black high-heeled boots . . . and everyone *had* to know where they could get one. I knew I was onto something.

I started mentioning glitter canes on social media, and then I began giving them out to friends like activist Haben Girma,

Australian singer Rachael Leahcar, and of course the blind baddies in my inner circle. Going viral followed. We'd done something no one had ever thought about doing before: made the symbol of blindness a fashion statement.

Then came the music video for "Bad Choices." With the signature lyric "There's no such thing as bad people, just really bad choices," the song follows a do-gooder who, receiving no reward for all the good they've done, turns to sex, drugs, and alcohol. For the video, I wanted a scintillating bad-girl outfit: a sequined black dress with silver sequined shoes. Arthur suggested I tie it all together with a cane covered in silver rhinestones. What an upgrade! The combo stopped traffic like a Princess Diana revenge dress. The rhinestone cane was now more than an accessory; it was a centerpiece.

Glam Canes were born. People advised Arthur and me not to try to sell them, because blind people wouldn't be a viable market. By now, you know what happens when someone discourages Lachi from doing something: Lachi builds a website and starts selling Glam Canes. Two Blind Brothers—a company run by (you guessed it!) two blind brothers who sell Braille-embroidered socks and shirts—were making it work swimmingly, so why couldn't we? Immediately, we were overwhelmed with orders, in part because Arthur was making them by hand, one at a time, in our backyard, all while managing a hefty Team Lachi schedule and heading up operations for RAMPD. But he was also quickly overwhelmed because word of mouth spread like wildfire.

My heart grows three sizes when I see people posting about their Glam Canes—from a girl going on her first date, to a grandfather attending a graduation, to Swifties and Barbz taking canes to concerts and premieres, to busy professionals buying them to match their suit jackets. But Andrew Barkan's cane story takes the cake.

A children's music composer and fellow blindish, Andrew kept his vision loss private because of social stigmas, since he was able to get around as sighted passing . . . sound like anyone you know? One day a friend (actually, Grammy-winning children's artist Lucy Kalantari) insisted I meet this amazing children's music duo Andrew and Polly—particularly Andrew. By this time my greatest joy had become radicalizing people into loudly and proudly proclaiming their Disability identity from the rooftops—and the more mainstream-minded or ableism-influenced the person, the better. So Andrew, Polly, and I got on a call, and before long Andrew mentioned he didn't tell anyone he was legally blind because he didn't want to take himself out of the running for professional opportunities.

That rang true for me. I channeled all my years of hiding, of essentially going commando and playing sighted, reexperienced the joy I felt at embracing my true, whole self, and said to Andrew, "My guy, if someone looks at your rocking pedigree and doesn't want to kick it with you because you're blind, well, they can go kick rocks. Money has no eyes, ears, or legs. It just has value, and you are valuable in this industry." I told him about how my Glam Canes helped me get in front of and celebrate my blindness. "I can get around in dark rooms, but my cane is also a light, non-inspiration-porn-esque conversation starter," I said. Andrew beamed.

A couple of months later, he flew into New York from Los Angeles, and of course we met up for coffee. He told me he'd been nominated for a Grammy and wanted the magic of the Glam Cane to honor this momentous achievement, to celebrate himself as a legally blind artist and advocate in his own way.

Girl, you know I was all the way here for this. I needed pix of a hot guy walking around with one of my canes, and here was Andrew! We were looking at each other like total growth opportunities, which is how everyone should look at everyone else all the time. We made Andrew a cane, and damn if that guy didn't strut through all the Grammy week parties in dapper-ass suits, fitted fedoras, nice ties—and a matching Glam Cane! Everyone complimented him, going bananas over the cane. Icing on the cake: We both got to stroll the official Grammys red carpet, posing for the cameras with smiles, our Glam Canes, and bold unapologetic Disability joy.

At the 2024 Grammys, RAMPD saw a few wheelchairs, prosthetics, and Glam Canes out on the carpet. When I caught up with Andrew at the after-party, his first words to me were "This cane has changed my life." I smiled ear to ear. "I can get around," he continued. "I can simply go up and talk to people. It photographs so well. But also I'm advocating as a walking billboard for Disability Pride." Posting about his experience on Instagram, Andrew wrote:

> So I came out as a cane-user at the #Grammys. I thought it would help make my disability visible and support @rampd_up i.e. be mostly symbolic (and stylish!) But it was actually way more useful mobility-wise than I would have guessed? I found myself high-fiving @pollyhall repeatedly as we discovered the benefits:

- *don't feel awkward when I can't look at photographers! high-five!*

- *didn't fall in a fountain!*

- *even the most self-important partiers part ways when we need to get through! high five!*

  Socially, I never know when I'm noticed or not noticed. I never know when I'm welcome or unwelcome. I overstep when others have clear indications to slow or disengage, and I can't imagine how many invitations to engage I've missed . . . Gratitude to @glamcanes by @lachimusic—SO MANY COMPLIMENTS!

After reading that post, in that moment, just days after the Grammys frenzy, I felt what I always feel after gifting someone the Glam Cane experience: a dope, positive transfer of energy. It took me my whole life to finally embrace my blindness, combat my own internalized ableism, and walk proudly—nay, *confidently*—in my disabled skin. Because of these Glam Canes I was able to give that same gift to Andrew and to scores of iced-out Swifties. That's progress.

So why have Glam Canes got people so hyped up? Well, it's not just the bling, but what the bling represents. As far as mainstream sentiment is concerned, luxury, beauty, fashion, and sparkly things do not mesh with disability.

Well, as I say after a full and productive day of shoe shopping, there's a lot to unpack here. First, society at large already regards indulgent pleasures—the first sip of an artisan IPA at a new brew-pub, the soothing vibes of sinking into a bubble bath surrounded by scented candles—as irrelevant to people with disabilities, so much so that we're often overlooked and even excluded as a consumer base. But that line of reductive thinking ignores the fact that we are complete, complex beings, and we're silently everywhere. We're foodies, movie buffs, tequila connoisseurs, audiophiles, and metalheads, and we love a good fart joke like the next person.

Popular culture, from daytime TV to advertising, defines Disability identity based on suspect and outdated tropes, trophies, and tragedies. Thus, a fear of judgment keeps a large contingent of people with low vision from using their prescribed cane, perpetuating the erasure that fuels those misguided tropes.

¡No gracias¡ ¡No mas¡ Glam Canes works to replace erasure with celebration. A Glam Cane user is saying *Because I believe I'm worth it* while walking down the street or into any room without having to utter a word.

We choose how we define ourselves based on what we want, own, and drive, who we wear, where we live, who we love, and how we waste our money. (By the way, yes, wheelchair users drive. Remember the scene from *There's Something About Mary* in which a Bostonian sports a "How am I Driving? Call (1-800) Eat-Shit" sign on the back of his wheelchair? The Farrelly brothers cast Danny Murphy, an authentically disabled actor and authentic Boston asshole, for that role. Chef's kiss!)

There's economic and social capital in marketing to consumers with disabilities. In fact, the robust luxury industry we see in America today owes a lot to a mogul with a disability: billionaire casino developer Steve Wynn, who exploded the Atlantic City and Las Vegas strip casino and resorts industries and who has retinitis pigmentosa, a degenerative eye disease that slow-walks into blindness. Sir Richard Branson, founder of the Virgin Group (which includes more than forty companies in areas like travel, telecommunications, and entertainment) is another mogul with a disability, rocking dyslexia, to which he ascribes much of his innovation and success. I definitely understand the "Life won't wait, so go live!" fire the Bransons of the world are out here sporting. Hence the whole skydiving thing.

Bottom line, moguls with disabilities can be ambitious and can have wealth. Case in point: Arthur and I figured that out of eight billion humans, there had to be other people with vision loss who, like me, were willing to pay for a luxury cane to celebrate their swagger. We put zero marketing dollars into Glam Canes, yet still got nearly thirty orders a month right from the start from yuppies, teens, boyfriends, moms, and our older debutantes. They're not simply buying canes; they're embracing sophistication and glamour. We're now expanding beyond mobility canes, selling Glam Cane walkers, quad canes, clips, bags, and T-shirts. Imagine what could happen with an ad budget, a national media campaign, and a few celebrity endorsements! It would be a red-letter day in the Disability economy.

Getting Lucky

So if we're gonna talk about the vices, spices, and everything nices à la disability, well—as Salt-N-Pepa demanded of all of us back in 1991—let's talk about sex, baby. When it comes to sex and disability, society tends to ricochet between taboo, extreme discomfort, and a semi-repulsed curiosity. Overwhelmingly, society sees people with disabilities as nonsexual. Incorrect. Plenty of us (including yours truly) are hella sexual (yes, I said *hella*, and I apologize). There are sex workers making bank off extensive rosters of clients with disabilities. This conversation takes me back to a quote by *Queer Eye* cohost Jonathan Van Ness, who, in a mock interview on Peacock's NPR parody *In the Know*, said, "As long as you're a consenting adult, honey, you're fuckable."

But disabled people can't even have sex, can they? you ask. I'm disabled and I have sex, so yes. Disabled people have sex. Next question. Despite the fact that mainstream media almost never portrays disabled sexuality or romance in even the mildest ways, we're out here showing it off on our own terms, on our Instas, Finstas, and OnlyFans. Sex is just mutual connection, communication, and (something we're total experts at) creative thinking.

The community's zeal for getting down and hooking up represents a sector of the Disability economy left mostly untapped by the gods of business and marketing. The condom brand Durex's 2023 #IHaveThisAbility campaign used video stories and testimonials with authentically disabled coeds to discuss their nice and naughty bedroom pleasure hacks, highlighting risqué lines like "I can't use my two legs, but I can use my third one." Wooh, it's getting hot up in here! Just as sex is a cornerstone of marketing to the general public, it should be a cornerstone of the Disability economy.

Part of the assumption that people with disabilities aren't sexually or romantically active stems from society's narrow definition of physical attractiveness. But Halle Berry is half-deaf. Toni Braxton has lupus. Dwayne "the Rock" Johnson has depression and had to quit football because of severe injuries and dislocations. That's just three gorgeous human beings who've been open about disability and who I wouldn't mind playing doctor with.

All bodies are unique works of art, and what may be unattractive to you may be beautiful to the next person.

The Blind community in particular is highly-with-a-capital-H sensual. Why? Touch is a vital part of communication for blind people, along with the sound of someone's voice and the smell of one's cologne. Quite the recipe for sensuality after a *blind* date. (Get it? Do you see what I did there?)

But let me say it again for the people in the back. When it comes to disability and sex, *consent is key*. A good number of blind people—especially women—can become targets of unwanted physical interaction. Far too often, people touch blind women without consent under the guise of guiding or caretaking. I go through this on a constant basis. People will grab my arm, touch my waist, or even grab my cane with zero regard for my privacy as a human, let alone as a grown woman—and I don't always have the energy to go all Harley Quinn on 'em.

Here's a helpful PSA that's good for all occasions: DON'T GRAB A BLIND PERSON! I really hope my publisher lets me keep this in all caps, because grabbing blind folks without asking is dehumanizing. I don't care if you have good intentions. I don't care if you're Mister *fricken* Rogers. Ask if even innocuous physical contact is okay, and if the answer isn't an enthusiastic "I said yes, dagnabbit!" then back it up. We are all adults and deserve dignity, autonomy, and the opportunity to consent. If you touch my hair, my cane, or my arm without consent, you are walking away with a shiner. I will happily pose for my T-shirt-worthy mug shot.

Now, speaking of consent, a question I sometimes get is whether a neurodivergent, intellectually disabled, or nonspeaking person can actually consent. Yes. If two or more adults can show their consent through whatever mode of communication they prefer, there you have it. Assuming a sober, conscious adult cannot consent based on their disability alone is classic infantilization.

I got to know comedian and TikTok personality Paris Campbell Grace after hearing her land this dead-on joke: "I didn't find out I was autistic till twenty-six, so obviously before that I was completely unaffected." I was immediately obsessed and I asked her about dating as an openly autistic comedian. She's now happily married to Laura Jane Grace, but Paris walked me through some of her more harrowing dating experiences.

"The biggest struggle I experienced was being fetishized, being infantilized," she said when we met up. "Some people were like, 'Aw, she's so cute. Oh, it's the 'tism.' Almost like, 'I want you to be my manic pixie dream girl' type of energy. I had someone say the most fucked-up thing to me once. I was going on dates with someone and things were going well, but I wondered, *Why doesn't this person make a move? Are they not attracted to me?* I brought it up, and he said, 'I didn't think you could consent.'"

Whaaa? I blurted out all of the expletives—and made up a few new ones—after hearing that creepy-as-hell story.

Other dating nightmares revolve around disclosure. *To disclose or not to disclose?* That is the question. If you don't disclose on the app that you're a little person or an amputee, are you catfishing? If your disability is non-apparent, does it even matter? If you do decide to disclose, will you attract the type of person who wants to take advantage of you, or a devotee who fetishizes disabled people? Yes, that's a thing. My friend Jillian, a little person, mentioned that men online often ask women with dwarfism—on first DM, no less—"Can you perform oral while standing up?"

Big yikes. What ever happened to the days of cheesy pickup lines like, "You're the only ten I see," "I'd put U and I together," or "They say dating is a numbers game, so give me yours"? Call me old-fashioned, but I'd prefer a cornball over a sleazeball any day.

But, okay, that's enough of the sketchier side of dating and disability. What say we palate-cleanse with some romance? Enter Cole Sydnor and Charisma Jamison, creators of the popular YouTube channel Roll with Cole & Charisma. The channel follows the relationship of Cole—who is white and paralyzed from the chest down—and Charisma, a young Black woman he met at the rehab facility where she worked.

While they get their share of online love for their videos, they also receive their share of uninspired comments, from the clueless (like how Charisma is "such an angel" for being with Cole) to the vicious (like people saying that Cole only settled for Charisma because no white woman would date him). *Really?* Do better, internet.

Cole and Charisma answer the eternal "How do you guys . . . do it?" questions, focusing less on the technical aspects of sex and more on the engine behind sex: *intimacy.*

I tapped Cole and Charisma for a Strut, then a short interview. Over Zoom, I asked about caregiving as an act of intimacy. "Caregiving does not hinder our growth or our love in any way, but actually strengthens it," Cole said. "We find a lot of moments for intimacy or fun or giggling together when we're caregiving. Back in the early days of our dating, we'd hang out on my parents' couch in the attic. That meant me transferring on and off the couch. A lot of times those transfers—I'd be resting my head on her shoulder and her arms would be on my waist—were us doing the transfer together. By the end, we had both fallen over giggling on the couch, just having a cute little moment, even though the transfer went terribly."

"A lot of times we're just trying to do our normal transfer and somehow Cole ends up on the floor," added Charisma. "I can either laugh about it or cry about it, and a lot of times I'll initially cry about it, but then moments later, when everything's okay, and Cole's alive, we'll laugh about it."

"Yeah, when I die, it's not as funny," Cole quipped.

Couples like Cole and Charisma or Jay and Pamela—the couple with osteogenesis imperfecta who star in TLC's *Jay & Pamela*—are out here showing folks that disability craves intimacy, and does what it's gotta do to adapt to bedroom challenges. Both Viagra and vibrators are assistive measures for intimacy. So let's just all agree that if something makes consensual, fun, satisfying sex possible, it's a good thing.

Intimacy matters. Communication matters. Mutual respect and consent are non-optional. Disabled people have sex and make scores of cute little snot-nosed rug rats who they love and nurture. What we all crave is intimacy and empathy, especially in a society that often separates and spectacles us.

Going Out

Speaking of Big Struts, I love to get dressed up just to be seen, to pregame with my girls before going out to the club, and to get hit on all night by guys everyone knows we're not going home with. Visible disability is often a forfeit of privacy, so listen, if they're gonna stare anyway, why not show off what Jim LeBrecht would call our "beautiful body jazz"? Humans are inherently social creatures, having evolved to form connections and develop shared memories. Gathering together and spending interpersonal face time with people we enjoy is great for mental health. People with sensory conditions, COVID-cautious coworkers, older couples, temporarily physically disabled folks, families with a neurodivergent kid—we all love to go out, whether to a bar, restaurant, concert, movie, ball game, or that bizarre murder mystery dinner Becky put together.

"I've always wanted to have a group of *Sex and the City*–style disabled girlfriends," I said on one of my first hangs with Victoria's Secret model and my Miami-hailing homegirl, Paula Carozzo. She and I have been known to get dressed up and hang out around town whenever she's in the city, just two disabled snaccs racking up stares and wolf whistles. "I want a group of friends that we travel with," I continued, "go out with, exchange sex tips with, and throw unnecessarily over-the-top parties for, where there's a dramatic reveal, someone ends up breaking a vase, the fire department is called, and there are bras and ice cream cake everywhere."

Paula responded with "Literally," and it was over.

We gathered together our wheelchair-using, prosthetic-wearing, dog- and cane-walking, signing, scootering, and free-thinking friends and began plotting outings. Making all gatherings as crip space as possible was pretty much baked in. Crip space, a concept defined by S. E. Smith's essay "The Beauty of Spaces Created for and by Disabled People," refers to a disability third space—a space where the Disability community can come together and enjoy ourselves with little to no ableist societal pressures. Like RAMPD's DisCo House parties, crip spaces are accessible, inclusive spaces where Disability identity is not just tolerated, but celebrated. My versions of Samantha, Miranda, and Charlotte and I started making the rounds, holding New York City hostage with our stilettoed-disabled-girl realness.

One of our bigger parties, the industry mixer and single release party for the song and video "Lift Me Up" in September 2023, was my first attempt at bringing music industry highbrows into a crip space not as spectators, but as industry players hanging out in a space built to celebrate disability. How hard could it be to satisfy both music industry gala-goers and disability thought leaders? All I needed was an accessible venue with a cool-off area, a step-n-repeat backdrop, booze, pizza, a DJ, and swag. I know it's not Kardashian-level party standards, but I just wanted to show everyone an intersectional good time, no NDAs needed.

Shout-out to Wandering Barman in Brooklyn, a colorful, spacious venue with a ramped entrance, integrated outdoor seating, accessible bathroom, and super-accommodating staff. With DJ Wheels on the decks, Paula as the emcee, and myself as the featured performer, singing "Lift Me Up," we put out the invite and packed the house. We had Grammy winners and music execs schmoozing with disabled public figures and TikTok stars, all drippin' Friday night glow-up for the step-n-repeat. Hands were shaken, numbers were exchanged, friendships were born, dance moves were danced, drunken spills were laughed about, all of it.

I did the dang thing. My first-ever DisCo House party. I threw a seventy-five-head, industry-standard party that accommodated a ton of disabilities, and I spent less than $5,000. Hold up, that means cost must not be the real issue when it comes to accommodation! Who knew? So what's really the tea on event producers, party planners, bars, and venues having to have the 101 discussion on disability inclusion time and again?

More patrons and passersby—and their families, after-work friends, and dates—would flock to bars, venues, festivals, and party spots if these spots accommodated disability. Festival producer and wheelchair user Austin Whitney mentions in a You-Tube video that the first time he'd smiled since his accident came after he attended an accessible festival with friends. But many party places, small or large, indoor or outdoor, don't often take or even know the necessary steps to make their venue more accommodating. This in turn makes it difficult for potential party-goers or performers with disabilities to turn up in the first place with their money . . . and their fans' and friends' money. Small business owners, lacking quick-fix solutions, can begin to view disability through the grievance model lens—more fearful of potential complaints than excited for potential business.

So why can't venues and events just *be* accessible? And don't tell me it's 'cause the building is old; the Colosseum in Rome has an elevator and that's literally *the* oldest building, period. Just get that ramp off Amazon, install a cute little doorbell, have a sign language contact on hand, repurpose a random alcove as a sensory area, and slap "ADA friendly" on the website. Done, right? While these are all good practices to look into, it's not that simple. *But doesn't the ADA legally require all accessibility measures?* Well, yes and no. Not enough people really get the ADA's rules when it comes to non-federal buildings. So let's course-correct on this.

First, venues generally just want money and bodies. They'll take a wealthy wheelchair user or a cash-rich crutch user over a nondisabled ne'er-do-well with a maxed-out Amex every night. But some lower-brow lawyers have been popularizing drive-by noncompliance lawsuits against independent, mom-and-pop venues and small businesses that aren't as accessible as the big guys.

These shysters prey on disabled individuals with limited incomes and use them to exploit ADA compliance laws to make bank while manufacturing a grievance culture between small venues and the disabled population. This type of litigation can sabotage venue operators' good-faith efforts to become ADA-compliant, since it's tough to lay out for a well-built ramp if you're also stuck paying legal fees.

The reality is that Title III of the ADA, which applies to privately owned public spaces such as restaurants, hotels, and bars, says that if a business would incur undue hardship to meet ADA requirements (determined on a case-by-case basis), they are encouraged to explore options that can still provide access for disabled customers. For example, asking a small restaurant with limited space to completely restructure its layout to accommodate a wheelchair user when there are possible alternatives for providing access would qualify as an undue hardship. But as long as a small venue is making a good faith effort to be accommodating, they're doing okay by the ADA. But not all small venues and not all disabled patrons know this, and most nickel-and-dime lawyers don't want them to.

Legal actions against larger, more established corporate spaces can be crucial for establishing the precedents that drive change, and many larger venues are proactively working to be more compliant. But making examples of well-meaning or unaware small business owners doesn't really serve anyone but the lawyers, and only widens the grievance chasm.

Organizations like RAMPD are trying to get in front of this by being proactive. We're working directly with local independent venues and spaces to train and consult on accommodation, inclusive culture, and low-cost, low-hanging solutions. There is no list of implementations that will serve every disability, so the key is to just be simpatico—have an accommodation concierge and be as hospitable to and inclusive of every individual's experience as you can. Businesses shouldn't feel that they *have* to serve their local Disability community; they should feel that they *get* to. The ADA is law, but a willingness to accommodate is *culture*.

Operating from a place of accommodation wouldn't only get folks with physical, chronic, or sensory conditions to turn up and get turnt up. It would draw older folks, a group of coeds and their one friend with temporary crutches, and nondisabled people who just like it better when the stairs are lit. Heck, accommodating for hybrid virtual and live events might rope in COVID-cautious folks and even the zillions of fur-baby and human-baby parents trapped at home bored out of their minds.

Also, inclusive vibes are good for bottom lines. That's not just speculation. A 2022 Harris poll found that post-COVID, a whopping 82 percent of consumers want the values of the business they patronize to align with their own values. Sustainability and inclusive practices have become just as important as quality and price. Just look at how the LGBTQIA+ community and its allies shun Chick-fil-A, no matter how crisp the waffle fries are. If people don't think you care about what they care about, they'll let you know with their debit cards. If they're feeling your moral alignment, they'll gladly swipe, tip, and even leave a Google Guide review with magazine-level pics of their drink. Point is, there's untapped money in valuing disability.

One last thing on this. I want to shout out my IDD family—people with intellectual or developmental disabilities. Mainstream culture has largely ignored the reality that people with IDD also like to have a good time, get wild, and be treated like autonomous adults. Then the 2024 "Hey Bartender" commercial went viral, in which model and actress Madison Tevlin, who has Down syndrome, says to a bartender, "Hey bartender, you assume that I can't drink a margarita, so you don't serve me a margarita . . . Your assumption becomes reality." She's one of many working hard to shift perceptions of the IDD community.

I sat down with actress Lauren Potter—a.k.a. Becky, the bully with Down syndrome everyone loved to hate from *Glee*—and her mother over Zoom, and asked her about this.

"I've been thinking a lot about this," Lauren said. "I want to have my life with my family, and I love where I am, and I love where I go. But in my heart my parents are saying to me, 'Get ready, get set, don't go.'" Lauren began to choke up, but her mother encouraged her to let it out. "I just want to be who I want to be . . . I just found out the good news that I'm going to have my own apartment in a protected group setting. I want to get married, too. And when I do get married, I just want my parents to be happy. Sometimes I just feel heartbroken because I'll have to leave my mom's nest. But I love to be on my own, watch movies, and be with friends."

I was right there with her, giving snaps on mute. The next time you see Lauren and me together, we'll be toe-to-toe with any bartender, bouncer, or barrier, because we're ready, we're set, and we are out here making waves.

Alls I'm saying is, businesses from bars to music venues to beyond need to build a way to take my money. I want to spend it at your spot. Get everyone feeling welcome, and not only will we show up, we'll pack the house.

Rocking Out

Let's transition from getting into the party to *being* the party, the glamorous gods onstage. Listen, there's partying, and there's *partying*. Ever since Jimi Hendrix coined the phrase "Wave your freak flag high" in the song "If 6 Was 9," the iconic counterculture elements of rock 'n' roll have crisscrossed with disability. Rock stars have symbolized rebellious freedom and counterculture solidarity that crowds eat all the way up, and many of them have been fueled by their Disability identities.

When we think legendary hip-hop rock star opulence, we think Lil Wayne, who's open about his epilepsy. When we think legendary gay rock star opulence, we think Elton John, who's also open about his epilepsy. Ever wonder why quintessential rock god Bono wears those iconic dark glasses? He's got glaucoma. Trevor Noah, rock star comedian with a dead-on impression of President Obama, joins Maroon Five's Adam Levine in crediting ADHD for his success. One of my personal favorites, Gurrumul, was a blind Indigenous Australian singer who transported global stadium audiences with his blend of traditional and modern sounds. And then there's BAFTA Award– and Academy Award–winning documentarian and Grammy Award–winning musician Questlove of The Roots, who sits among an all-star squad of showstopping autistic musicians like David Byrne of Talking Heads, Joe Walsh of the Eagles, and Dallon Weekes of Panic! at the Disco.

But this goes beyond just a great performance and into inadvertent, and sometimes purposeful, advocacy. In a *Forbes* article about rockers with disabilities, Ruth Blatt covers everyone from Johnny Rotten of the Sex Pistols, who "turned his signature hunch, blank stare and sneer caused by childhood meningitis into swagger," and Ian Dury of Ian Dury and the Blockheads, who lived with polio, joining the ranks of virtuoso concert violinist Itzhak Perlman, Neil Young, Joni Mitchell, and a myriad of others. In songs like "Spasticus Autisticus," Dury faced his disability head-on with tongue-twisting lyrics like "I'm knobbled on the cobbles 'cause I hobble when I wobble." That multidimensional realness is served up on a platter for authenticity-starved audiences by fast-rising disabled showboaters rocking the stage today: Deaf Super Bowl ASL performer Justina Miles; Natalis Rubero, a Latina vocalist open about her lupus; one-handed concert pianist Nicholas McCarthy . . . and yours truly.

Despite this flood of disabled talent, one in five performers with disabilities still report having to cancel a show after finding out the venue was inaccessible, according to an Attitude Is Everything survey. Yeesh. If a venue assures me the entrance and stage are accessible, but when my fans and I arrive it's not, I'm the one who loses my fans' trust. Whether in rock, country, hip-hop, or comedy, fans are screaming for safe spaces to celebrate acceptance and belonging in a society constantly forcing them to conform.

In *Forbes*, Blatt writes of disabled musicians, "Illness is not a source of stigma or fear. It is a source of artistic insight and self-expression. In many ways, they celebrated the eye-opening potential of disability. They recognized that it offered a lens into society that wasn't available." Snaps all around! It's past time for intentionally inclusive talent booking and the inclusion of accessibility on all performance riders. It's past time to get openly disabled, different, and divergent rockers headlining, opening for major tours, and sitting on talk show couches, because not only will disabled fans pack the house, we'll bring the house *down*.

Getting Cute

Disabled people love leaving the house looking fly. First off . . . comfort is everything. When your body's already putting in over-time just to navigate, the last thing you need is a full-on civil war with an itchy, scratchy, nails-claws-and-teeth beast of a dress. Give me a cute little on-again-off-again with soft fabrics and stretchy materials any day of the week.

That's where *adaptive fashion* steps back into frame. From styl-ish shoes, wraps, and dresses with easy-to-manage zips, Velcros, and magnets to chic accessories that scream *I will not be overlooked*, we're out here making a statement. Adaptive fashion—which de-signs clothing centered on the needs of people with varying body types, sizes, and degrees of mobility—has been around since Ne-anderthals sported couture animal hide, gaining its first stint of popularity with top brands in the 1950s and 1960s, when post-war bodies were expected to hurry up and look hirable.

Helen Cookman, a deaf designer, led the charge back in the day. In 1955 she developed Functional Fashions, a collection of sev-enteen items designed to help disabled people dress independently—including the now-iconic wraparound dress. A resurgence started in the 2010s when models with disabilities like Dr. Danielle Shey-puk began turning heads on social media (and eventually Fash-ion Week runways), and now brands like Nike, Kohl's, Tommy Hilfiger, and Zappos are joining Victoria's Secret in taking ad-vantage of the growing market, offering adaptive styles that make getting cute and dapper hassle-free, and working with our bodies, not against them.

If you're thinking, *So where is this growing market of fashionistas with disabilities?* take a look around. We're everywhere—older folks, folks with any form of mobility or chronic pain conditions, and people who just prefer comfortable clothes. We're just not represented on as many carpets and catwalks as we should be . . . yet. Seeing fashionistas like April Lockhart and Sofía Jirau killing it on top runways, or gorgeous veterans with prosthetics rocking Ukraine's 2024 Fashion Week mid-war, showing everyone the beauty, resilience, and ingenuity of disabled self-expression? That's the kind of representation we've been craving! When the pics from Paula Carozzo's 2023 Victoria's Secret Pink Adaptive shoot hit the streets, I remember seeing them all over my IG feed and thinking, *That right there? That's me! It doesn't look exactly like me, but that's me.*

I called Paula, who has mild cerebral palsy and uses a cane, to ask about her experience on the shoot for the fashion giant. "I am a disabled Victoria's Secret Angel," she said when we sat down to talk. "I feel like we're a set of new angels, new trendsetters redefining this new era of life in all the ways that it comes. Working with Victoria's Secret has been one of my favorite campaigns. For such a big brand that's been canceled for not being diverse and coming back trying to be more diverse, I think it's essential to include disabilities. Not just Victoria's Secret but any brand."

Paula went on, "For a brand to showcase a disabled body, it doesn't get more beautiful than that. I really want brands to think ahead and think deeper. Fashion consumers, we're dressing more relaxed . . . we want to wear pants with lots of pockets so that we don't have to carry bags. All of my winter coats have a bunch of pockets because I walk with a cane, and I don't necessarily want to be with a cane and a bag and my dog and her leash. I think brands need to get smarter, create functional fashion that everybody can use, and integrate the disabled consumer into that."

Beyond function and looking good, it's about feeling Sasha Fierce confident. Throughout grade school, I was bullied pretty heavily for being every definition of unpretty, so growing up I had a nonexistent self-image. And since Mattel's blind Barbie wouldn't come out until 2024, I had to lay the foundation of my own self-confidence brick by brick, using the two things that made me smile: music and style.

Style is a form of self-expression. So why wouldn't a person with a visible disability want to zhuzh it up, turn heads, showcase the guns, or serve a seductive look? Every unique body is its own work of art. That's why disability-centric fashion platforms like Cur8able and Sky Cubacub's Rebirth Garments are so important. Sky's mission is *radical visibility*—creating custom wearables that reveal not only the beauty of every kind of disabled and gender-expansive body, but the passion and spirit of the person in it.

We're all out here just tryna be seen. I sat down with Deaf advocate, sign language performer, and TV personality Raven Sutton over Zoom, and we kiki'd about the many ways she declares her Disability Pride. "I have a shirt that says 'Deaf' big and bold on the front," she said via her interpreter. "It's not something to hide. I feel very proud as a Black Deaf woman. Also, when I get my nails done, they're a French pink-and-white manicure. When I'm signing, it's like an extra flair on my fingertips."

When Raven was on the popular Netflix series *The Circle*, she was a cult-fave flirt queen, always getting her nails did, rocking that blue hair, and flashing her Deaf Pride for the whole world to see. Shopping, playing dress-up, getting *my* nails did, flirting—that's all a big part of my own love lexicon. Like Raven, my Disability identity brings me joy, and I celebrate and bring visibility to that joy through music, storytelling, and fashion.

Think about the evolution of "plus size." The plus-size section used to be a no-man's land hidden in a shadowy valley, where you would prowl low and speak with whispered voices betwixt looming blouses, only to scamper away empty-handed, praying no one noticed. Now it's just a section of the clothing department—one where I often find myself shopping, by the by, because when it comes to blue jeans, a Black girl eight and a white girl eight are two very different eights.

Point is, plus size went mainstream. Some designers, models, and advocates in the fast-growing adaptive fashion community are pushing for an adaptive section that would cater to different body and mobility types, as well as older folks, bigger folks, and people in recovery. I want adaptive fashion to have its moment, then become as commonplace as plus size. Let's make shopping inclusive of everyone who wants to give you their money. Get on it, Corporate America. I'm tryna help *you* out!

The Disability Economy

The deal is, from travel to entertainment to memorable death-defying experiences, consumers with every type of condition love it all, want it all, deserve it all, and will spend bucks to have it all. We want our identity to be stirred into the big, global economic stew. But often, we're afterthoughts.

According to the International Finance Corporation (IFC), many people with disabilities face "various barriers, such as inaccessible buildings and inflexible work environments which may hinder their full and effective participation in society," making them "more likely to experience adverse socioeconomic outcomes."

Joe Businessman is thinking, *Hold up, if disabled folk are worse off economically, why would I market to them?* Well, Joe, it turns out that, according to the IFC, the global disability market is nearly as large as China. You remember that more than 1.3 billion people around the world report living with some form of disability, right? Well, those folks together have around $13 trillion in annual disposable income. For perspective, that's three times the GDP of Japan.

The disability market stretches far beyond individuals with apparent disabilities. A 2015 Disability Belongs report stated that more than half of Americans have a family member or close friend with a disability (that's a lot of other people who wanna buy cool, trendy, or random stuff *for* the disabled population). We also need to remember where America's wealth concentrates. In 2023, CNBC reported that Americans in their sixties and seventies have the highest net worth. Also, according to Global Disability Rights Now, 50 percent of U.S. adults sixty-five and up have a disability. Let's do some math. Half the Americans in the group that has the most money have a disability. And because a lot of those folks are retired, guess what they also have? Lots of leisure time to take cruises, buy accessible RVs, and fine-dine in accommodating restaurants. Joe Businessman, don't sleep on these rich-ass older folk.

While individuals with state-defined disabilities often have lower education rates and levels of employment because of discrimination, collectively we're an undeniably large consumer group. Add family members, friends, caregivers, and the countless scores of consumers who *do* have a disability but don't identify as such, and there's a massive economic opportunity being left on the table.

Recording technology company Native Instruments (NI) is a great example of what's possible. The company sells products that are accessible to blind and low-vision audio-tech consumers, a community that has been booming since the 2010s and is notorious for sharing information online and building its own audio add-ons. In the 2010s, NI released a music production keyboard and accompaniment software package called Komplete Kontrol, and can you say "game changer"? The tech gave users auditory feedback when they pressed buttons. If a producer or engineer had their laptop connected to the board, it detected the laptop's text-to-speech software and gave the user *spoken* feedback. Later, when the company crunched its user data, it found that 5 percent of all Komplete Kontrol users reported as blind or low vision. Not just 5 percent of disabled users, but 5 percent of *all* users. *That's* how you capture a market.

"That's significant, as it's one of our major products," said NI's VP of product management Tim Adnitt, when we spoke on recording technology access. NI now leans heavily into accessibility, especially for Komplete Kontrol, working closely with its blind and low-vision customer base. "There's still a lot to do there," Tim said, "but it all came from that place of 'Let's do this, because it takes us from nowhere to somewhere.'" NI's story proves that if you build it, and they can access it, they will come.

It's time we folded the disability economy into the larger mega-economy. Everyone from retailers to tech giants to wellness gurus to ticket brokers would respect the fact that Americans with disabilities have a half-billion dollars of discretionary income to spend every year and are aching to spend it in ways that make us look and feel good. Corporations would learn to fear the power of our wallets. They would design marketing campaigns that get us, include us, and are created in boardrooms where disability has a seat at the table. They'd compete to be the first "fully accessible" this or "crip friendly" that. It would be disruptive, grasping, greedy, good ol' American capitalism.

Yes, I do recognize the contradiction inherent in saying "Your system is oppressive and deserves to be dismantled" and "Please include me in your system" at the same time. But I don't care how much you can't stand Becky and weren't planning to go to her party anyway. It's always nice to be invited, and world-shattering when you aren't. If someone's handing out free samples of ice cream at the supermarket, you want one, even if you're lactose intolerant and just one bite will mean spending the rest of the day cutting silent-but-deadlies and looking around innocently, when you and everyone in the vicinity knows damn well it was you. But in that moment of truth, we all just want to be a part of the ice cream club, because when I scream, and you scream, we all want to scream for ice cream!

Being relentlessly marketed to is an initiation rite into mainstream culture. For consumers with disabilities and other chronic conditions, having our lives invaded by YouTube ads, AI spam, and direct mail postcards would be the larger world saying, "You're in the club! You made it! Now buy tons and tons and tons of crap!" On the flip side, not being sold to equals economic erasure. We deserve independence, comfort, access, and the power to shape the economic landscape with our spending choices.

Luxury evolves and means different things to different people. For many people with disabilities, access, inclusion, and autonomy are luxuries. We often pay extra for adaptive add-ons or devices to access or navigate the same technologies and spaces. It's called the Disability Tax, the extra costs people with disabilities incur to live with the same quality of life as people without those disabilities.

In her book, *The Anti-Ableist Manifesto*, author and organizer Tiffany Yu breaks it down. "While the disability tax includes financial costs like medical needs, adding accommodations to our homes or vehicles, grocery delivery, or buying one-handed cutting boards," she writes, "it also includes costs like the extra time we need to get ready and leave the house, the mental energy needed . . . a slower pace of progress, and poor job performance." We're paying extra, financially and sociologically—and oftentimes on lower wages—for basic necessities, when we should be spending extra on recreation, fine silks, finer wine, and top-tier service at the kind of restaurant that calls a waiter a *garçon*.

It's worth emphasizing that it's been *legal* for employers to pay disabled people subminimum wage (less than the federal minimum) under the Fair Labor Standards Act. This practice devalues disabled workers and doesn't lead to competitive or integrated employment. Activists and elected officials have been working tirelessly to phase out these practices.

"We are striving to be part of this market so that we are equally paid and are seen as equally valuable," Paula said toward the end of our chat. "For me, I love the finer things. I love the finer fashion. I love sex. I love partying. It's my taste. Part of my mission is educating people that, yes, I am disabled and yes, I do have pleasures . . . I think society just really has to be woken up. We are valuable enough to have the same experiences that a nondisabled person has."

Amen, sis!

As intellectual disabilities advocate Ricardo Thornton Sr. said in an address to the U.S. Senate, "When people are given a chance to grow and contribute, they grow and contribute." The cycle breaks when the stigma breaks. See us as valuable customers, and we'll *be* valuable customers.

Chapter Six

Innovating 'stead of Waiting

On April 9, 2024, I learned the one thing you need to master the art of the entrepreneurial pitch: *confidence*. Experts will say you need a pristine, color-themed PowerPoint deck with graphs and a polished finances slide that looks like but doesn't look like you made it on Canva. Nope. Experts will say you need a perfectly pressed dark (but not black) suit, looking like Steve Harvey at Sunday brunch. Nope. While you *should* have those things, the only thing you *need* is confidence.

The occasion was the 2gether-International Pitch Competition, sponsored by the National Disability Institute. I stepped to the *Shark Tank*–style plate in front of an enthusiastic audience of community members, fellow entrepreneurs, and potential investors to take a swing at $10,000 for RAMPD. I was competing against four other talented, hungry founders, all with disabilities, to convince the judges that the barely two-year-old RAMPD was a winner. Well, ya girl knocked it out the park. We got the ten large, thanks 100 percent to confidence.

But if you thought Big Boss Energy with a smile was always

my go-to growing up, think again. I didn't settle into that big-chested, "If I lose, it's their loss" swagger until I began witnessing the traction of my vision with RAMPD. That pitch win wasn't close to the beginning of my story as an entrepreneur—more like a thousand pages into a middle chapter. Like most entrepreneurs from across the spectrum, my journey started when I realized I had to solve a problem because no one else was gonna solve it for me.

Put on your N95 mask and travel with me (if you dare) back in time to the dark days of 2020, when New Yorkers were either gathering on balconies every evening to cheer on frontline workers or huddled in their co-ops marathoning *RuPaul's Drag Race* and lamenting the end of twenty-four-hour bodegas.

Right up until quarantine, I'd started gaining momentum, becoming better known and getting into better recording sessions with bigger names. I'd been hiding my Disability identity for the most part, tripping over wires and bumping into the glass doors of vocal booths (my archenemy). But as industry folks started recognizing my talents, so grew my confidence. I figured what the hell, why not let folks know I've got vision loss and how they can accommodate me to get my very best performance at their session. So I did. Some studios made it their personal business to create an accommodating environment, but when I hit up larger organizations, productions, and venues on how they were addressing disability inclusion, I got the crickets. When COVID hit, I relied pretty heavily on my home studio, which I'd already pimped out for optimal productivity.

Then came May 2020 and the horrific brutality of George Floyd's death. I remember not sleeping for days on end, afraid to dream, fearing a lack of control in a country where I already felt like I had to apologize for existing. Then came Black Lives Matter, and then Black Disabled Lives Matter. And for the first time in my life, I started feeling unequivocally, unapologetically Black. I started feeling unapologetically Black disabled. It was the most in line and lockstep with my communities I had felt up to that point, and though I hadn't had any physical contact with anyone other than Arthur, a silent but raging fire within me had been kindled.

It started with me standing alone on a corner of my very white Upper East Side neighborhood every day at 5 p.m., holding a marker-written "Black, Trans, and Disabled Lives Matter" sign. While I got nasty stares, snide remarks, and the occasional chucked water bottle, I held my silent protest for about three weeks, until I started attracting press. I had zero interest in press involvement, so I changed gears. I began attending webinars on diversity and inclusion. Through the webinar chats and Discord/Clubhouse side sessions, I conjured up some impactful connections and conversations. I started to feel a real, visceral sense of community.

But while I was finding Black and female community, I wasn't finding Disability community. In my women's community, I didn't fit all the way in because I was Black. In my Black community, I didn't fit all the way in because of my vision loss. I needed *Black Disability* community, but settled on searching for Disability community. I began copying and pasting Wikipedia and CDC articles on disability—charts, infographics, and all—into webinar chats only to receive a tepid "Oh word?" from other attendees. When I pulled a chat takeover on a webinar put on by the global nonprofit Women in Music, someone high up noticed, and in September 2020 Women in Music asked me to moderate my first disability-centered music industry webinar.

Around that same time, I made my way onto the Recording Academy's New York Chapter Advocacy Committee thanks to boss lady, industry mentor, and committee co-chair Sharon Tapper. The committee advocates for music professionals with local officials and Congress. My first day on the committee, someone messed up and gave me the floor, so I shot my shot. I made my pitch, advocating for accessible spaces and a more disability-accommodating music industry. Sharon asked how I wanted to engage the chapter on the issue, and I said I'd love to do a virtual panel. "Put together a proposal," she said. After googling "How to put together a proposal," I did.

In April 2021, we put on that virtual panel exploring what the Recording Academy could do to support music creators and industry professionals with disabilities. I'd brought together some notable disabled music leaders to participate, including touring violinist and Broadway composer Gaelynn Lea, a wheelchair user, and the legendary Siedah Garrett, a Grammy Award–winning singer-songwriter with multiple sclerosis, among other panelists.

The panel was chaired by then–chief of diversity and inclusion of the Recording Academy Valeisha Butterfield Jones, moderated by yours truly, and streamed on the Grammys' national platforms. The event was well attended and flowed perfectly. We presented our perspectives, experiences, and asks passionately and authentically, eye to eye with the topmost leaders in the industry. At the end, Valeisha thanked us for the opportunity we'd given the Academy to learn and grow, and then said, "I'm listening. I've noted all of our action items. We are ready to get to work."

Wait, what?

Who was gonna hold a mammoth like the Recording Academy accountable for walking their talk? Us? After the panel, musicians and professionals from across the globe started flooding my DMs and inbox, saying things like "Lachi, this is exactly what we need. How can we join this movement?" or "Where can we learn more about your organization and about bringing disability inclusion to the music industry?"

Movement?

Organization?

But the fire had already been lit. Someone needed to catch the music industry up with disability inclusion. But did that someone have to be me? My longtime manager, Gary Salzman, had recently passed away because of COVID. I was just starting to regain my footing in the business. I didn't want to start a movement on top of all the recording, writing, and vocal producing gigs I was juggling to feed those hungry Upper East Side rent envelopes. Especially not a movement that no one before me had believed in enough to start themselves.

I went to bed, and when I woke up, the acronym RAMPD—Recording Artists and Music Professionals with Disabilities—was ping-ponging through my head like Suni Lee on the uneven bars. *Whoa.* Had the visionary fairy dropped a dust deuce in my ear while I slept? That was it. The spark. I knew I *had* to create RAMPD.

I didn't exactly know where to start, but to quote the great Celestine Tate Harrington, "When you are born without the use of your limbs and you have the will to overcome, you learn to improvise." So I did just that.

First I called Judy "Queen of Organizing" Heumann. After some small talk, during which I hooked her up with some styling tips and designers for her Oscars look, I finally asked her how to start an organization. Her comeback was classic Judy: "Call all your friends. Now you have an organization." Copy that.

I started with the folks from the panel, then turned to the Clubhouse app to connect with more disabled music professionals. After speaking with nearly fifty folks one-on-one about music industry access issues, I noticed that everyone was singing a variation of the same two tunes: *isolation* and *stigma*. I thought, *How come all fifty of us are feeling isolated? Let's get together!*

That led to biweekly Zoom meetings. We were passionate disabled and neurodivergent songwriters, producers, instrumentalists, and industry-side professionals who were excited, awake, and ready. Word got out, and groups like the National Independent Venue Association, Women in Music, and of course, the Recording Academy began offering us a platform to get our message out. Clearly, we needed to put RAMPD together and fast. It wasn't just artists and industry folk who wanted this. The big guys, the labels, and the trade associations were tapping in.

This was 2021, so when people weren't talking Lil Nas X, *Squid Game*, or #FreeBritney, they were talking DEI. But still, no one in the industry was talking accessibility. Why would they? It's expensive, uncomfortable, and kinda sad, right? Then from out of the shadows emerges this self-assured, competitive group of real cats putting together a disability-centered power-building platform—for the industry by the industry—that's about everything *but* the inspiration trope. The corporate music world flocked to us like a babysitter to Cocomelon. It was go time!

We were receiving grants before we even had a bank account and quickly put together an executive body. By January 2022 the RAMPD website—built with accessible-first design—was live and we had a mechanism for new members to join. A live-streamed online launch event on January 22 coproduced by Gae-lynn Lea and me did the trick, along with live music, words of endorsement from prominent partners, and opening and closing remarks live from the Grammy Museum Experience at the Prudential Center in Newark, New Jersey.

Hundreds attended the live stream with a couple thousand trickling in shortly after. The whole thing, from concept to carry-out, went so undeniably well, amplifying our talent, solidarity, mission, and joy, that *The New York Times* covered it. *Billboard* followed, and then *The Hollywood Reporter.* As the coverage flooded in, so did inquiries about memberships and partnerships.

It's still hard to believe that everything came together so fast. The Recording Academy panel happened in April 2021. By April 2022, the Recording Academy became RAMPD's first official partner, collaborating with us on highly visible disability-inclusive measures at the 64th Annual Grammy Awards.

We advised them on how to make the awards ceremony more accessible to and inclusive of all disabilities. We advocated for audio description and captioning, a visibly accessible stage (the circular, ramp-accessible dais that's now a staple of the show), ramps throughout the media areas, and most notably, American Sign Language on the red carpet—which made for some nice viral moments and subsequent write-ups. Oh, and did I mention that during this time, I was burning the other end of the candle on a thesis for my master's degree in music technology at New York University? (By the way, apart from my NYU thesis on tech access for blind producers and engineers, there are only a handful of studies on the intersection of music and disability in the U.S.) Either way, I'll sleep when I'm dead.

We built up our client and partner catalogs; got early grants from the likes of the Ford Foundation's Creativity and Free Expression fund, Borealis, and the Loreen Arbus Foundation; received recognition from the U.N.'s Zero Project, Adcolor, *Ad Age*, and the Music Business Association; and received the Judith Heumann Innovation & Entrepreneurship Award from 2Gether-International, all while growing our member numbers. Today we've supported over one hundred of our peer-vetted professional members—those vetted as working professionals in the industry—and serve more than one thousand of our community members in more than a dozen countries, offering industry opportunities, resources, networking events, and visibility with and through our industry partners. Talk about a wild ride!

That's how RAMPD became a thing. By the 2023 Grammys, *The Hollywood Reporter* described us as "a global network of talent and industry." A *global* network! Makes me sound like a James Bond villain. By the 2024 Grammys, we had wheelchairs, Glam Canes, and prosthetics gracing the official red carpets and had collaborated or consulted with dozens of major music entities, including Live Nation, Netflix, Tidal, the National Association of Music Merchants (NAMM), and the Country Music Association. After I snagged the Adcolor Innovator of the Year Award, Adcolor and Disney even displayed my face and the RAMPD name on a digital billboard in Times Square. (There's something surreal about a blind woman looking over the city, something very "Mwahaha!")

By the 2025 Grammys, we were at it again, bringing sign language to the red carpet and, for the first time ever, to the Premiere Ceremony (a special presentation where the majority of the night's awards are given out), while getting our professional membership onto the Recording Academy governing boards. We'd put on massive DisCo (Disability Community) House parties offering swanky industry crip spaces from New York to L.A. RAMPD is a bona fide industry leader, supporting music creators and industry professionals by equipping the music and live entertainment ecosystem with disability-inclusive solutions, resources, and programming.

Big Diʃ Energy

Any entrepreneur will recognize the beats of this story. An opportunity to solve a problem. A heavily compressed timeline. Crushing feats you didn't know you could crush. Mentors and besties stepping up to support. Flying the helicopter while gluing on the propellers. Pop quiz time! Ready? An entrepreneur is:

A. Someone who sees an unmet need and creates something to meet it.

B. Someone willing to take the risks needed to turn a product or an idea into a business.

C. Someone who recognizes their physical or neurodivergent differences as unique assets and leans in.

D. All of the above.

By now, y'all know me well enough to know the answer is D. A BBC Bitesize article posits that the four characteristics of any competitive entrepreneur are creativity, risk-taking, determination, and confidence. Kelsey Miller's 2020 Harvard Business School article on entrepreneurship adds adaptability and focus to that list—and we all know how I feel about a high adversity quotient. These traits combine to create the type of visionary personality capable of founding and leading a successful venture. But to me, being adaptable, determined, creative, and focused are innate to anyone who leans into their Disability identity. That's that Big Dis Energy.

Entrepreneurship is one of the most lucrative, accessible options for work-age hustlers with disabilities. It turns out, many celebrated C-suite executives, tech entrepreneurs, and visionary innovators are disabled or neurodivergent. Apple founder Steve Jobs navigated his way through life with dyslexia, as did Henry Ford and Ingvar Kamprad, the late founder of IKEA. Paul Orfalea, founder of Kinko's, has ADD, as does Justin Timberlake, while David Neeleman, founder of JetBlue, famously celebrates the benefits of his ADHD. Then there's my good friend Louis Posen, CEO of Hopeless Records, one of the most successful independent record labels in punk rock history. He is blind.

Okay. We're all thinking it. *Damn, Gina, that's a lot of straight white guys. How about some page space for some women, some color, and some queerfolk?* I got you. There's a growing cadre of disabled and neurodivergent entrepreneurs and leaders across the identity spectrum kicking ass, taking names, and bringing receipts. Dona Sarkar, chief engineer at Microsoft (women in STEM, let's gooo!), and Emma Grede, cofounder and CEO of clothing brand Good American, are open about their dyslexia. Gena Harper—cross-country skier, rock climber, and former senior VP at Morgan Stanley—attributes her success to the focus and drive her blindness has given her. Google's global head of disability innovation, KR Liu, recognizes her hearing loss as an advantage, a sentiment that also rings true for Caroline Casey, the founder and executive behind the Valuable 500, who takes pride in her vision loss. Proudly disabled and queer, Andrew Gurza is the founder and CEO at Bump'n, a popular sex toy brand by and for disabled people. Sangita Desai was born with missing digits, and after 2006 floods destroyed her busy Mumbai fashion design studio, she pivoted toward her innate entrepreneurial talents and cofounded Raw Nature, India's largest all-natural cosmetics brand.

Now let's go Black. Grammy Award–winning empire builder Will.I.Am, reality TV and music icon Ray J, and Dr. Raven the Science Maven have all attributed aspects of their success to their ADHD. Ruby Taylor—founder and CEO of Financial Joy School, a platform successfully building generational wealth for Black and Brown families—credits her stuttering and brain injury for shaping her trajectory. Harvard MBA Jessica O. Matthews, a multi-patented inventor with lupus, is founder and CEO of sustainable infrastructure company Uncharted.

This list wouldn't be complete without Daymond John, the force behind FUBU (For Us, By Us), the international brand and groundbreaking hip-hop fashion movement. A series-regular judge on *Shark Tank*, John has spoken openly about his dyslexia and how it drove him to think beyond the ordinary. More recently, he developed hearing loss, and in a spirit of fashion-forward Disability Pride, said of his hearing aids, "I wear red hearing aids because I want people to ask me about them. Normally, hearing aids are flesh tone and blend in. My custom red ones stick out, and that's why I love them." Dude, I 100 percent relate.

Dang, Lachi, that is a fire list. Exactly! It proves unequivocally that a disability does not preclude someone from being a kick-ass innovator or wealth creator. In fact, an openly acknowledged well-accommodated Disability identity can actually *enhance* people's entrepreneurial badassery. That's that Big Dis Energy. Let's talk about it.

As a blind neurodivergent woman, I've always had to be crafty, driven, and hyperfocused just to keep up. I was undeterred by the "nos." I worked to turn them into "not yets" while wielding a sharp Big Dis Energy sword—and a fierce Big Dis Energy team. And when I wanted to interview someone about running a driven disability-led team, I immediately thought of Jenny Lay-Flurrie, chief accessibility officer at Microsoft. Jenny, who is deaf and hilarious, started our Zoom call talking about how time tends to butt in and toss on disabilities as we age, and about how her proudly autistic daughter never fails to slay.

She then segued into how on her watch Microsoft has become more welcoming for employees with disabilities, with a self-identification rate of 9 percent—twice the national rate of corporate disability self-identification, according to Disability:IN. This was exciting to hear, as RAMPD has worked with the Recording Academy to include self-identifying disability questions in the questionnaire it sends out to its membership of more than fifteen thousand music industry leaders.

Then I asked her whether leaning into accessibility has made Microsoft more successful. Her simple answer? "Yes." Then she elaborated.

"The mission of this company is to empower every person and every organization to achieve more," Jenny said. "That's the mission that we ground to every day. One of the truest gifts I've had is that this isn't just me banging a drum. Satya, the CEO, is actually the sponsor of the disability employee resource group. He's a member of our gang, he's an ally, he's a parent of a kiddo, and I've had the honor and pleasure of working with him since 2012 on this topic. Then you go through the organization all the way from top to bottom.

"Every single person here is grounded to and talks about publicly and internally why this matters and how it's making a difference," she went on. "This is a company movement. It has garnered hearts and minds, and it enables us to work with customers and empowers them to do the same thing because this technology ends up in their hands. Our best practices—whatever we learn, we publish. Then we consume what's out there, so it is a cyclical learning motion.

"I want to see more people in accessibility. I want to see more people with my job title," Jenny concluded. "Remediating isn't the right way to do accessibility. We need to build it right from the start and learn how to do inclusive designs and embedded accessibility. Yes, we're a big company, but any company can and should be doing this. A lot of these tools are free. It's a thinking and a culture that you need to embed and grow. We've got big goals. I really want to change the disability divide. This gap in societal inclusion is prevalent and real, and I think we've got a part to play in changing that."

Jenny's words made it clear to me that not only are companies with big footprints—like Microsoft—key players in convincing more people to self-identify with disability, helping end stigma, but that working on accessibility also makes them engines for innovation. "One of the other things I run is the Ability Summit. That one started with twenty people," she said. "It's grown over the years, to the point where we had it in March this year and had seventeen thousand people attend. There are so many people invested and interested in this space who are looking to learn more, be an ally, be inclusive, and who just want to nerd out. This area is cool, and we know the interest is there in creating a culture where you can see yourself.

"We always start off by telling everyone, 'Disability is all around us,'" Jenny finished. "It's stuff you may not realize. It's cancer, it's lupus, it's dyspraxia, it's ADHD, it's mono. It's Ehlers-Danlos syndrome, it's anxiety, it's PTSD. This is bigger than you think . . . and we consider this a strength and an asset. Your lived experience is going to inform what we do."

Safe to say businesses and their bottom lines need more Jenny Lay-Flurries.

The Curb-Cut Effect

Tables, chairs, and clothing were all once forward-thinking adaptive solutions. Products originally created for people who navigate the world differently tend to be the most innovative and also tend to benefit everyone, regardless of their Disability identity. For example, audiobooks (originally Talking Books) were designed to enable blind folks who couldn't read Braille (fewer than 10 percent of blind folks do read Braille) to enjoy trashy romance novels. Text-to-speech, cruise control, and the motorized scooter were all created by and for disabled people. Then there's this thing called the internet, which has proved sorta useful. Well, thank Vint Cerf, the deaf engineer who cocreated ARPANet, the precursor to the internet, for the Department of Defense back in the 1960s. He's frequently called the "father of the internet" and is still with us in his eighties, so you might want to drop him an Amazon gift card or something as a thank-you.

And of course, curb cuts, which make it easier for everybody—walking, wheeling, pushing a stroller, pulling a rolling suitcase, or locomoting by any other means—to navigate sidewalk corners. They came about after World War II, when disabled veteran and lawyer Jack Fisher installed the first one in Kalamazoo, Michigan, to help other disabled vets and anyone with a disability manage curbs. This innovation inspired its own concept, the curb-cut effect. Coined by Angela Glover Blackwell, the phrase describes when features originally designed to be accessible to people with disabilities are used by and beneficial to a wider group of people.

As Dr. Joshua Miele, Ph.D., a blind adaptive technology designer and winner of a 2021 MacArthur Genius grant, says, "Disability drives innovation. It's undeniable." Josh developed a software called Tactile Maps Automated Production (TMAP), which generates tactile street maps that can be printed with at-home Braille embossers. He even designed a set of tactile maps for every station of San Francisco's BART rail system, making it compatible with an audio smart pen, allowing blind travelers to virtually explore and plan their routes.

People who navigate through the world creatively are uniquely suited to entrepreneurship and are top-notch innovators for the same reason we're resilient in the face of unnerving obstacles: We have to be. It's just what disabled people do. We MacGyver that shit. We adapt, and we keep it moving. We're masters at thinking around corners, and we have hustle baked into our DNA. We're used to challenge, rejection, and solving problems from a unique perspective. These are all traits that make for an ideal entrepreneur.

Imagine what we could do as a society if that resilience and that adaptive, problem-solving mentality were applied to all things in life on a daily basis, to serve everyone's needs. One example: In the summer of 2024, the K. Lisa Yang Center for Bionics at MIT announced that they had developed bionic prosthetic limbs that some amputees can control with their brains—and their lead scientist, Hugh Herr, is a double amputee. If we just brought that consistent, rapid-fire innovative sauce that comes with the Disability identity to the world of technology, life-changing inventions could be prototyped, tested, and released to the public in one year, not ten.

Don't Hate, Accommodate

With the right resources, entrepreneurship and small business ownership can be a more viable path to economic empowerment for doers with disabilities than the working-for-the-man route. A 2024 Department of Labor article, "Business Ownership, Self-Employment and Entrepreneurship Among People with Disabilities," maintains that entrepreneurship and self-employment offer unique benefits to people with disabilities, including greater access, independence, flexibility at work, economic stability, and the opportunity to reduce or eliminate traditional workplace barriers.

However, entrepreneurship is not the path for everyone. In an ideal world, the traditional workplace would value the uptick in productivity, retention, and reputation points that comes with an inclusive culture, allowing employees with disabilities and neurodivergence to openly identify as such, customize the optimal environment they need to work effectively, and find purpose and wellness in the place where they spend most of their good hours. But this would take businesses viewing the disability experience as an asset, recognizing accommodations—including remote work—as a core value, and investing in ongoing, culturally inclusive training.

There are some pretty swank nontraditional workplaces, some with hybrid and remote options, and others embracing assistive AI tools like predictive text, voice recognition, and adaptive interfaces. But unfortunately the typical workplace these days is no five-star experience for anyone, especially someone identifying as disabled. The post-COVID "quiet quit" storm is proof. Many work environments don't suit anyone's needs, let alone those with a disabled or neurodivergent body-mind or a chronic or mental health condition. Say you've got to commute to a physical location by any means necessary (whether you've got to swim or tightrope-walk, ain't no mountain high enough), get up to a thirtieth-floor office, and then deal with interpersonal workplace theatrics, politics, and *Sister Wives*–level drama. Given all this, it's a tall order for someone to drum up enough mental fortitude to maintain that innovative self-starterish-ness they had on day one. And then having to code-switch or camouflage on top of all that? Nondisabled, neurotypical people aren't even feeling it, so imagine the added barriers and negative attitudes for workers with disabilities.

Case in point: I came across this 2023 Reddit post the other day: "I was in McDonald's today and a customer was complaining that most of the sauce was on the outside of the burger. He asks for a new burger. The guy who made his burger then hands him his new burger and he's clearly disabled. Idk if it was dyspraxia or something, but he didn't have fine motor control in his hands. Anyway I overhear the customer saying to his wife, 'People like that shouldn't be allowed to work here.'"

I'll bet you five McBucks that the guy who made the burger was not made to feel comfortable asking for assistive devices or any other accommodations because of the watchful eye of the grievance model. Instead, he had to stiff-upper-lip it through the stares, comments, and exclusion from customers and coworkers alike, then traverse home through an inaccessible transit system. Pardon my French, as I'm a little rusty, but *fudge that!* People with disabilities are not the problem. We're the problem solvers. To that McDonald's employee, let's you and me start Saucy Burgers and give McDonald's a run for its McMoney.

Many of the 160-plus comments under that Reddit post were from disabled and neurodivergent folks validating the experience of the McDonald's worker. I get it. I, too, was once a nine-to-fiver. As I'd talked about on PBS's *Stories from the Stage*, despite my love for music, I was encouraged to walk the safe, day-job path. I worked at the U.S. Army Corps of Engineers for more than three years, but while I excelled at the job, I was very much unfulfilled. Though I kept my head down and my mouth shut, I was routinely singled out not just for being a woman and being Black, but for being not quite normal. Senior colleagues and management would ridicule or chide me for things like my hair, my clothes, or (my favorite) "getting an attitude." *Homey, I haven't said two words since I got here three years ago!*

Back in the 2010s, I didn't have words like *ableism* or *misogynoir* (the unique, racially enhanced gender discrimination faced by

Black women) in my lexicon, but I *did* know that somehow I felt both overwatched yet ignored, unacknowledged yet a burden, admonished for not speaking up yet also admonished for my consistently misconstrued self-advocacy. I *did* know that my unmet accommodation requests were keeping me from doing what I loved: succeeding.

I *did* know that looking in the mirror and not seeing a creative and bright jokester reflected back felt wrong. I *did* know that being made to write an official apology to a white senior male staffer for provoking *him* to yell at me in front of the entire office (mind you, this was back in my shy and silent days) meant it was time to pack my four Commander's coins and bounce. The moment I quit, my life began. I redefined what power meant to me. And now here I am. A proud, decorated artist and CEO, occasionally showing up at the White House, winning lifetime achievement awards, and hanging with celebrities and world leaders, simply because one day I decided to recognize my worth.

Disability-Owned

Entrepreneurship is an accessible, flexible path for free thinkers, problem solvers, and people who prefer to design their optimal productivity environment. Disabled entrepreneurs are clearly built to live that lifestyle. We just need opportunity. So why don't we get it?

A big obstacle is *stigma*. Disabled people don't fit the cookie-cutter image of what an entrepreneur looks like: a ruthless, independent tech go-getter (usually white or Asian and male) who, when he's not elbow-deep in the Silicon Valley start-up grind at

Y Combinator, is knee-deep in ketamine-fueled number crunching. We're not who the average investor sees when they close their eyes and picture Joe Entrepreneur, so our ideas don't get a hearing.

In 2022, the Kauffman Foundation published a paper that showed not only that women-, Black-, and Latine-owned businesses each receive less than 3 percent of available venture capital but also that data on funding for entrepreneurs with disabilities doesn't even exist. The Disability & Philanthropy Forum estimated that foundations only invest one tenth of one cent out of every grant-making dollar on disability rights and social justice. Despite the obvious value we bring and how hard we work to bring it, founders leaning in on disability often remain excluded from the investment and grantee ecosystem.

But now imagine a thriving, disability-embracing middle class that leverages its problem-solving prowess to steer capitalism in the direction of an authentic, diverse, and equitable system. What if there was a resource that could help side-hustlers with disabilities leave dependency behind and acquire the skills and knowledge to chase their entrepreneurial dreams without the need for ketamine? (Unless you're into that. Judgment-free zone here.)

There is. I give you . . . 2Gether-International.

Diego Mariscal, the founder of 2Gether-International—the leading accelerator serving entrepreneurs with disabilities—has supported more than one hundred disability-led start-ups that have raised more than $81 million, and has been changing the game since 2012. Born with cerebral palsy, Diego is a tireless champion for entrepreneurs with disabilities.

Diego and I were both Judy Heumann disciples and became friends after I participated in 2GI's BIPOC cohort. So I was determined to speak with him for this book. We spoke over Zoom about his background growing up in Mexico, and then we pivoted to disability and entrepreneurship. "A lot of my work focuses on how we foster Disability Pride and identity in service of entrepreneurship or as a means to entrepreneurship," he said. "For me, success looks like an entrepreneur with a disability not only thriving in their respective field but also leaning into their disability as a source of strength, inspiration, and resilience. I think that's where Disability community and Disability Pride intersect with entrepreneurship."

He continued, "Yet the entrepreneurship community and the innovation community don't yet recognize disability as a source of innovation, creativity, and frankly, some of the most groundbreaking innovations in the world. The fact that it is not recognized that way—rather, it's recognized as something that needs to be cured or fixed, very much the medical model—puts a huge burden on disabled entrepreneurs. Not only do we have to convince investors and funders about the market, but also about our own skill level and capabilities as founders."

Diego went on to say that he often has to coach people in his accelerators to ask for more money. (That wasn't exactly a problem for me—I got ninety-nine problems, but hesitating to ask for "Is she serious?" amounts of money ain't one.) "Oftentimes, we go to pitches and we'll have founders come in asking for ten thousand or twenty thousand dollars, when you have nondisabled people asking for a minimum of a quarter million," Diego said. "And it's because they can't fathom asking for what they really need."

But Diego's most revealing statement came when he spoke about how fitting the image of an entrepreneur means swimming upstream against your own internalized ableism. "Oftentimes [entrepreneurs] don't lean into their disabilities because it's seen as something that will get in the way of success. That's why a lot of the things that we do through 2Gether programming is to say, 'Lean into your disability as a source of strength and a source of power, rather than as something that needs to be fixed or cured.'"

Amen.

Fortunately, things are starting to change for the better. Conversations about finding ways a disabled entrepreneur can lean in with their chest out are being had at the federal level. A bill—S.3528, the Supporting Disabled Entrepreneurs Act—was introduced into the Senate in late 2023, sponsored by New Hampshire Democratic senator Jeanne Shaheen.

Yay, look at us! We're part of the Deep State!

Caps and Gaps

RAMPD's fast growth was due to a combination of risk-taking, adaptability, and creative vision, alongside a strong "no" tolerance; an energized, well-maintained network; and a passionate, disability-empowered team. When the RAMPD snowball started avalanching down the mountain, a lot of people wanted us to slow down. Instead, we doubled down.

We weren't like anything out there. RAMPD doesn't serve the Disability community; it serves the music industry as a professional Disability Culture consultancy group and affinity network. It is disability-led, with no caregivers or parents holding any staff-level or member-level decision-making power, though they can totally support or get involved tangentially.

As disability advocate Emma Farley commented on one of my LinkedIn posts, "When nondisabled people continue to hold power, even if they involve disabled people in the process, it suggests a reluctance to relinquish the control and benefits that come with their privileged position . . . ultimate decisions are still made by those who are not directly affected by the issues at hand." RAMPD is here to power-build. So we only hire and support the professional with the disability or neurodivergence.

When the industry sees RAMPD, they see a growing music industry staple connecting, developing, and prioritizing authentic, competitive talent while granting them the opportunity to jump on board the Disability Culture revolution. For instance, we run songwriting camps and industry accelerators for members. For partners, we offer trainings and a suite of resources that help ensure that a venue, festival, artist team, or music industry entity is culturally disability-inclusive, is accommodation- and sensory-friendly, and values an accessible and safe environment for their staff and all members of the music ecosystem.

We also offer hands-on support in getting our professional members out to music conferences, festivals, and hobnob galas to keynote, panel, or perform through our Ambassadors on DEC (Disability Equity and Culture) program. This brings RAMPD and the professionals greater visibility, offers them career development and opportunities, and fosters disability inclusion and awareness at the event. It's a win-win-win.

While it's an honor to be able to support music creators with various conditions in this way, we've also witnessed firsthand the difficulties some really dope artists face on their journey to financial stability. Similarly to Diego, I found that the main big bad barrier to entry is that same systematically conditioned fear of money that many within the disabled population feel.

What? Who wouldn't want money? Well, at the time of this writing, a good number of Americans with state-defined disabilities receive a government-subsidized income through the Social Security Administration that puts a cap on how much income that person can earn before becoming ineligible for Medicaid. *Institutionalized dependency* is one of the big hurdles for building wealth as a disabled person. I've seen fierce performers turn down lucrative gigs, fearing that if they earn too much, they won't be able to get their meds, they'll lose their home health aide, or they'll run out of oxygen. They're trapped in the cycle. But if they didn't have to choose between wealth and health, some of those same talented, educated folks could lift themselves into the middle class.

Two bills—S.2767, the SSI Savings Penalty Elimination Act, introduced in the Senate in 2023; and H.R.7138, the Supplemental Security Income Restoration Act, introduced in the House in 2024—would bring about some much-needed reform to this system and work to dismantle this cycle. Dear Government, get it together, and act now.

Still, most Americans on the disability and neurodivergent spectrums don't receive government disability benefits, according to a 2022 Social Security Administration report, and as we've discussed, even more don't recognize or identify with their disability. So where does this "income anxiety" come from? Mostly from a collective internalized ableism that whispers *You're not worthy of wealth* and keeps us from taking the big-girl risks.

Tiffany Yu—who, apart from being a vocal Disability Pride advocate, is also the founder of Diversability and a RAMPD Advisory Board member—and I are in the same boat here, because we're entrepreneurs who generate income for our businesses and aren't afraid to celebrate it. Through Diversability, Tiffany works to empower both the disabled and nondisabled ecosystems to see that they're worthy of the same access to work, money, life, liberty, and the pursuit of decadent, chocolate-level luxury.

Finally, some within the disabled population avoid wealth because they've been conditioned to believe they must play the charity card to receive opportunities, or, on the flip side, they fear being accused of taking advantage of the system. I get it. People be judgy. Those who throw side-eye generally tend to be the ones who see me strutting down fancy streets, being interviewed on fancy shows, or speaking at a fancy gala, and think, *A disabled person should be poor and pissed off, not better off than I am, so I'm not into it.* How dare I be bold, loud, flashy, and proud?

This is why platforms that offer power-building paths to financial freedom for disabled entrepreneurs are super important in our mission to achieve Disability liberation. Apart from 2Gether-International, other disability-powered entrepreneurial accelerators include Synergies Work, Remarkable Accelerator Program in Australia, Access to Success in Canada, and the Global Disability Innovation Hub, which offers global support. This is what change looks like, and it's just the beginning.

Investment in disability-led entrepreneurial ventures is crucial. We are the ones on the ground, moving to shift the stigmatized narrative of disability, so that when folks inevitably dive into the deep end and join our ranks, the water will be just fine. Designing with disability in mind is universally beneficial, and we—the designers, entrepreneurs, and inventors with those disabilities—are best poised to understand the problem and how to solve it, and we have the passion to follow through. All we need are the right people, the right resources, and the ripe opportunity.

So, dear venture capitalist, invest in us. The Disability community is driven, persistent, and perceptive because we play this game every day at boss level. I'm not saying, *Help us fit in.* I'm saying, *Recognize our big-ass differences as big-ass assets.* Those who aspire to fit into a mold may make it to "mediocre," but we disabled folk don't do mediocre. Outsiders, mavericks, and visionaries have always been our culture-shifters and change-makers, the ones moving innovation forward. They are us. We are who historians will write about.

Chapter Seven

The Drama with Big Trauma

My mother says I began my music journey in the womb. Where other babies would kick, I played the keys against her stomach. I have no idea how I had a keyboard in there, but I've since taken Mom's word for it.

For the more conventional take on my start in music, it began when a guitar player and I opted to head down to South by Southwest back in 2009 to play a small side-street gig we booked on our own just to be a part of the hullabaloo. Now a hangout for corporate suits and AI evangelists, SXSW was once a vibrant indie music mega-festival in Austin, Texas, where up-and-coming bands got discovered overnight. Before heading down, I cold-emailed a pageful of record label executives, informing them of my non–main stage performance, urging them to check me out if they happened to be in town, knowing full well that's not how the industry works. But this story wouldn't be in this book if one of the execs hadn't shown up, which—you guessed it—he did.

After the guitarist and I finished pouring our hearts out for a daytime half-empty Austin hole-in-the-wall, a label A&R (artists and repertoire) manager walked up to us and said, "I love what you're doing. Call me when you're back in New York," and handed me a card. Between me being low vision and the guitarist being totally blind, it took us a while to figure the whole card thing out. It turned out he worked at an imprint under then-major label EMI Records. This was big! Not long after, I was a signed artist.

I put a band together—some folks from the local blind community—we recorded an album, and we started touring. The other shoe dropped when I found I was being marketed as "blind singer Lachi," and everyone from fans to blogs began describing me as brave and courageous, and praising me for overcoming some thing or another. (For many people navigating an inaccessible world, courage is a necessity, not a compliment. Saying "You're so brave" to someone for just existing is giving me thick layers of *Aw, your struggle is so cute*.) Some articles even mixed up my disability, describing me as deaf, because my actual Disability identity didn't matter.

I spoke to the label about not liking this PR angle. The term *inspiration porn* hadn't hit the streets yet, but it all felt very "bless-her-heart." I was talented and didn't need to pull at people's heartstrings for them to enjoy my art. But the label insisted they knew what they were doing. Eventually, I decided I was done and dipped out. I would not return to music in a significant way for a couple of years, adamant that I would never speak again about my disability.

But don't you talk about your Disability identity all the time? You are Lachi, right? Yes. After a lot of work and Rhonda Byrne–level visualization, I was able to overcome not my disability, but the ableism, the charity-case narrative, reshaping my own story from a place of power, strength, and pride.

Fast-forward to the spring of 2024. I spoke at a conference in Los Angeles that centered on LGBTQIA+ folks in the music industry. I knocked the talk out of the park, and at the after-party these two young women started following me around, sticking to me like Ben Affleck to Matt Damon, firing off questions like "How do you walk around in those heels? Where did you get that sparkly cane? Who picks out your clothes for you?" With Arthur's help, I deflected them as good-naturedly as possible while praying someone, anyone, would get these girls a stiff drink, no ice. Instead, they cornered me the second Arthur disappeared to use the men's room.

Being an out-and-proud blind New Yorker, I've taken home the gold more than once in the "Smile While People Say Uninformed Things to the Disabled Person" Olympics, so my spidey sense told me these young women were about to step over the line from enthusiastic to cringe. One of them tossed off a compliment about my nails, so I replied, "Why, thank you. I think this conversation is going quite well."

To which the woman said, "How can you tell this conversation is going well if you can't see me?"

The telenovela camera zooms on my flabbergasted face. *Really?* My shoulder angel tapped me and whispered, *Don't say it. Don't say it.*

But of course I said it, no prodding from my shoulder demon necessary. Flashing my famously charming wit, I quipped, "I can tell it's going well because you're not punching me in the face, stealing my purse, and running off to a getaway car."

As if on cue and without a clue, the other woman chimed in. "So you can just feel and hear people's reactions and automatically *know* what to say and do next? How do you do that?" *Aaand facepalm.*

It's called being in a conversation, y'all! She was equating me to some kind of mystical being with supernatural powers—Blind Girl Magic, if you will. Bruh. I'm not automatically a mythical oracle because I'm blind. Everything I do, say, and predict is correct because I'm an *Aries.*

All kidding aside, in a way, I get it. They had just witnessed me, a successful blind woman, deliver a smart, effervescent speech filled with positivity, empathy, and pride, and it fried their circuitry. They couldn't process that a blind person could build a happy, fulfilling life by working hard, getting good at my craft, and being all-around tenacious, so the only alternative had to be that I was a glammed-out magical Tinker Bell making fairy-tale dreams come true with just one wave of my magical cane.

By now we've spent a fair amount of time together and sorta become ride-or-dies. If I've done my job, your nerve endings have become attuned to unconscious ableism and are standing on end. Because underneath is an unspoken, unacknowledged belief: *Disabled people don't get to be average people, even though the average person interacts with disability all the time.*

Not every disabled person is jumping out of planes. (Again, I did it because I'm an *Aries.*) Most folks with apparent disabilities long to be seen as average, mundane, middle-of-the-road students, professionals, or moms and dads. As long as we are afforded the basic accommodations we need to navigate the world independently and with dignity, we all just want to do our laundry, go to work, raise our kids, argue over politics, and lie awake for nights on end wondering how the hell Idris Elba only ranked number six on the UK's 2024 "Sexiest Men Alive" list.

But the reality is, there's coin to be made, virtue to be signaled, donors to be tear-jerked, and Hallmark originals to be green-lit, all off charity narratives and trauma tropes. We can't have "normal" disabled people out here being ordinary commuters, office workers, lawyers, and baristas. We have to push every cultural lever at our disposal—television, movies, music, books—to make sure that whenever someone encounters a disabled or neurodivergent person, the person gets the pity feels, the "they're so braves," or the stop-and-stares. From corny news article headlines to popular Groupon experiences like "Dining in the Dark" and "Dialogue in the Dark," the powers that be seem to be selling a certain disability narrative.

(Have you heard of these Groupon experiences? Companies are out here offering blindness simulations. This involves blindfolding oneself to experience what it's like to be blind. While it is designed to foster empathy, it exploits the trauma of *going* blind right then and there, rather than demonstrating the fully fleshed-out lived experience of *being* a blind citizen.)

Now hold up, isn't empathy a good thing? Yes. But this is *disploitation*, a term I use to describe when third parties try to capitalize on the disability experience by portraying it as a trauma trigger. The goal of disploitation is to evoke not empathy, but *sympathy*. Empathy involves understanding someone else's situation and often results in support. Sympathy is a sense of "there but for the grace of God go I" relief that you're not the one in that situation, and it leads to othering. When someone rains down well-meaning-but-deleterious sympathy, they're implying that living with a disability is like being Sisyphus forever trudging up the hill with an immense boulder and no carabiner clip. *Incorrecto.*

(Speaking of mythological figures, Hephaestus, the Greek god of artisans, blacksmiths, sculpture, and volcanoes, walks with a limp. Norse god Odin rocks one eye. Ebisu, one of the Seven Lucky Gods in Japanese mythology, has cerebral palsy and hearing loss. Sedna, the Inuit goddess of the sea, has no fingers. No word on whether Mount Olympus is accessible, though.)

Having a disability is nothing more or less than experiencing the world in a different way from someone who does not live with that condition. My blindness isn't about my limited vision; it's about the different way I experience the world and people around me. A person who is hard of hearing has their own unique experience of the world, as does someone who has asthma or on-again, off-again back pain. Our experiences are often richer and more authentic than those of someone who does not recognize or acknowledge their own Disability identity.

But that's not how the folks dog-paddling through the mainstream narrative ocean see disability. In the eyes of mainstream culture, if you're a blind person, especially a blind Black woman, and if your life is anything but tragic, you *must* be some sort of mystical savant. Those are the rules. It can't be that you've worked to develop your skills, find accommodation, self-advocate, seize opportunities, and build a comfortable life. These two narrow lanes of disploitation—inspiration porn and trauma trope—are how disabled and neurodivergent people are widely portrayed, and they're so visceral that people are willing to open their wallets to make the guilt and other icky feelings go away.

The irony is that most people whose lives openly intersect with disability are average Joes who live in an invisible third lane where they're just going about their daily business, trying to get by in a world not quite built for them. This applies to anyone with any condition under the vast disability umbrella, including anyone who denies, doesn't understand, or is unaware of their Disability identity, has had a temporary disability, or cares for someone with a disability. That third lane beyond inspiration porn and trauma trope is the one the folks who make the rules don't want you to know about when it comes to the disability narratives they're peddling.

By the way, who makes the rules? Who creates the disploitation industrial complex in which the masses are manipulated into paying away pity? Those would be the folks I call "Big Trauma."

Big Trauma

Starting in 1966 and going all the way to 2014, millions of Americans, too struck with food comas from their Labor Day weekend barbecues to venture outdoors, would settle in front of their TVs with a cold one for the annual spectacle of saccharine celebrity charity antics known as the Jerry Lewis Labor Day Muscular Dystrophy Association Telethon. Trigger warning: cringe.

Picture a glittering stage adorned with more sequins than King Tut's wardrobe (yes, homeboy was dripping in gold sequins, henny) and a roll call of A- to Z-list celebrities awkwardly yet shamelessly pitching viewers to give and give generously. The ringmaster of the pageantry was Jerry Lewis himself, hamming it up like a Vegas lounge act, getting more and more tearful (and, I suspect, more inebriated) as the twenty-one-and-a-half-hour live broadcast went on. Back in the 1950s, Lewis was a bankable comedy actor, but gradually, he became all about inspiring people to "Save Jerry's Kids."

As part of the telethon, a steady parade of kids with muscular dystrophy would file onto the stage using walkers or wheelchairs. Jerry would prop the kids in front of the TV cameras and dare the viewing audience not to pick up their phones and donate to the Muscular Dystrophy Association (MDA), which would use the funds to find a cure and *definitely* not to pay for private jets to the Augusta National Golf Club. The kids would smile gamely while (I assume) they itched to get out of the klieg lights and away from the creepy dude in the tux and back to watching *He-Man* or playing with Etch-a-Sketches or whatever kids did before iPads.

Was there ever any meaningful dialogue during those broadcasts about what it was like to build a career or raise a family while living with the condition? Not that I know of. I *do* know that network executives flooded TVs around the globe with these Jerry's Kids, tugging at the sympathy wallet and raking in that cold, hard charity cash.

In 1981, Evan Kemp Jr., a then White House official who lived with muscular atrophy, was the first to criticize MDA's fundraising strategy, writing in *The New York Times* that the use of a "pity appeal" using poster children encouraged "stereotypes that offend our self-respect and harm our efforts to live independent lives." In 1991, a group named Jerry's Orphans, led by Mike Ervin, a former Jerry's Kid, began protesting the telethon, denouncing the use of pity narratives and the lack of disability representation within the leadership of the MDA.

In a 1990 essay for *Parade* magazine titled "If I Had Muscular Dystrophy," Jerry Lewis imagined how he'd feel and he actually wrote, "I realize my life is half . . . so I just have to learn to try to be good at being half a person," referring to a wheelchair as "a steel imprisonment." As expected, this outraged many adults living with muscular dystrophy, but it wasn't until Lewis used an anti-gay pejorative on a hot mic during a 2007 telecast that his days became numbered.

Lewis hosted the telethon for more than forty years, prompting some to call the broadcast an American tradition. According to a 2009 *Los Angeles Times* article, from its creation to the 2009 broadcast, the MDA Labor Day Telethon had raised $2.45 billion in donations. *That* is what I mean when I refer to Big Trauma.

Big Trauma—think along the lines of Big Pharma or Big Tobacco—refers to any enterprise that exploits the disabled population as objects of on-demand sympathy to manipulate an audience into parting with money. It's the whole "If you don't fork over the cash, you are personally responsible for this human suffering" pitch in action. It's when a high-powered bigwig convinces us that donating billions to disploitation is as American as NASCAR and the Fourth of July.

Big Trauma consumes pop culture, often incorporating mass broadcast and celebrity endorsements into the recipe. According to Big Trauma, the best way to make sales, win awards, or get folks to like and subscribe is to lead with a heartstrings-plucking traumatic disability tragedy—or as I like to call it, a *traumady*. After all, if he hadn't been diagnosed with ALS in the middle of a Hall of Fame baseball career, would we remember Lou Gehrig as anything more than one of the guys who played with Babe Ruth? Instead, he's the American hero who told a weeping Yankee Stadium crowd, "Today, I consider myself the luckiest man on the face of the earth."

Big Trauma is everywhere. It goes beyond disability, so long as the mark (you, the viewer) is convinced that there's human suffering they can alleviate with a credit card and pin number. Those ads about starving kids in Africa. Those Wounded Warrior commercials. And who could forget those ASPCA spots with Sarah McLachlan singing "Angel" over footage of sad-eyed dogs and cats? By the way, who is standing around with a camera crew filming homeless animals while they're freezing or suffering? Really, y'all?

Don't even get me started on Telethon 2.0, otherwise known as the Shriners Hospitals for Children ads that seem to air twenty-four-seven with the tagline "Love to the Rescue." Those guys are Big Trauma black belts and world-class Jedi masters of manipulation. For $19 a month, I'm told, I can save Tiny Tim from cancer! No shade to you, Timmy (I loved you in *A Christmas Carol*), but when I see those ads, all I can think is, *Someone is spending hundreds of thousands on these ad campaigns. I'm pretty sure my nineteen bucks ain't going to little Timmy.*

According to its IRS tax filing, Shriners Hospitals for Children had $10.8 billion in assets in 2023, so this is not a church bake-sale operation. Donors are paying the ads' directors, writers, producers, and film crew; paying for airtime, the set design, location costs, production and postproduction costs, the ad agency commissions, and maybe even a kickback or two to some good ol' doctors.

Everybody's seeing some green. But is little Timmy?

Okay, let's get into it.

First off, the hospitals are owned and operated by Shriners International, a Freemasonry order formerly known as the An-

cient Arabic Order of the Nobles of the Mystic Shrine, with its
men-only members called Shriners. I mean, does that not just
scream good-ol'-boys industrial-complex tomfoolery? *The New
York Times* thought so. Back in 2007, with the help of a whistle-
blower, they did a deep dive into the Shriners and found "a picture of lax accounting procedures and oversight under which
money earmarked for the hospitals instead financed temple activities."

In 2008, *The Times* revealed an internal Shriners report that
highlighted improprieties at a number of the local temples, "including the commingling of charitable and non-charitable assets
and the disappearance of money raised for the hospitals."

But that's ancient history, right? Yeah, not so much. In 2023
PETA accused Shrine Circus—also run by Shriners International—
of animal cruelty, misogyny, and anti-trans rhetoric. PETA also
reported that the ticket sales for those circuses "aren't actually
charitable donations. Instead, the profits are generally used to
maintain the club's premises and fund its activities."

To gain some insight from the inside, I caught up with TV and
film actor RJ Mitte—who played Walt Jr. in the hit TV series
Breaking Bad—about his thoughts on Shriners. "I was diagnosed
with CP at two," he said on our call. "We had a single-parent
home, so I worked with the Shriners hospital, who gave me a lot
of tools at a very young age up until eighteen.

"The reality is," he continued, "half the world cares and half
the world doesn't. Because Shriners hospital doesn't turn you
away if you can't pay, the money for care needs to come from
somewhere. So Shriners hires PR companies to get those donations and meet those quotas so they don't have to shut their doors.

They're targeting those rich single moms and parents who otherwise may not care. That's why they do those types of commercials. So it's essentially not the entity itself, but their PR."

I maintain that the way an entity presents itself publicly *is* who they are. I asked RJ what we as a society need to do to break away from charity model trauma tropes. "People fear disability," he said. "So they create these inaccurate ideas and tropes to protect themselves. And when they see the kids in these hospital commercials, they think all kids with disabilities are exactly like that. We have to flip the coin from inspiration porn characters to more characters like Walt Jr.—real people who live with disabilities."

Agreed.

Okay, so to be fair, Shriners hospitals do some good work. But raising big bucks by leveraging disability, and then skimming liberally off the top, while maintaining a do-gooder public face? That is Bowser-level Big Trauma. I'm no Ronan Farrow, so I'll leave the rest of the digging on that to John Oliver (John—huge fan—Ima need on-air credit).

But honestly, I wouldn't care as much about whatever financial buggery the Shriners engaged in if it wasn't also engaging in a forward-facing, systematic exploitation of Disability identity—of my identity.

For instance, why can't the kids in their ads look like they're enjoying life like the folks in the TV spots for psoriasis or arthritis medications? Those people in the Skyrizi and Rinvoq ads are supposed to have debilitating chronic conditions, and they're taking cooking classes, hiking trails in polo shirts, and crewing sailboats like it ain't no thang! They got me turning up the volume like *Wait, what are these people taking?*

The key is that the consumers of those medications wouldn't

part with their money if *they* were portrayed as trauma tropes. Instead, they're totally cool with being portrayed as everyday people navigating life a little differently. Disploitation is not about portraying a disabled person enjoying life. It's not even about curing a disease. Disploitation is about convincing you that paying the "man" will make your internalized ableism go away. As Kemp wrote, "Playing to pity may raise money, but it also raises walls of fear between the public and [disability]."

Every industrial complex sustains a web of systemic influence—socioeconomic, political, and pop cultural. For instance, Hollywood. More than twenty nondisabled actors have won Academy Awards for playing characters with disabilities, including Al Pacino (*Scent of a Woman*); Jack Nicholson (*As Good as It Gets*); Colin Firth (*The King's Speech*); Eddie Redmayne (*The Theory of Everything*); Anne Bancroft (*The Miracle Worker*); Jamie Foxx (*Ray*); Tom Hanks (*Forrest Gump*); Hilary Swank (*Million Dollar Baby*); Jon Voight (*Coming Home*), of course, Dustin Hoffman for *Rain Man* and Daniel Day-Lewis for *My Left Foot*, and the list goes on. Oh, and the vast majority of these films reinforce traumadies, a narrative y'all know would never reach the screen if I—or anyone from the Disability community—was wielding the pen.

I came across an article by *IndieWire* editor Anne Thompson suggesting an Oscar-nominated actor who mimicked physical or mental disability had nearly a fifty-fifty chance of going home with a statue. So let's not ignore that Big Trauma is all about making bank by exploiting disability as inspiration porn or trauma tropes, because it totally is.

It might be tempting to think, *Those are just movies, and the actors are just acting, what harm can they do?* Someone pass me my bullhorn. When an actor portrays the lived experience of an identity that is not their own, it's not master-level dramaturgy. They are mimicking, and when that identity is Disability, they are cripping up, taking away jobs from trained actors with those Disability identities.

Hollywood has an enormous impact on global culture. These films, shows, and ads are often the first time millions become aware of the idea of disability as a lived experience, and the tropes that are portrayed become accepted norms. Like I said back in chapter 3, directors, producers, and showrunners who live with disabilities should be the ones creating Hollywood's blockbuster disability stories. We've lived them, and we'll get'm right.

Exploiting Thyself

I'm actually not against exploitation when it means leveraging your unique self and your talents. Go get you that bag, sis. I leverage what I got whenever I Strut with my Glam Canes for the For You Page, but I do it for me, my brand, and to shine a light on Disability joy, not to help line the pockets of Big Trauma. In fact, plenty of creators, like queer-disabled content creator Spencer West and entrepreneurs Blair Imani and Keely Cat-Wells, have leaned into the unique talents and stories related to their disabilities in order to build and educate a following.

I'm all about the disability-centered, disability-led amplification of Disability Pride through profit-generating content. Add a healthy serving of diverse creators with disabilities to your daily content diet. You know how you trust a restaurant frequented by locals? Well, follow the disabled leaders who people in the Disability community are following and learning from if you really wanna get it right. I guarantee you, every $19 you spend on a disabled creator's Patreon will do a lot more to support the Disability economy than if you donate that same $19 after falling for a Big Trauma ad. It's like sending a few bucks to supposedly help starving kids in Africa versus investing in a Black-owned business accelerator fund: Both are important, but only one is actually going to Black folk.

People have asked Arthur and me if our r/MakeUpAddiction subreddit posts are exploitative. For the unaware, back in 2020 my longtime makeup artist stopped coming into the city because of what we were calling "the 'Rona." But I still had remote gig obligations, and I had to come cute. Arthur stepped up and began testing out makeup tips he found on r/MakeUpAddiction. He posted his first photo to the subreddit in August 2021, saying, "My SO is visually impaired, through Covid I've been learning how to do her makeup . . . how can I improve?" The post received dozens of polite critiques and suggestions that Arthur implemented and presented in subsequent posts. After a year of this, we went viral with a post showing off a red, white, and blue look I wore to the White House. We've since built a return following of folks invested in all of my appearances, looks, and faces. Our 2025 Grammys look became the most-viewed and highest-rated post in the history of the subbreddit up to that point. The whole thing has become so massive that we're constantly spotted and stopped on the street.

We receive hundreds of comments per Reddit post that are some variation of "She looks amazing! You're such a sweet man for doing that for her!" So wait, isn't that saccharine exploitation using a disabled person as a prop? Yes. But it's disability-led, because y'all know I'm out here cosponsoring the entire endeavor, and Arthur himself is neurodivergent and color-blind. It's disability-centered because we not only spark conversations on disability, love, and beauty, but we also promote accessibility through our use of alt text.

Everyone wins. Arthur receives earnest makeup pro tips and the praise he deserves for being legit good. The subreddit benefits from thriving community engagement enthralled in a pop-cultural relevant narrative. I benefit by getting to show off my professional-glam-chic-happy take on Disability joy to a growing community. And the cultural model of Disability benefits because a bunch of everyday beauty lovers are now learning about, supporting, and looking into disability from a place of "Wait, this disabled girl is pretty dope, lemme look more into what she's about" instead of from a "How much money do I need to throw at this sad image to make it go away?" perspective.

It's about agency. People yell "Exploitation!" when they see little people participating in Micro Wrestling events or on Lifetime's *Little Women*. They might be a part of the disploitation complex, but they are choosing to audition for the roles. However, it does get sticky when we look at who really is and isn't benefiting here. Yes, a disabled actor is authentically cast, is probably getting some coin, and is maybe building a platform. Executives and network heads are building an ad-watching audience. The audience is getting its spectator sport. But the power-dynamic isn't even. I think charges of exploitation or stereotyping lie at the feet of those writing the checks, not those trying to get ahold of them. Former circus worker turned documentarian with dwarfism Aubrey Smalls agrees with me.

"In general, I tend to blame whoever's in charge," he said

when I asked him about modern-day disability exploitation. "Who's making the decisions at the top? Who is given the ultimate say? I do try to be lenient with little people who exploit themselves, because it's tough out there. The job market is not great, and I think that's a bigger discussion about disabled people in the workplace."

Do we have a right to self-exploit if it's our choice? Of course we do. It's unfair to lay the responsibility for dismantling an oppressive system solely on disabled actors, who are out here just trying to pay mounting medical bills.

Like most uncomfortable pieces of American history, Big Trauma has origins in transatlantic slavery. The Lynchburg Museum notes that America's first documented traveling sideshow popped up in 1738, in which a woman with dwarfism kidnapped from West Africa was put on display. The freak show, the for-profit enterprise of exhibiting people with physical and behavioral disabilities for audience amusement, soared in popularity throughout the nineteenth and early twentieth centuries. This was seen as an acceptable part of American entertainment.

Around this time, people with disabilities were often institutionalized in asylums so appalling that it took an undercover reporter to reveal how *American Horror Story* season two they were before folks would act. Or they were otherwise hidden away in accordance with the U.S. "ugly laws," which prohibited people with apparent disabilities from being in public. Becoming part of a freak show attraction was one of the only ways many citizens with disabilities could make a living. While the real money makers were the nondisabled show owners, some of the acts, like Charles B. Tripp, a nineteenth-century painter, carpenter, and calligrapher with no arms, made a good name and good coin by hustling the sideshow game. But the less white and male you were, the more exploited and disparaged you were.

In the 1850s, an enslaver named James Bethune began hiring out the eight-year-old son of two enslaved people, a blind, piano-playing prodigy (will no one rid me of this meddlesome trope?) named Tom Wiggins. "Blind Tom," who was also believed to be developmentally disabled, gave concerts all over the country, including for the likes of Mark Twain. He was even the first Black artist to perform at the White House, playing for President James Buchanan. He was so gifted that he often played back, note for note, complex pieces he'd heard for the first time and would sometimes perform three songs simultaneously—playing one with his left hand, another with his right hand, and singing a third.

Blind Tom was one of *the* biggest sideshow acts in the world throughout the nineteenth century. During a performing and composing career that lasted more than thirty years, it's estimated that he earned about $750,000 for the Bethune family—equal to more than $20 million today—making him the highest-grossing pianist (not Black pianist or blind pianist, but *pianist* pianist) of the nineteenth century. Of course, not a shilling went to Tom or his family. Even when Tom reached adulthood, the Bethunes treated him like a child, all the while working him relentlessly. This kind of celebrity exploitation through conservatorship continues to permeate Hollywood today, as evidenced by cases like those involving Britney Spears and TV personality Wendy Williams. Tom Wiggins's mother, Charity Wiggins, fought tirelessly for her son's freedom, but the Bethunes sued to keep him under legal custodianship for life, ensuring they controlled all his earnings well past the end of slavery in America.

Again, it's the essence of Big Trauma. Audiences turned out in droves to watch this strange Black disabled savant do tricks while his owners raked in the cash.

Cure Chasing

Big Trauma claims to be about entertainment, charity, telling inspiring stories, and "finding a cure." But if we scratch just beneath the surface—not too deep 'cause I'm not reapplying these nails—we find disploitation that continues to paint everyday people as a tragic burden on society. All for the sake of profit. Because that's how Big Trauma do. It's all about the Benjamins.

Consider the charity model. Charities will package up a traumady—the more tragic, the better—to wring out donations by stoking guilt instead of fostering understanding. But shade doesn't all go to the major nonprofits like the MDA or the ALS Association, because they *are* funding necessary research, and research is knowledge and knowledge is power. In recent years, the MDA has even begun steering its messaging toward more lived-experience-centered messaging as it brings in some leaders with muscular dystrophy.

Some shade *does* go to some of the nonprofits run by the parents of disabled kids, the ones with names like Donny's Hope Foundation. They often center traumady and are sorely out of touch with Disability community power-building. The truth is, parents will never fully grasp the reality of actually living in the body-mind of their disabled kid, and proximity to a disability is not expertise.

Again, LinkedIn friend and advocate Emma Farley puts it well. "When nondisabled people retain leadership positions in disability-related spaces," she writes, "it often perpetuates the existing power imbalances and allows them to continue benefiting from the privileges that come with being nondisabled . . . it maintains a system where nondisabled people are making key decisions about what is best for disabled people—a process that, regardless of good intentions, often fails to fully meet the needs of the Disability community." Pro tip: When a cause makes the do-gooder the hero of the story, you're in the belly of the charity model.

Side note, big shout-out to parents *with* disabilities. I see you! But also, a shout-out to parents without disabilities who just want the best for their disabled kid; I see you, too. Parents hit me up all the time with deep, beautiful, engaging conversations. They'll say, *Lachi, you've said that as a kid you had ADHD and several other learning disabilities, were severely shy, and stimmed heavily.* (Side note to the side note: "Stimming" refers to self-stimulating or self-soothing repetitive acts, like rocking or humming, that neurodivergent people use to cope with stress.) These parents then ask the most common question I receive: *What did your parents do to help you turn things around and get to where you are now?*

I tell them what I tell my caregiver audiences, who have the same question. My parents valued my autonomy. My mom was adamant that I be as independent as possible when I was young, teaching me how to work a stove and cook simple meals or to always make mental notes of which direction things were in. She would go as far as encouraging folks to "Ask her" when people would ask her about my needs. So when it was finally time for me to break out and try this thing called disabled life on my own, my inner child already knew how.

By the way, most folks I know who receive disability benefits don't want charity or to be income-capped. The disabled population ultimately wants an end to stigma and shame. We want the freedom to live with dignity. We want the basic tools and access to compete with our non-disabled counterparts on a level playing field at school and in our careers. But those things aren't glamorous. They don't get wealthy donors to limber up their debit cards. Big Trauma dictates what money goes where when it comes to the perception of disability, and making the world more accessible goes directly against Big Trauma's mission of raking in that cake, cheddar, and bacon.

But Big Trauma's real harm lies in tricking society into believing that disability is inherently traumatic and that living day-to-day with a disability is a fate worse than death. Sure, a disabled life is different and can be challenging when accommodation is hard to come by, or when people are jerks. But last time I checked, everyone has lives that are challenging and can be frustrating from time to time, especially when people are jerks. For the majority of us, life with a disability is just . . . life. We're not meandering around traumatized because of our diabetes, Tourette's, or lupus, because many of us have never known anything else.

Emily Ladau says it better than I do. She writes, "I don't have a burning desire to walk or run or climb or jump like a nondisabled person, because such actions have never been part of my life to begin with. Since I was born with my disability, I don't feel that anything was taken away from me. It's simply not possible to miss something I never experienced . . . My disability is my normal state."

Big Trauma says disability is traumatic, should be put on display, and should be used to manipulate people into opening up their wallets. We, the Disability community, have counternarratives we've been living for decades, and it's time we got the masses talking about those big ideas instead.

Big Acceptance

If I wanted, I could have much better vision, at least in one eye. It's true. Because a good deal of my vision loss is a result of my corneal gobbledygook, I could wear fitted scleral contact lenses over my corneas to straighten them out and significantly improve my vision. I wouldn't be able to fly fighter jets, but I wouldn't be mistaking mannequins for store clerks and *might* be able to sink a three-pointer, Steph Curry–style.* I literally have those contacts in my desk drawer right now. But I choose not to wear 'em.

If you're a sighted person, odds are you're mouthing, *Uh, hellooooo,* Jimmy Fallon–style, saying, *Lachi, your blindness is cured! Wear the damn contacts!* But if you're Disability kinfolk, you're probably like, *Comme ci, comme ça.*

First and foremost, don't fix me, fix society. You can't cure perfect.

But really, some of the reasons I don't wear the contacts are mundane. They're expensive and a hassle to obtain, and putting them in all meticulous-like is one more thing to do in the morning that takes time away from hair, coffee, and slow-cycling on the Peloton for my morning Instagram scroll. But again, through magnifiers, screen reading, audio description, my canes, my dude, and the support of my platform, I've made my world accessible enough that I don't need them. My blindness has made me who

---

* NBA sharpshooter Steph Curry actually has a version of keratoconus (one of the eye diseases I have) and wears scleral lenses to manage his vision.

I am, and I love my life. I ain't broke, so what are we fixing exactly?

I remember those images that flooded the interwebs after Stephen Hawking died, with him in heaven standing next to his wheelchair with captions like "Now he can be happy." Steven Hawking's wheelchair was part of why he was such a Big-Dis-Energy, change-making, breakthrough-getting badass. My vision of heaven, of bliss, is not being nondisabled. In fact, my poem, "Heaven Is Not Sight," portrays my idea of heaven not as a place where who I am and how I was born have to change in order for me to live well, but as a fully accessible world that accepts me exactly how I am.

That's one alternative to Big Trauma: *Big Acceptance*. Acceptance is the antidote to stigma and the highway to pride. Accepting (or in my case, welcoming) one's Disability identity doesn't mean resigning oneself to a lesser life; it's not a defeat, but a victory. Acceptance is peace. It is empowerment. It is boldly owning your one-of-a-kindness in interacting with the world with a singularly unique body-mind and spirit. It is being wrapped up in the group hug of the Disability community. It's a rebellious declaration of self-worth that says, *I'm here, I'm whole, and I ain't got time for your pity.* Call it *DIS-education.*

Big Acceptance is an important starting point for facing off against Big Trauma because it claps back not only at the trauma narrative but also at *curism,* a term I use to describe the obsession with "finding a cure" for disability. Countless foundations and organizations prattle on endlessly about a cure, often at the expense of recognizing the value and dignity of an individual's current lived experience. Spending one's life cure-chasing, waiting on a cure that might come . . . someday, maybe . . . is a form of copium. It's a distraction from advocating for equitable inclusion, embracing who we are, and living a full life right now.

Curists are disciples of the medical model, hoping for that miraculous scientific breakthrough that will fix them. Girl, I don't need a cure in ten years. I just need this book in large print *today*. Curists are the church folk who try to lay hands on me and pray that God will heal me. (A church family came over to pray for me once. I asked if I could pray for them first. When I was done, they weren't tryna pray for me anymore.) Like Amy Kenny says, "My body is not a prayer request." Obviously, if God is perfect, disability is perfect.

Curism is Uma Thurman wiggling her big toe in *Kill Bill* and willing her injury away. It implies that for my life not to be a tragedy, I've got to wiggle my Blind identity away. Curism is erasure, and the Deaf community has a lot to say about that. There is such deep pride in being born into Deaf culture and having a rich Deaf ancestry that many Deaf folks couldn't care less about cochlear implants. With curism, the story starts being about the cure and stops being about the person.

People aren't going to say about me, *Her sight was restored, so she could finally begin living her life.* My life began after I quit the Army Corps of Engineers—actually, after my first listen to Lauryn Hill's *Miseducation* because, hello, "Doo Wop."

Don't get me wrong; my issue is not with research for a cure. In fact, bring it on. If a person wants to alter something about themselves and ease some tension or pain, you do you, queen! Some chronic pains, sensory overloads, or unexpected temporary disabilities may be more than one can handle right then, and a quick and easy switch-up would be nice. We live in a beautiful world of self-love and implants, body positivity and body sculpt-ing, and access to choice is the ultimate liberation.

Most people want a cure because they're scared, but often they're scared because of the Big Trauma message that "Unless I'm cured, everyone else will see me as a Tiny Tim traumady." So, the issue is not *you*. The issue is Big Trauma disseminating internalized ableism and curism as viable alternatives to self-advocacy and self-acceptance.

Big Acceptance means respecting those who want a cure while understanding that many don't. Big Acceptance is recog-nizing the atypical as an asset—recognizing disability as part of someone's rich life story, not as a problem to fix. Again, Emily Ladau nails it, writing, "As tough as certain aspects of my life have been, and though I know I will continue to face disability-related challenges throughout my life, I wouldn't trade my life for a minute. My disability has given me a place in a community and a culture; it has been the reason why I've had amazing adventures and unforgettable experiences. To walk freely up and down stairs for one day would never measure up to the things I've done *because* I have a disability."

Big Gratitude

Emily hints at the next Big Trauma alternative: *Big Gratitude*. She's grateful for the life her unique body-mind has given her and wouldn't change it. I'm right there with her, as are many who lean into their Disability identity. Talk to folks from across the community and you'll hear lots of variations on "I'm good. If there was a cure, I'm not sure I'd take it."

Just like the women's rights movement ain't about becoming men but about ending sexism, disability movements aren't about being cured. They're about ending ableism. They're about being treated with respect, dignity, grace, and empathy. John the wheelchair user isn't pissed because his legs work differently, he's actually pissed because he can't get into buildings, and because people tend to treat him like a burden, an expense, a potential grievance, or a charity case instead of a human being just tryna grab a beer and some hottie's phone number after work. It's never been about fixing his legs; it's about being able to go into a pub and grab a pint with his buddies with dignity.

People like me, and lots of folks in the Disability community, view our disabilities as a big part of our raison d'être. I'm a different musician than the one I would be if I didn't create art from this unique body-mind. I certainly wouldn't be as outspoken, energetic, and purpose-driven. Nearly every artist, business owner, and content creator with a disability that I know—many of whom I interviewed for this book—broadly maintains that their disability gave them purpose, gave them community, or helped them see life from a deeper, richer perspective, making them better at what they do and fostering an enjoyable, whole, fulfilled life. Big Gratitude is Disability joy—a form of resistance and self-acceptance, challenging the notion that the Disability identity solely encompasses grief or grievance as opposed to joy.

But Big Gratitude goes even further, crossing generations. Some folks with autism have said if they have children, they prefer their kids to be on the spectrum as well, because they understand what it's like, recognize the benefits, and will be better able to relate to their kids.

Raven Sutton articulates this feeling better than almost anyone I know. "I'm fourth-generation Deaf on my dad's side," she said in our interview. "I just feel connected to that identity . . . Deaf people have our own culture. We have our own language, and we've been fighting to show that. Deaf people are a unique group of people within the Disability community, because we want our kids to be Deaf just like us. Not everyone in the Disability community experiences that same type of culture that they want to pass down."

Is it shocking that a parent with a disability might want their child to be born autistic or Deaf? It shouldn't be, because they don't view their disabilities as traumas, but as traits. We treasure those traits and regard them with pride; why *wouldn't* we want our children to feel that same pride?

"If you provide me with what I need, I am able to navigate through this space, through this life, through this situation, just fine," Raven says. "But when you refuse to do that, that's where the impact on me is negative—not because of a disability, not because of hearing loss, but because you can provide me what I need and you're not. Even when I was young, I used to tell my mom all the time, 'I'm happy God made me Deaf.' I've always been this way, and I've never wished to be hearing."

There you have it, folks. Big Gratitude at its finest from a reality TV star. *Well, of course someone born with their disability can find and feel identity pride,* you say? Challenge accepted. Gaining a disability later in life can be positively transformative, as Wesley Hamilton can attest. Wes, the bodybuilding wheelchair user who appeared in season four of *Queer Eye*, has used his platform to become an advocate for accessible fitness facilities and an empowering disability mindset. He's also a great example of Big Gratitude.

On his episode, Wes confessed that prior to acquiring his disability, he wasn't much more than a street thug, packing heat and doomed to die young. But after becoming disabled, he discovered physical fitness, lost one hundred pounds, became a champion CrossFit athlete, and found both a new purpose as an activist and real joy in his life.

A spinal cord injury from a gunshot put Wes in a wheelchair back in 2012. In his *Queer Eye* episode, he met up at a Kansas City bar with the man who shot him, and he relayed how he's truly thankful for the way his disability has given him the opportunity to remake his life, especially since he's a single father to a daughter.

"Am I grateful that I have to wake up with a spinal cord injury every day and deal with all the things the spinal cord injury comes with? Maybe not. It's a lot to deal with," he said in our interview. "But I am grateful for the opportunity that life has given me, because I do have another chance. I have another chance to be more aware, more proud, more free because of my disability, because that's not who I was before. I was a product of my environment before."

Better dad. Better leader. Better public figure. Wes became all those things *because of* his Disability identity, not in spite of it.

For those who aren't quite there yet when it comes to Disability Pride or Disability joy, Michael J. Fox puts it best: "With gratitude, optimism is sustainable." Gratitude is appreciation, and I appreciate the opportunity, community, and liberation my Disability identity has given me. People have asked me, "How can you be blind and also so joyful?" Boo, if you've been defrauded into believing that if you ever lost your sight, you'd automatically become unhappy, *that's* the real tragedy.

Big Average

You know about the CDC reporting that one in four American adults has some form of disability? Again, I'm suspish. What about the rest of y'all who ain't reporting, or who don't know you have a disability? Let's finally address this elephant. How many folks with dyslexia, anxiety, long COVID, ADHD, IBS, fibromyalgia and other chronic joint and muscle aches, or even low vision don't view themselves as having any form of disability? How many Black and Brown people are actually reporting they have a disability in the first place? How many are even surveyed?

I believe everyone has Disability identity—"Gooble gobble, gooble gobble" and all that—but because it doesn't disrupt their ability to work or find love, they don't disclose it, and some may not even realize it. They don't request accommodation, or simply don't need it. By this logic, the average person lives with some form of big-umbrella disability on a daily basis—some people with higher needs, some with fewer needs. But because they don't think of themselves as having a disability, their condition doesn't look like trauma, tragedy, inspiration porn, or spectacle. It looks like an everyday person navigating life a little differently.

Instead of Big Trauma, most people with disabilities (maybe even you, dear reader) are really looking for what I call *Big Average*. We're all just people who should be able to live our lives however we show up. We might have different access needs, need different accommodations, have different challenges, and like different TV shows. But we're all just examples of different ways to be human. Most people with disabilities don't drive in the inspirational trope lane, with people giving pats on the back and participation trophies just for coming out in public. Most people don't drive in the trauma trope lane, either, with folks saying "You poor thing" and trying to "save" them.

In a Big Average world, people who identify with their disability would drive in the middle lane with everyone else. Everyone would have the access and accommodation we need to thrive because those things would no longer be overlooked or treated as inconvenient add-ons. With Big Average, accommodating people's access needs would become routine for performance venues, workplaces, schools, and airports. We'd all be invited to the party, brought into the conversation with our rich and unique stories. We would no longer feel the need to ask for permission to take up space or apologize for existing.

In our Big Average future, demographics surveys would recognize self-identified disability as a categorical identifier for understanding access needs. The made-up medical-model fear of violating HIPAA as an excuse to exclude the self-identifier would be a thing of the past. Like with gender and race, response options under the Disability Identity heading would include the more common disability subcategories along with a write-in and a "choose not to disclose" option. This would get society thinking about, talking about, and eventually formalizing and normalizing Disability as an identity spectrum on which everyone is sliding.

Where Big Trauma "others" us, Big Average recognizes that we're all dignified human beings with different wattages, spottages, crossed *T*s and *I* dottages. It's all about embracing each other's unique needs with appreciation and gusto.

What would that look like? Two examples.

The first is the ever-viral "Escort instead of stripper" story that exploded on Reddit and remains one of the most-commented-upon Reddit posts of all time. In r/AskReddit a user asked, "Strippers of Reddit, what's your weirdest story while working?" In a reply, an escort details that one of her clients would take her out to dinner once a month, simply to have conversations that helped him work through his extreme stutter. She explains that outside of these dates the man would speak by writing things down because no one had the patience to listen, and that she was his seventh escort because the others refused to return for a second date.

While the goal on paper might have been to work on his communication, the real crux of the matter was the man's isolation and having to feel less-than due to shaming and stigma. The man and the escort remained in touch long after she left the job, and (presumably because he had someone he could talk with comfortably on a consistent basis) his stutter became far less pronounced. Ten years later, he's living his best life, fulfilled and happily married.

The comments blew up as many folks focused on the escort being such a good person. But it's more likely that the other six escorts had simply been duped by Big Trauma's ad spend. What I *do* like about this story is the mundanity of it. A guy paid an escort to hang out. He had an issue with self-advocating, so came up with a creative way to self-accommodate. Pretty routine for a person with a disability. The escort showed up and viewed him as a person—not a charity case or trauma case, but a client who paid for and received a couple of hours per month of companionship. But what makes this story stand out is the relationship they maintained afterward. He's just some guy. She's just some woman. They built a rapport of mutual dignity and respect.

Now for the anything but mundane: Coldplay's *Music of the*

Spheres world tour. Coldplay has long been one of the most fan-inclusive bands in pop music history, going to great lengths to make sure their fans across the disability spectrum have an incredible concert experience rivaling those of their nondisabled fans. After lead singer Chris Martin developed tinnitus, his then-partner, Dakota Johnson, gifted him a SUBPAC—a vest that allows wearers to physically feel sonic vibrations—which inspired Martin to make Coldplay concerts more accessible to fans who are hard of hearing and beyond. The band is now all about recognizing the value in their d/Deaf or disabled fans' experience and addressing it with creativity and care.

Team Lachi is honored to be great friends with Team Coldplay, and we love that they have a person on staff dedicated to accessibility. Lauren Rauch, management coordinator and director of merchandise for the band, is involved with the substantial accessibility and accommodation that go into Coldplay's shows, and she sat down with me via Zoom to talk about the work the band does to make its disabled fans feel not only accommodated, but welcomed and valued.

"We currently have an additional riser on the floor where we welcome our blind and visually impaired guests, our deaf and hard of hearing guests, and guests who may not want to be on the wheelchair riser but still need a safe and accessible viewing area," she said. "We open it up to anybody who feels like they need that safe space."

She continued, "Aside from the separate riser, we offer SUBPAC vests, the vibration-delivering vests that get a live audio feed. We welcome all SUBPAC guests to watch the show from the same place. This is where the sign language interpreters are if guests utilize sign language."

She already had me at hello, but there was more. "We also do touch tours, quasi-backstage—well, technically under-stage—tours that take place as soon as the doors open," Lauren said. "We walk the group around the stage, talk about the different show elements . . . and they have an opportunity to feel the stage. They have an opportunity to meet bandmate Jonny Buckland's guitar tech, Matt McGinn. Matt talks to them about what he does, and they are welcome to feel and play some of Jonny's guitars. After we speak to Matt, we visit Neil, the piano tech, and Neil walks everybody through the different elements of the piano."

Lauren also told me about specific accommodations for neurodivergent people and those with sensory disabilities. Coldplay's shows are designed to offer people with sensory issues multiple ways to engage with the experience, so they can choose what's comfortable for them. "We have kinetic floor dance parties throughout the show," she said. "This show is so immersive, from the confetti, the light-up wristbands, the painting around the stage, the painting on the stage floor, and the instruments, which all have custom paintings on them."

Coldplay invited me to experience the magic of their touch tour and show at Allegiant Stadium in Las Vegas. Boy, did they not disappoint! An environment of music, inclusion, joy, and love, where fans with disabilities aren't afterthoughts but priorities. Where every performer, patron, and passerby is given the same dignity, consideration, and respect, not to mention an equitable shared experience with the person rocking out next to them. Where the average experience is an exceptional experience. That's Big Average. At these concerts, no one treats fans with disabilities as trauma victims, tragedies, or inspirational tropes, but as valued fans whose needs, while different and unique, are important and worthy of attention. That's because the antidote for Big Trauma is being seen, being invited to the party, and knowing you're just as welcome as any other fan to get blissed out on the music, be sore from dancing, and burn up your credit card on overpriced merch. It's not being treated as "special." It's being treated as an individual.

Once we stop feeding into the mass manipulation and profiteering of Big Trauma, we'll see disability for what it is.

Humanity.

Chapter Eight

Shame on Who, Exactly?

I 've found that the more I "un-normal," the higher my quality of life. Remember those miracle contact lenses I could wear, but don't? Here's the backstory. It was 2018, and I was taking the first baby steps toward accepting my rapidly diminishing vision (even though I wouldn't fully "come out" until the pandemic). When my ophthalmologist told me about the contacts, of course I said, "Tell me more," because who wouldn't? But after doctor visit after doctor visit to get the things custom-fitted, honestly, I just got kinda bored. I would be sitting in the clinic for the third time in a week, thinking, *I could be performing, I could be recording, I could be day drinking, I could be doing literally anything but waiting around in a waiting room. Yawn.*

Meanwhile, as my contacts were being manufactured, I had finally started using a cane—just the traditional white cane; the rhinestone-bedecked showstoppers were still to come—and becoming more familiar with readily available assistive technologies like magnifiers, dictation, screen readers, and every blind person's ultimate war hammer, the keyboard shortcut. I was getting everything done that I'd been hoping to do after I got the contacts and was quicker, more efficient, and far less frustrated than I'd ever been. So what exactly did I need the contacts for?

Then the contacts arrived. I put them in . . . and I suppose it should have been a YouTube moment when the music swells, a child points and yells, "Mommy, Mommy, look! She can see!" Julie Andrews breaks into song as I marvel, teary-eyed, at how clear and beautiful all of my favorite things are now. But there were no heavenly choirs singing or angels weeping. *Underwhelming* springs to mind. Once I got past the first couple of days of piercing headaches, my vision was definitely clearer, but my reaction to the whole experience was very much *Meh.* It would take up precious time and energy to put the damn things in, take them out, clean them, mentally adjust, and navigate our busted-ass healthcare system to have them refitted as my eyes evolved. Seeing was a *hassle.* So I took the contacts out and kept it moving.

If you're like, *Dude, not using those contacts to improve your vision makes zero sense,* then you might also be part of the 52 percent of Americans who—according to a Reuters poll—would rather die than live with a disability. (Believe me, we'll come back to that.) Here's the deal. I had all the tools I needed to work hard, play hard, rinse, and repeat at pace with any sighted person, which meant I had options. For me, it was *not* better to have clearer eyesight with all the strings that came attached to it. So I said "Screw it" and never looked back.

I'm aware that I had the privilege to say "Screw it." I had the health insurance to cover, at least in part, the cost of the contacts and doctor visits. I had the money for cabs and Ubers to get to and from the visits on my own. If I lost my sight completely, I had family and friends who would support me. I had Arthur, I had a rainy day fund, but most important, I had good credit. Not everyone has those things. I did, so I could afford to say a polite *thank you, next* to something that, for someone else, might have been indispensable.

But that wasn't the only reason I decided to ditch the contacts. It had taken me years of swallowing tears, wearing fake smiles, and being a brave little toaster to get to a point where I was relatively immune to the entrée of shame society tried to serve me whenever I dined at its table. For so long, I'd felt a deep-rooted shame at being legally blind, and that shame informed my decisions and contributed to my anxiety. But as I grew older and more confident, I started to feel pride in my talent, at who I was becoming, what I was capable of, and how I was showing up in the world. But I *was* still blind. So obviously the blindness was never the problem.

Let's be real. I hadn't been considering the contacts so I could see better, but so I could be more acceptable to society—be more "normal."

So my 2.0 self chose to dump those contacts, to live and give Blind Queen Energy, and to lean into all the competitive advantages that come with my Disability identity. My OCD gives me sharp alertness, acute communication, and studious punctuality. My ADHD powers hyperfocus and follow-through on my many whimsical ideas, along with abundant energy, spontaneity, and the drive to take action. My anxiety fosters excitement, critical thinking, and analytical skills while also bringing empathy, self-awareness, and growth. My PTSD keeps me transparent and considerate of others' needs. My maladaptive daydreaming—which is what it sounds like, excessive and vivid daydreaming, often to escape internalized stigmas or to cope with anxiety or depression—had involved me conjuring epic sagas for several hours at a time, even to the point of skipping meals, but eventually the ideas coalesced into my sci-fi thriller, *Death Tango*. My blindness grants me creative problem-solving, driven focus, a bunch of unique life experiences, self-determination, and yes, dope-ass Glam Canes. When it comes to my built-in life hacks, I choose pride.

Not everyone does. The flip side of pride is shame, and if you're looking for the Mother of All Afflictions permeating the disabled population, shame got game. Let's you and me break it down.

Macro- and Micro-Shame

Stigmas, barriers, and exclusion don't happen because of our conditions but because of our *conditioning*. Every person with any form of disability, neurodivergence, or chronic condition has felt the sting of shame. We feel it when the kids in our class pick on or avoid us, and when teachers get exasperated for needing to repeat things because we don't learn like the other kids. We feel it when Becky in accounting sighs heavily at having to hold the elevator door for a slow-moving cane user. John the wheelchair user (who still just wants to enjoy a beer) isn't ashamed that he uses a wheelchair; his shame comes from how others exclude or patronize him for being in the chair.

No one experiences shame quite as viscerally as people with disabilities, and it's the distinct product of ableism. Ableism and shame go together like gin and tonic, Bordeaux and stinky cheese, control + C and control + V. Now, who can refresh our memory on what ableism is? Yes, you in the back of the class. Very good:

Ableism is prejudice against individuals with disabilities based on the belief that they are inherently inferior to people without those disabilities.

A more thorough working definition comes from lawyer and community organizer TL Lewis. Lewis describes ableism as a means of assigning value to people's bodies and minds based on the societally constructed standards of beauty, productivity, intelligence, fitness, and what it means to be normal. Lewis also contends that those ideas are rooted in dominance ideologies like eugenics, anti-Blackness, misogyny, colonialism, and capitalism.

I also appreciate writer and organizer Vinay Krishnan's plain-language definition. In his *Medium* article "The Sick and the Well," he writes, "What ableism comes down to is this—I'm healthier than you are. There's something inherently wrong with you that is right with me. If there's a fire. If there's a flood. If only one of us can make it out alive. It should be me. This isn't just the thought in the minds of bigoted people—something to be combated with knowledge and experience. This is the ethos of whole systems."

Ableist biases often show themselves through *microaggressions*, pocket-size acts of everyday-isms like mansplaining, whitesplaining, and straightsplaining (which is when a straight person drives a chat with a queer person into a ditch by saying something like "I know exactly what you mean. I have a gay friend who . . ."). Ableism also shows up in the daily indignities that disabled people endure for having the temerity (a good Atticus Finch word) to want to use the bathroom or grab a drink at a bar.

During the lead-up to the Great Diddy Unraveling of 2024, I, like every red-blooded Black human, was privately popcorn-bingeing *RealLyfe Street Starz, Art of Dialogue,* and *The Breakfast*

Club on YouTube for to-the-minute updates like they were a dirty little secret between me and my Android. During this time, I came across a well-meaning yet harmful brand of ableism.

The hip-hop community hasn't had many prominent anti-ableist voices, so I definitely find it necessary to grant some grace as we grow and find our empathy, language, and humanity. A few incidents stood out to me, but a particularly interesting one transpired on RealLyfe's video podcast *So Let's Talk About It*, episode 20, with special guest Jaguar Wright, a personality and former background vocalist. At the top of the episode, host Angel White introduces herself as "the baddest albino entertainer," and Jaguar's smile fades.

"You see yourself as albino?" Jaguar asks with concern in her voice.

"I am," Angel responds, alongside a few nods from others in the studio.

"You're light-skinned to me," Jaguar says. "I don't understand what you're talking about." The room then gets awkwardly quiet as Angel smiles and searches for words. Jaguar continues with, "I love you just the way you are. I hate labels. Just beauty," ending with a quiet "awww" purr.

Angel begins to say something, then settles on an "I appreciate it," and quickly moves the conversation along to get the show started.

Let's break down the well-meaning microaggression. First, Angel demonstrates a healthy dose of identity pride as a woman with albinism. Jaguar's reaction and statements, though well-intentioned, are harmful. Her question, "You see yourself as *albino?*" displays a negative association not only with the word, but with the state of being. Subtext: "Why would you associate yourself with an identity that is self-limiting and shameful?" My identity is my identity; it's *society* that ascribes shame to it.

Jaguar's statement "I love you just the way you are. I hate labels" is giving me "I don't see color" vibes and hints of traumady. Clearly, Jaguar is a friend to Angel and meant her no harm as an individual, so Angel doesn't press the issue and graciously moves things along. A keen viewer would see Angel as the protagonist, a proud woman and gracious host. But there could be many young girls with albinism who watch the episode and think, *Maybe I shouldn't proudly say I'm a badass woman with albinism because I would be so embarrassed if someone said* aww *to me under their breath.*

A few friends cautioned me to watch what I say about hip-hop as it pertains to disability. To that I offer these bars: *Let 'em break my legs. To try to hold me back. I'm already moving steady in the Dis track! Whether I'm running or I'm rolling, as long as I'm breathing, Ima keep on going. Best believe it.*

Point blank, period. New paragraph.

These types of microaggressions can also be far less subtle, can be far less well-intentioned, and can happen at any demographic intersection. Actress Kiera Allen, who we heard from several chapters back, has vivid recollections of the micro-shaming she's experienced since becoming a wheelchair user. When we met in Manhattan, she recalled, "One of those shames the world tries to impose upon disabled people is the subtle message of *You shouldn't be outside of the house. The sidewalk isn't for you. This building isn't for you.*"

She went on, "Before I go to a restaurant, I always google its accessibility. I call the restaurant and ask, 'Are you wheelchair accessible? Are there any steps to get in?' Even then, there's only a fifty percent chance that it actually is accessible even if I get all the right answers to those questions. One time I came to this restaurant with two friends who I had known for less than a year, and I was still afraid that these accessibility issues were going to come up and they would say, 'This is too complicated. She's not worth it.'"

"We came to this restaurant and there was a step up to get in. I said, 'Hey, you said you were wheelchair accessible.' They brought out a tiny little ramp and seemed so put out by having to put it there. I was so worried that I would never see these friends again. I have lost friends like that from them becoming overwhelmed and not wanting to go out with me anymore, which they never admit. They just disappear."

What Kiera is describing here is *social avoidance*—losing a friend, a gig, or one's social standing as a result of ableism or any other form of prejudgment. Another form of micro-shaming is *spotlighting*, singling out a person with a disability under the guise of helping them, which ultimately leaves them feeling uncomfortable and on display. Examples include over-the-top praise, loudly admonishing others (e.g., *How dare you not help her!*), or making a Tony-worthy show of your effort when assisting someone with a disability.

"I rarely take the bus because I've had so many experiences with bus drivers blowing up at me for asking them to put down the ramp," Kiera concluded. "I have every marker of wealth, privilege, and whiteness, and still I get treated like this. I can't even imagine what it's like for people who don't have all those privileges."

Ableism cuts across every other societal marker. It doesn't matter your race, gender, sexual preference, income status, or size. If you're epileptic, a crutch user, or nonspeaking, or you don't read as fast as others, you might be shamed because of it. It's the weight of this societal shame—not the disability—that makes people feel othered, like we'd rather duck and cover than face another eye roll or patronizing "aww."

It's why many people with non-apparent disabilities do what they can not to disclose, to "pass." According to Attitude Is Everything, 70 percent of music performers keep their disabilities hidden for fear of damaging a professional relationship. That's why for years I stumbled over steps, squinted at screens, and missed deal-making waves: I feared disclosure. Since going public about my Disability identity, that fear now seems silly. But hindsight is twenty-twenty. When you live in fear of someone discovering your secret Disability identity, that shame towers over you like Godzilla—the original, not the remake.

Arthur, my business manager, confidant, partner, makeup artist, and veritable ginger chew, experienced this, too. Today, he's a proudly big and tall neurodivergent mover and shaker in both the music industry and the Disability community, with way too much red hair. But when he was young he and his parents were at war, struggling to find an answer, a diagnosis to explain his hyperactive behavior. While soaring academically, Arthur had been on different medications throughout his middle and high school years, and nothing seemed to work for him the way the airbrushed Big Pharma commercials said they would.

The meds were supposed to make the issues at school and at home go away—to make him understand the world and the world understand him—but they didn't. As a result, he lost trust in everyone from his parents to his teachers to his therapists and psychiatrists. He was an overstimulated, misunderstood kid consistently sent to detention or time-out as punishment for not conforming to the rules (something I can dead-ass relate to). One day, in his early teens, he was sent up to his room for a time-out and decided he wouldn't come back down for days. He found peace in choosing to view the time-out less as a punishment and more as an escape. When his parents asked him to come down for supper, he pulled a full Max from *Where the Wild Things Are* and told them through the door that society was dead to him, so he was going to stay in his room forever, and they could feed him if they wanted.

Eventually, his parents played the "escalate quickly" card, committing Arthur to an adult psych ward for a weekend. He spent the day confined, watching old men rocking, frothing at the mouth, polishing themselves off—terrifying stuff for a kid. Arthur asked a nurse, "How do I get out of here and never come back?"

"Fake it," she said. "Pretend to be normal, and you'll never have to come back."

The experience scared him straight. From that moment forward, he started pretending he was "normal." He began watching shows like *Friends* and *Frasier*—a.k.a. "white people stock footage"—to learn how to be like the normies, and he stopped fighting so much with his parents and acting out in class. He went to boarding school, then college, and got a job, all the while burning beaucoup energy playacting as a combination of Martin, Niles, Ross, and Chandler—he never really figured out Joey. When we met up and became friends in college, I convinced him to be more himself—less Chandler and more Arthur. This freed up so much pent-up energy. He eventually followed me headfirst into the depths of my Disability identity acceptance journey.

But the shit didn't hit the fan until he went with RAMPD to our first Grammy Awards run instead of going to a mandatory mid-pandemic, in-office work meeting. He ended up snapshotted for an article covering RAMPD's involvement with the Grammys that was re-shared all over LinkedIn and outed him to his employer. Oops. With the horse out of the barn, Arthur walked away from his high-powered, nine-to-five, executive recruitment gig and went all in on disability inclusion, equity, and self-advocacy, using his newfound surplus in headspace to empower other neurodivergent professionals to do the same.

I'm super proud of Arthur for stepping away from the energy-sucking void of shame and denial and into the light of authenticity and liberation. Still, he wasted twenty years of his life playacting as someone else. That's the power of shame.

Shame vs. Empathy

So what is, and why is, shame? First, a disclaimer. While I've certainly felt shame because of childhood trauma and internalized ableism, my heritage does not include the generational trauma of American enslavement.

I am a second-generation Nigerian, a direct Igboland descendant. My father is a chief of the Isu people, repping the Umuoparadim village within the Nwangele local government in Imo State, Nigeria. His father, my grandfather, was a hardcore, old-fashioned hunter; it even says "Hunter" on his LinkedIn profile. He would literally take a spear, go out into the wild, and hunt wild game. That's me, except we're hunting opportunities, baby! My grandmother on my father's side was a farmer and worked in the trenches, just like I do with RAMPD, so my dad's side gave me grit and work ethic.

My mother, Dr. Marcellina—also a chief as of 2024 (one of the few women chiefs hailing from Imo State)—is an award-winning humanitarian who has worked as a community organizer, church leader, university professor, and college dean. Her father, raised in the Isu village of Umuorlu, was a suave, savvy, handsome man who moved to the city and became a chef for wealthy folk. He then convinced those rich folk to invest in him, leading him to eventually go into business with his wife, my mom's mom, a tall glass of drop-dead gorgeous, in the business of manufacturing and reselling fabrics. So I guess you could say my mom's side gave me my passion for community building, my business acumen, my fearless sense of style, and my eyelash-waving charm.

So I identify as a smooth-talking hunter from Africa, and there's something real to that.

But while I recognize that my heritage protects me from certain generational traumas, I would be remiss not to acknowledge that many parts of my home country, as well as much of continental Africa, have historically abandoned infants with disabilities. Disabled adults have been outcast, disowned, or hidden away for fear of disgracing their families, all because of a combination of superstition and shame. My parents immigrated to America in the 1970s to get Western educations. By the 90s, they'd moved to the suburbs to raise their kids. We lived a very immigrant life, rich in heritage, pride, Igbo language, and fufu. My parents weren't ashamed that I had a disability. They had more of an "Every one of our seven children is going to win at this thing called America, or else why did we come?" vibe. My mother took advantage of the services America had to offer me, but none of this shielded me from the stares, the avoidance, and the whispers I faced every time I set foot outside our home . . . or from internalizing that shame.

Verywell Mind expertly defines shame, and differentiates it

from guilt: "Guilt is a feeling you get when you perceive you did something wrong . . . Shame is a feeling that your whole self is wrong and it may not be related to a specific behavior or event." It's the difference between feeling bad for what you did and feeling bad for who you are and how you show up.

As society as a whole encounters Disability identity, acceptance, and pride more often, I predict that the correlation between disability and shame will start to diverge. Take eyeglasses. I call the selective acceptance of certain disability accommodations the *eyeglass concession* (sounds like the title of a bad Jason Bourne novel). Millions of people wear eyeglasses so they can read, drive, and otherwise function in their daily lives. Without them, many of those same people wouldn't be able to follow a recipe, read a street sign, or navigate their computer screens. So why does mainstream culture not consider glasses wearers to be disabled? Eyeglasses, even the readers you can buy at CVS, are an adaptive device, aren't they?

While folks were once teased for wearing them, eyeglasses have become commonplace and are now a socially acceptable access need. No one looks at a person wearing glasses and thinks, *You poor thing*, or avoids them out of some belief that near-sightedness is contagious. Other examples of the eyeglass concession include hearing aids for older people, some performance-enhancement pills, and slings, casts, or other solutions that suggest a disability is temporary. The point is, people with eyeglasses are not considered disabled because glasses are socially acceptable, while disability isn't. It's that simple.

Because all the big dogs, from media, to religion, to the corporate world, to cruel fourth graders, paint disability as socially unacceptable, few people with disabilities willingly and openly identify with that part of their identity. Why does mainstream society treat disabilities, neurodivergence, and chronic health conditions with such skyscraping levels of fear, intolerance, and avoidance?

I have an answer, but I feel like I'm making a case in court, and I probably would've made a fun TV lawyer, so let's go full-on *Law & Order* on this thing. I have some power suits that would look awesome in a courtroom.

Ladies and gentle-peoples of the jury, the real reason the world shames and shuns disability has nothing to do with the costs, inconveniences, or even the fear of infirmity or mortality that disability can represent. The true reason is a concept I call *empathy blockage*.

Empathy blockage is emotional armor that protects you from the guilt that comes with finding out that you are part of the problem. Suppose you're coming back from dropping off a load of recyclables. You're feeling all virtuous and planet-saving, thinking, *Wow, I make the world better just by being in it!* Then you cross paths with a wheelchair user who's experiencing a pretty darn humiliating lack of accessibility—say, they can't safely board a commuter train because the gap between the platform and train is too wide. You're now faced with this burdensome feeling:

I see you, and it's painful to consider how hard your daily life must be. I feel a rush of shame for the continued inaction of society—myself included—to improve your situation. Thinking about how hard my life would be if I were you is exhausting, and knowing I'm not doing anything about it is even more exhausting, so I'm just gonna go about my day like you don't exist.

These unbidden thoughts and feelings flash by in a split second, but they culminate in a feeling of deep discomfort related to the disabled individual. Instead of offering to assist that wheel-chair user in boarding the train, you do what most people do when we confront uncomfortable feelings: put on a suit of armor to protect you from the source of the discomfort, and then put as much distance between you and it as quickly as possible. In this case, you speed-walk past the wheelchair user and board the next car over so you won't have to see them and be reminded of their difficulty. That's empathy blockage.

The burden in this scenario is not the disabled person. It's the wall of denial we build to keep out the remorse that creeps in when we're confronted with the reality that we could (and should) act to make things better for a disabled individual or the entire community—but *don't*. The resulting emotions include pity, anxiety, anger, and fear. The subsequent feeling of "Screw you for making me feel this way!" leads to avoidance, bullying, and in-fantilization. Essentially, it's blowing an empathy fuse, because actual empathy would require learning and growing beyond one's comfort zone.

Empathy blockage goes beyond ableism, though. It can be found in the movement looking to scrub hard truths about Black history from education, in movements looking to ban sex ed or reproductive rights, the "Don't Say Gay" laws, and initiatives seeking to purge supposedly woke terminologies. These acts give credence to the quote often attributed to the great Mallory O'Meara: "To the privileged, equality feels like oppression."

But what sets disability apart when it comes to empathy blockage is that disability is inevitable. Thanks to aging, injury, accident, and social BS, there are only two categories of people: those who accept their Disability identity, and those who will eventually *have to* accept their Disability identity. So when you come across a person with a disability and part of you whispers, *Thinking about you and how we as a society have failed you is exhausting,* you're saying that to your future self. That's heavy. When faced with that visceral truth, some folks see disability inequity as too big to fix. *Isn't it the state's problem? What could I possibly do?* Thus the avoidance, awkwardness, and, most telling—the apologies. People often apologize when they learn of a person's disability. Their "I'm sorry" is shorthand for "I'm sorry, I recognize the world is inaccessible and non-inclusive, yet I am doing nothing to help remedy that for you or my future self. All I can offer are my condolences."

Even disabled people can be apologists. We might apologize for being in the way, for existing in a non-inclusive world, for self-advocating—all attempts to relieve someone else of the potential burden of empathizing with us. According to 2014 research by Scope, 67 percent of people feel uncomfortable when talking to a person with a disability. They fear saying the wrong thing or have no experience with disabled individuals.

Ask your doctor about empathy, for the treatment of empathy blockage. Side effects may include seeing that disability really ain't that tragic, no longer centering or referencing nondisabled people when defining disability, not being afraid to confront your own Disability identity, and working within the Disability community to help power-build and make the world suitable for everyone—whether disabled or not quite there yet.

The Evolution of Ableism

True empathy for disability looks like a push for acceptance, dignity, and autonomy. Millions of Americans today are living with non-apparent disabilities, so a good portion of that 52 percent who'd rather die than live with a disability are enjoying nice lives with a disability and don't even realize it.

The *Havamal*, a collection of Old Norse wisdom on proper conduct from the Viking age, reads, "The halt can manage a horse, the handless a flock; the deaf be a doughty fighter. To be blind is better than to burn on a pyre: There is nothing the dead can do." Back in 900 AD, the Vikings, OG masters of commerce and war, valued living with a disability over death. So why is disability so tied up with shame today? Are there historical shifts? Is there an evolutionary component? Let's put on our readers and take a quick look.

The influence of disability on how a society views itself has shaped human culture throughout history. First, an authoritative body sets the tone for how disability should be regarded. Next, society follows that decree until another authority pops up and says, "Actually, let's look at disability like *this* now." But before we can get into authority structures, we have to fire up that Wayback Machine and set the dial for about 200,000 years back.

There *were* disabled Neanderthals. *Psychosocial Aspects of Disability*, by Irmo Marini, Noreen M. Glover-Graf, and Michael Jay Millington, says that archaeological and anthropological evidence suggest that people with spinal, hip, and other mobility disabilities lived during the Old Stone Age and that, with no evidence of adaptive aids, loved ones likely took care of their disabled members, carrying them from place to place.

For our first authority structure, let's jump forward to the culture where the concept of bodily perfection ruled. The ancient Greeks introduced the concept of the ideal form, and the notion that a blemished body meant a blemished soul. In 440 BCE, artist Polykleitos sculpted the *Doryphoros*, a tall warrior serving as the canon of perfect physical appearance and proportion. Plato then sanctioned disabled infanticide for eugenics purposes, while Aristotle followed suit, writing, "As to the exposure and rearing of children, let there be a law that no deformed child shall live," for the purposes of ridding the state of disability's economic burden.

Then there's the long-standing authority of godly punishment. Marini, Graf, and Millington go on to mention that ancient Hebrews viewed disability as unclean as decreed in Leviticus 21: "None of your descendants who have a defect may come near to offer the food of his God . . . no man who is blind or lame, disfigured or deformed, no man with a crippled foot or hand or who is a hunchback or a dwarf, or who has any eye defect . . ." Once Christianity took over during the Middle Ages, clergy and monks viewed citizens with disabilities and mental conditions as possessed and "cured" them with a complex recipe of prayer and exorcism. During the Renaissance, the manifesto *Malleus Maleficarum* (a.k.a. *The Hammer of Witches*) identified how to spot a witch by their impairments, and again society fell for it, leading to torture and death for tens of millions of women with disabilities.

Let's skip to the Industrial Revolution, where capitalist America decreed that human worth was defined by one's ability to produce. Everyone darted off to factory jobs, often becoming disabled by heavy equipment and then being like, "Wait, what? No services or nothing?" In response to the growing need, hospitals, schools for disabled people, and even workers' compensation coverage started popping up . . . and then along came Chuck Darwin to rain on the parade with a new voice of authority. In his 1871 book, *The Descent of Man*, he kicked off eugenics with this gem:

"Our medical men exert their utmost skill to save the life of everyone . . . thus the weak members of civilized societies propagate their kind . . . this must be highly injurious to the race of man." The rise of Social Darwinism eventually led to the legal sterilization and euthanasia of hundreds of thousands of citizens with disabilities in several countries, including Nazi Germany and the United States.

And how could we forget those ugly laws? From the 1860s all the way up to the 1970s, many U.S. cities enacted laws making it illegal for unsightly or disfigured people to appear in public, forcing many disabled people into institutions. My momma always told me, "Don't leave the house without combing your hair," but sheesh. Again, a societal authority sanctioned the oppression of disability.

Things started to get better in the 1970s. In 1973, the U.S. passed the Rehabilitation Act, prohibiting discrimination by federal entities based on disability. This paved the way for the 1990 Americans with Disabilities Act, which introduced a new kind of authority—a disability authority—called litigation. That bad boy *worked*. Lawsuit after lawsuit started forcing everyone, from corporations to educational institutions to shopping centers, to chill out on the whole disability oppression thing. But now the pendulum is swinging back as the burden of the grievance model begins to make some folks feel ashamed to self-advocate and causes others to lead with a "No, I'm fine" mentality so as to not rock the boat and keep others comfortable.

From way back when to now, one authority or another has dictated how society views disability, often building that narrative around shame. But today's authority is built on pop culture and evergreen social media content. If we're going to reframe the disability narrative, we're going to have to do it by wielding the power of authentic stories—one disabled series regular, neurodivergent executive producer, deaf TikToker, or blind award-winning recording artist at a time.

Disclosure Therapy

Not gonna lie; it feels sooo good to be out and proud about my Disability identity. It has been the ultimate liberation. If we want to start seeing everyday people step out of their "No, I'm fine"-ness with dignity and pride, we need to see more portrayals of Disability joy, acceptance, self-determination, and community—not just on the screen and behind the scenes, but IRL. When celebrated figures have authentic, public discussions about disability and neurodivergence, they can change how millions of people see Disability identity with one IG story or post.

For example, Brian Wilson, cofounder of the Beach Boys, was half-deaf and lived with depression and schizoaffective disorder for most of his life. His mental health conditions were known and accepted in the industry, which led to Barenaked Ladies recording the song "Brian Wilson," in which singer Steven Page speaks to the effects of mental illness and the power of artistic outlets to bring inner peace. Electropop vocalist Halsey has been famously open about living with bipolar disorder, EDS, postural orthostatic tachycardia syndrome (POTS), and several immunodeficiencies, engaging in full-on online dialogues with fans who have similar diagnoses. Dance-pop vocalist Bebe Rexha has been open about her anxiety and depression. My hope is that more people with platforms will see their conditions not only as an individual experience, but as a part of a collective identity, and engage with their Disability community. Things aren't so scary when we face them together.

I remember sitting in the tenth row at the *I Am Celine Dion* Amazon Prime premiere at Lincoln Center and watching *thee* Celine herself speak to us live about her struggle with stiff person syndrome (a neurological disorder characterized by muscular rigidity). She said that her biggest struggle was the isolation, and I remember my heart going full hug emoji like, *Damn girl, I coulda been there for you. WE coulda been there for you. The Disability community is here with open arms.* It reminded me of the late actor Chadwick Boseman, the lead in *Black Panther,* and how he, too, dealt with his cancer alone. If only we lived in a society where anyone could freely open up about their disabilities and the rest of the world was down for the pivot.

But of course, the disclosure journey is different for everyone, and the need to maintain a certain status or persona can make that journey arduous. Plenty of people with non-apparent disabilities, whether small-town girl or big-city celebrity, fear that if they disclose, they'll lose job opportunities, romantic partners, party invites, and what have you. So they stay hidden in the shadows, going through life in lurk-mode, doing what they can to conform in order to avoid being or feeling othered. Take Rosemary Kennedy, JFK's younger sister. She lived out most of her life in an institution after her father sought to cure her intellectual disabilities with a botched lobotomy. Her conditions and whereabouts remained hidden so as to not damage the family's political careers.

Everyone has disclosure questions. *If I disclose on a dating app, to a confidante at work, or randomly in my Instagram stories, will my life be over, or will a new life free of this secret solitude begin?* I spoke with blind *Master Chef* champion Christine Ha about her disclosure story. "I used to be ashamed of my disability, and I would always try to hide it," she said in our Zoom interview. "I wouldn't use my cane in school, and I would try to find the restroom and end up in the men's room instead of the women's room. Then after being on national television, suddenly everyone knew about my disability. It was so freeing, like, 'Well, I'm glad that happened because it got ripped off like a Band-Aid in one swift motion.'"

She continued, "Now I'm very proud about my disability because *Master Chef* was the impetus. Society's not really in a place that fully accepts a lot of disabilities, but more and more people like us are being public and loud about it, and saying, 'This is okay, it's empowering, it's not a weakness, it's just that we're different. Look at all the things that we're able to accomplish if we get some adaptations.' I think that that empowers more people and gives the next generation of Asians who have disabilities in their family the courage to be more forward about their disability, talk about it, and not sweep it under the rug."

The Reference Man

On our call, Christine Ha mentioned how Gordon Ramsay treated her like everyone else, lightheartedly teasing her about things like walking face-first into a test kitchen wall, while also pushing her to be her best like he did all the other contestants. That's a recipe for a good experience, but it's not always the case. Some people are reluctant to embrace Disability identity because they don't want to deal with the condescension that comes with the Big Trauma–induced ingrained stigmas. I've seen people talk loudly to a wheelchair user like they're deaf, or use baby talk with a neurodivergent adult.

I spoke with Icelandic philanthropist and tech entrepreneur Haraldur Ingi Þorleifsson (Halli), who had a very different experience than Christine on his journey to acceptance and pride. Today Halli is known for installing more than 1,500 ramps across Iceland, releasing music about life with muscular dystrophy, and a viral, public back-and-forth with Elon Musk over his Twitter employment, during which Musk questioned Halli's disability and need for accommodations. But Halli's success was born of a hard past.

"I started using the wheelchair when I was twenty-five," he said on our Zoom call. "I had a different walk to other kids and was very self-conscious about that, so I built up a lot of defenses. I have internalized ableism, feeling disconnected from my own body. I didn't want to be vulnerable, so I did everything I could to be successful at all costs . . . this need to succeed to prove that I'm a worthy human."

I felt that in my gut flora. Success gunning has generally been my defense mechanism against ableism, both internal and external.

"I felt that I wasn't enough . . . I felt a pressure from society in general to be strong and that any kind of weakness will be used to push me down even further," Halli continued. "There's the actual physical disability and the problems that come with that. But often bigger are those societal implications of not being able to participate, being seen as other. We build our world around a particular type of ability and a particular type of person, and everyone that doesn't fall into that mold is stack-ranked and is treated differently because of that."

Since time immemorial, every person in a society has been compared to some ideal—and discriminated against based on how sharply they deviated from that ideal. In ancient Greece, the ideal was *Doryphoros*. In Renaissance Rome, it was Michelangelo's *David*. In mid-twentieth-century radiation safety, it was a concept called the "Reference Man." This was the theoretical model of a standard, "normal" individual—the model used to calculate safe radiation doses and against which scientists would measure deviations. The 1975 version of the Reference Man was a healthy, young adult Caucasian male between twenty and thirty years old. This was the ideal human being, so deviations included skin color, age, gender, fitness . . . and perceived ability.

Today, the Reference Man has infiltrated every corner of mainstream culture. To millions of people, he is what's "normal" and "acceptable," and anyone who doesn't fit within his narrow parameters is, by definition, abnormal or unacceptable in some way. This one-size-fits-all marker of normality has penetrated hiring practices, corporate promotions, and Hollywood casting. The Reference Man has become the definition of good, successful, strong, intelligent, and a leader. This is why for decades, every action hero was a tall, iron-jawed, presumably straight white guy, and why we had to wait for 1990s Will Smith before we got a mainstream Black action hero.

Society has led us to believe that the more we look, behave, think, and do like the Reference Man do, the more likely we are to win at life. But y'all already know what I say to that. The more power you find in those deep parts of yourself that society expects you to push down, the more you win at life. Period. The cure to internalized ableism—from internalized body shaming to accommodation guilt to negative self-talk—is internalized Disability identity pride, the proud acceptance of one's whole self. That Big Dis Energy.

The next step is community. Many in the disabled population don't consider themselves part of the Disability community or even acknowledge that there *is* a Disability community. Instead, they think they're just a little off or a bit different. That's how I felt for a long time. Out of self-preservation, I differentiated myself from folks with higher-access needs or more limited mobility with an *at least I'm not them* mentality, but that's just more empathy blockage. I am the most liberated version of myself I've ever been because I built community around my difference. Finding that difference, that thingy, that puzzle piece, that spark in you, and then seeking out community and allowing yourself to bask in a greater sense of collective liberation—that is freedom. That is success.

"Four years ago was the first time I posted a photo of myself publicly showing that I use a wheelchair," Halli said. "There's still a lot of shame . . . but it is a fascinating journey."

Disability Badassery

Tell me a story you've come across about disability that isn't sad, saccharine, or full of inspirational tropes—a story celebrating disability without shame. If you're my people, you've got tons. But if you can't think of any right now, there are a handful in this book and millions more out in the wild: in the grocery store, in the park, on your socials, all around you, and even within you. All without shame, all waiting to be heard.

Here's the thing about shame: It's not a life sentence. It can be overcome. If you want proof, look no further than Illinois Senator

Tammy Duckworth. Duckworth (phonetically pronounced "bad ass") is a former Iraq War Black Hawk helicopter pilot turned congresswoman turned senator who lost both legs when an enemy grenade hit her chopper. She went on to become the first Thai-American woman elected to Congress, the first woman with a disability elected to Congress, and the first senator to straight up give birth while serving in office. Senator, you had me at Black Hawk helicopter pilot.

I'd first heard of Senator Duckworth back in 2016 (and have since met up with her briefly at White House events). Then in the House, she'd been one of the few sources for smartphone footage—which Republicans wanted to embargo—of a raucous protest by House Democrats over gun legislation on the House floor. A few years later I learned of her service, valor, and disability and knew I had to speak with her. Today, she's widely known for being a dauntless legislator, but she shared her experiences before gaining her disability, when she felt she couldn't match the physical performance of the men in her army unit. Since becoming part of the community, she's rediscovered her pride. She told me about her experience during our interview.

"In many ways, identifying as a person with a disability makes me feel stronger than before, because I took my abilities for granted before," she said. "If anything, I was often frustrated by my own inability to do physical things. I couldn't run as fast as the men in my unit. I couldn't do as many push-ups as the men in my unit. And the bane of my existence, I couldn't do pull-ups like the guys could. So even though I was very athletic, I always felt my physical ability was limited compared to the men that I served with, where I was often the only woman in an all-male unit. By gaining my disability, I came to appreciate all the things that I can still do, and the things that I do now that I never would have done before. I've done a whole bunch of Chicago Marathons. So, in a very roundabout way, I feel more appreciative of my physical abilities as a disabled person than I ever did as [a nondisabled] person."

To me, what really makes the senator a leader is her attitude that people with disabilities have a right to be wherever we want to be, and therefore have a right to have our needs accommodated—no shade, no shame, no fear.

"Well, I think we need to set the standard, and you have to first value your place in the organization," she said. "I had to value that I was a congresswoman, just like everybody else. My constituents voted for me to be in Congress, just as they voted for me to be in the Senate, and I have as much of a right to be here as anybody else. And if I do, then I have a right to have my needs accommodated for. So it starts off with valuing your place in the organization and not just being grateful for being there. So what I tell the folks is set the standards and they will make accommodations for you, because you have every right to be there, and they value your input."

I also wanted to know if the senator's disability had influenced her pivot to politics, and if she herself had folks to look up to coming in with a disability. "Acquiring my disability did not impact my decision to run for office, because I never planned on running for office," she said. "But it opened up the opportunity for me to run for office because that's how I met Senator Durbin." (Senate majority whip Dick Durbin, also of Illinois, heavily encouraged Senator Duckworth to run for Senate, and has since teamed up with her on several disability initiatives.) "It forced me to look for a new mission in life because the experience of getting my disability meant the end of the main mission of my life, which was to serve in uniform. When I found out I couldn't fly Black Hawks for my country anymore, I was, like so many veterans, lost. It was Senator Durbin who pointed out to me that I could become an advocate for veterans."

When I asked the senator to recount a badass "disability moment" while serving in Congress, I had to hold on to my eyebrows. "Back in 2016 when I was serving in the House of Representatives," she said, "some of my Democratic colleagues and I held a sit-in to protest the lack of action by our Republican colleagues on gun violence. Then-speaker Paul Ryan was confiscating phones at the door, so I hid my phone in my prosthetic leg and snuck it onto the floor with me. And I'm glad I did, because when House Republicans called a recess and stopped the official broadcast, I was able to take to Twitter and share videos of what it looked like from the inside." So *that's* how that happened? Epic.

That's pride. That's the antidote (or, at least, one of the antidotes) for shame. In today's society, authentic pride is a blade you need to continually sharpen. Every once in a while, your crown will slip sideways and you've got to put it back on straight. But the thing about pride is that we're constantly told that we shouldn't feel it—that we should, to quote K. Dot, "Be humble, sit down," and forever wait our turn. But I bet nobody told Bill Gates, Steve Jobs, or the guy who made Linux to wait their turn. Nobody told Genghis Khan to sit down, so why should I?

Well, Genghis Khan was a conqueror. Bitch, I'm a hunter! We're all just different flavors of the same soup, and we all deserve to feel that peace that comes with identity pride.

On its own, shame is *powerless*. The only power shame has is the power we give it. When we believe we don't deserve accommodation or we're not worthy of showing up ten toes, whole self, chest out, that's when we cower, duck our heads, and mutter things like, "I'm sorry, I hope my need to breathe didn't inconvenience anyone too much."

There's a difference between feeling and fact, and the fact is, we take back our power by confronting our shame. Stand up for yourself to yourself. You are worthy and can do hard things. In the words of the great Celine Dion in *I Am Celine Dion*, "When you like yourself, you walk better. You perform better."

I learned that, among many lessons, from my fearless mentor, Judy Heumann. Because of her impact on my life, I've begun mentoring, finding future music industry legend mentees through Women in Music, Grammy U, and RAMPD. One of the lessons I teach is to bring your authentic disabled, neurodivergent, unique-AF whole-self swagger to the table, make 'em set a plate for you just the way you like, and let 'em know you'll be bringing five friends.

Confidence is contagious and sexy. A big chunk of mainstream society expects people with disabilities, people of color, or women and non-binary folks to keep our heads down and back away from confrontation, using shame as a shield. I keep my head up, take big steps when I walk, and speak with bass in my voice, because that's what it takes for someone like me. The professor or HR person or venture capitalist or competition judge is going to assume you'll fold, but you keep your pride shining. Some days you may wake up feeling like an impostor, but I've found that the cure to impostor syndrome is taking responsibility for the space you take up.

Own your shit. Know your worth. Let's do the hell out of this thing. Fortune always favors the bold, the authentic, and those who stay ready so they never have to *get* ready. Be trained up, armed up, and show up. There's no such thing as luck. When the thing comes—the meeting, the audition, the pitch—you're there, you're ready, and winning is just a matter of time.

It's so fulfilling to watch my mentees start walking the walks, rolling the roles, taking the meetings, and doing big, hard things, not only because *they're* so proud, but because they've had the chance to swagger in front of bigwigs and, in doing so, literally change someone *else's* entire worldview.

Once you love and embrace the deepest parts of yourself society expects you to hide, you level all the way up. It's like the power-up mushroom in Mario Brothers. You have a condition that doesn't quite fit "normal," so you overcompensate to avoid dealing with the potential shame. That overcompensation can reveal some of your greatest strengths. But it's not always easy to recognize those hidden strengths. You wind up feeling like your body-mind isn't quite as good as everyone else's, so you crash out, act up, or go to war with yourself, because that's better than being shamed. But that's internalized ableism. And it's okay. Everyone is going through it. Everyone is feeling the exact same way. Everyone has internalized ableism.

Once you accept and see the beauty in that part of yourself, that unique freckle that is the deepest cause of your adversity, life becomes beautiful, too.

Shame Busting

One of the key ways we can slay shame and stigma is to boost the visibility of amazing, cool, successful disabled people throughout mainstream culture. We've hit on representation in pop culture, but that's only a piece of the multilayered cake. We need to be holding elected office, running public corporations, landing on the moon, sitting on the top of the *New York Times* bestseller list (hint, hint), and headlining at major comedy clubs. The more normal it is to see un-normal, the faster the myths and misconceptions will disappear.

One person already taking her turn at center stage is multi-hyphenate Cat Cohen, a comedian-actress-writer-singer (whew) who's performed her own Netflix special. She also cohosts a podcast on mental health called *Seek Treatment*, where the hosts joke about their own mental health challenges and speak openly about the stigmas and misconceptions in order to shatter them. A fellow general-anxiety-disorder baddie, Cat spoke on our call about how freeing it's been to talk openly on *Seek Treatment* and onstage about trauma and mental health.

"The joke is that my cohost, Pat Regan, and I are the ones who really need the treatment, and we've basically been just spilling our guts for five years," she said. "I feel like it's created this community of people who really feel like we're all friends, and who I adore when we meet in real life. It's a ton of discussion about our mental health journeys. Whenever I go somewhere and people have listened to the podcast, it's like this immediate familiarity."

I asked Cat how she thought other people experiencing mental health conditions could turn their own trauma into lighthearted humor. "It starts with talking about it with people close to you," she said. "I'm lucky to have friends who are open-minded and a community of people who I feel I can dish to. I start by talking about it with Pat on the podcast, then maybe I talk about it onstage for a hundred people. Then I'm like, *Okay, maybe I'll talk about this in a bigger venue.* The more comfortable I am talking about something, the more I think about what Pat once told me: 'It'll be funny when the shame wears off.' The more comfortable you are with what you're discussing, the shame sort of sloughs away. It's about becoming comfortable enough with those dark parts of yourself that the funny stuff starts to shine through." I heard that!

Ableism is often unintentional, while some have difficulty taking responsibility for the ableist harm they've caused because of how they were confronted. I'm all for educating people, myself included, with a smile and the disarming catharsis of humor. But we can't talk about the effect of positivity, music, and culture to emanate real change without mentioning the one and only Warren Snipe, better known as Wawa—a Deaf rapper, writer, actor, and dancer who's performed artistic sign language at the Super Bowl. We talked via Zoom and he told me about helping others move past the notion that disabled, neurodivergent, and d/Deaf people can't do everyday, basic tasks.

"You are looking at the impossible made possible," he said with a wide smile. "Some people just can't seem to get that through their thick heads. Driving was impossible. Flying was impossible. Now it's possible. When are people going to wake up and say, 'Oh, snap, everything is possible'?

"We have a disability; people think it's a problem when really it's not," Wawa went on. "We open their eyes, we open their minds, we open them up to things that they never thought about. Also, we welcome them when they end up with a disability in the future, because that's inevitable. They might feel alone or left out, but people with disabilities are already here and we're like, 'We've got you.'"

All anyone wants is dignity, autonomy, and empathy. To see someone else without those things, attempting to live the same life you're living, is scary. Knowing that but for the grace of God, that person could be you is *scary*. What could you possibly offer that person other than your pity, your prayers, or your avoidance? Well, how about an invite to hang, talk, or meet your other friends? How about a paying gig (she said with a wink)? What about a conversation on access needs, proper identifying language, or anything non–trauma trope oriented? What about an opportunity for us to learn more about each other and how we can work together to make the world not so scary?

So let's talk. All of us. Those of us comfortable in our Disability identity and those of us not quite there yet. I'll provide the drinks, the audio description, and the captions. You provide the snacks. Let's have conversations online and in person about what it means to embrace one's Disability identity, what it's like to live with a disability, neurodivergence, or a mental health or chronic condition day-to-day, and anything else that will help free up any empathy blockage. We can even talk about your fears about your unacknowledged disability, or acquiring a disability one day.

Silence is not the answer to shame. *Dialogue is*. The conversations may get a little uncomfortable, but so what? We're all friends here, and friends are real with each other, so here's the real. I was blind and ashamed. I am still blind, and I am liberated. Ergo, my blindness wasn't the actual source of my shame. Wanna talk about power? Embracing my Disability identity is the single most powerful thing I've ever done.

Chapter Nine

Our Symbol—a White Guy in a Wheelchair

The president complimented my outfit," reads the carefully crafted caption under my well-traveled White House lawn photo with President Joe Biden. But the picture—which still gets me, the blue T.W.I.N. blazer, and the matching makeup recognized on the streets—is definitely worth a lot more words.

The September 2022 ADA anniversary celebration marked thirty-two years of the Americans with Disabilities Act, and also the first of many Glam Cane Struts through the halls of the president's residence. Congressional leaders, prominent activists, public figures, and notable influencers gathered in the Rose Garden as Dr. Jill Biden and her husband spoke on the history, growth, and needed improvements re: the ADA.

My stylist, a.k.a. Arthur, styled me face to shoelace in red, white, and blue eleganza. From the fit to the cane to my hair and nails game, we were on a mission to turn heads since getting the invite. Y'all already know that a huge part of my advocacy is expressing my culture, identity, and pride through my style, which manifests in my canes, cornrows, and blind-girl-walking-better-than-you-could-in-seven-inch-heels stride. It's about letting the people in the back know that you can be confident, cute, funny, smart, successful, Black, and disabled. Speaking of which, we bumped into Claudia Gordon on the lawn—the first Deaf Black female attorney in the U.S. and White House adviser on disability issues (she and I low-key compete for best dressed, and she does give me a run for my money).

After the presidential address, and after all the DC types got their presidential handshakes in, I sashayed up to the president like it was a Memorial Day cookout. We exchanged brief all-smiles courtesies, which ended in me waving a Vanna White–style hand in front of my fit and saying, "Okay, real talk. What do you think of the outfit?"

I kid you not, the commander in chief did not miss a beat. He stepped back, slightly lowered his sunshades, and said, "It's sexy." I was close enough to witness the whole thing with my own vision. Of course, in a classic main-character rush of excitement, I turned to the crowd of onlookers, press, and guests waiting to speak with the president, grabbed his hand, pumped our fists to the sky, and declared, "America, the president called me sexy!"

The audience responded with a mix of light laughs, a gasp or two, and a smattering of photographs. In classic Biden style, the president muttered what sounded like a lighthearted "whoops," "yikes," or "uh-oh" under his breath. I left the White House on cloud nine. Not because of the president's words, but because my brand of advocacy, my self-expression, and the confidence that emanated from me had reached the highest office in the land.

However, outside the gates, a few of the DC K-Street types who'd been in attendance approached Arthur and me and advised us not to repeat what happened. If we must say something, they suggested, we should say, "The president complimented my outfit." An older woman, whose name I did not get, cautioned that it would be a bad look for me as a woman of color, which stuck with me. I get that it would be quite the look for ol' Uncle Joe, running around calling people sexy out here in these streets, but there was something in the pedantic way these folks were cautioning me. They exuded a strong "It's wrong for a Black disabled woman to be called sexy" vibe with an undercurrent of "Black disabled woman, we know what's best for you."

But I am sexy. Disability is sexy. Everyone in the Disability community is sexy. We are also tough, talented, outgoing, and stylish. I, a generally happy-go-lucky woman of color with a sense of humor and flair, represent disability. Yet I do not see myself in the symbol used to portray disability—a white male in a wheelchair, stick-figure thin, and while I haven't asked him, I'm pretty sure he's straight, too. One thing he isn't? A reflection of me. He's not even a reflection of most white disabled people, let alone anyone who deviates from that. This sentiment is echoed in the way society views disability.

I'd already been feeling some type of way about this before the White House episode. Nine months earlier, in January 2022, Laura Zornosa of *The New York Times* sat with me to discuss RAMPD's ambitious goals and eventually published a beautiful, in-depth piece that landed on the front page of the Arts section. It was my first national-print article working in the disability space, and it generated a healthy influx of new traffic and inquiry for RAMPD. Somewhere in the article, I said, "It's paramount for folks to recognize that disability has color, that disability has gender, that disability has sexual preference, and

that disability is not just straight, white, middle-American male."
I gave Laura reams of other provocative quotes, but that particular sentence caused (and still causes) some real inbox rancor.

Some people went as far as to question whether Caucasian
males were allowed in RAMPD. Some content collaborators and
bloggers cut out sections where I mention my cornrows or my
Blackness, and when I asked them about it, they said they didn't
want to sound divisive. Which is interesting because there are
times when I find myself relating more to non-Black disabled
folks than to nondisabled Black folks. If we learned anything
from the Luigi Mangione incident, it's that white, middle-income
men can be disabled and fed up, too. But the reactions to my *New
York Times* statement have been what they are because disability
is already hard enough to sell to the Endies (again, my nondisabled NDs), so we can't be out here offering up a notion of
disability that's even further away from the Reference Man,
right? Certainly not a queer disabled woman of color.

Even as disability rises out of the shadows, becoming more
active and visible, when people think of a disabled person, they
overwhelmingly think of a fit, upper-middle-class, straight, white
wheelchair user. When advertisers cast disabled characters in
their ads, they overwhelmingly cast a fit, upper-middle-class,
straight, white, wheelchair-using dude who's "just like you and
me, but in a wheelchair!" No disrespect for being straight, white,
a dude, or a wheelchair user, but homeboy is literally not just like
me, nor does he represent the majority of what disability looks
like. This makes it difficult for the mainstream public to recognize the Disability identity within themselves.

Here's a great example of what Disability community looks
like. Back in 1977, three women—Judy Heumann, Kitty Cone,

and Mary Jane Owen—organized the longest sit-in in a federal building to date, a twenty-six-day protest at the federal Department of Health, Education, and Welfare (HEW) building in San Francisco to demand the enforcement of Section 504 of the Rehabilitation Act.

But it was because of the support of a Black guy and his very Black crew that they were able to pull it off. The protesters were mostly wheelchair users (and yes, I know there's a joke in there that goes *Of course wheelchair users would organize the longest "sit"-in, rim shot!* I'm still sorting out the delivery). There were sit-ins at nine other HEW regional headquarters, but because many of the disabled protesters needed essentials like oxygen and insulin, not to mention food and water, the other sit-ins dissolved pretty quickly . . . all except for Judy's.

Or, should I say, Brad's.

A Black wheelchair user with multiple sclerosis named Bradford Lomax convinced the Black Panther Party (and the nearby Glide Memorial Church) to show up for the San Francisco sit-in. They came through, providing supplies and one hot meal every day to each protester—and I don't mean a quick bowl of lentil soup, either. The Panthers brought homemade meatloaf, fried chicken, salad, and ribs daily because they were cooking for family. Now, the Panthers are a capital "B" Black movement, so Brad, who had co-founded their Washington, DC, chapter, had to convince the San Francisco Panthers that Section 504 was a fight worth fighting, and that Black people needed to come together with this mostly white movement. He was the linchpin, the GOAT, the Muhammad Ali who made this high-risk, high-stakes movement all work out.

The sit-in was a success and legislators eventually caved because of it. We have the Americans with Disabilities Act, which came in 1990, the UK's subsequent Disability Discrimination Act (DDA) in 1995, and similar laws around the world throughout the 1990s, all because of a coalition between white women and the Black Panthers and the power of home-cooked soul food—really, all because of Brad Lomax, a Black disabled man.

Brad is my truest ancestor in disability because he saw a need, saw an opportunity to address that need, and acted. He didn't do it for the name or the fame, but to bring about change. His action brought about one of the strongest shifts for disability in history. But Brad's best work, including laying groundwork for the beginnings of a Black independent living movement, has been shelved and overshadowed.

The Disability Rights movement has a history of preferentially acknowledging and supporting the dignity and autonomy of more privileged disabled or neurodivergent people, leading to an imbalance in whose stories get told. That disparity paved the way for a newer, more holistic, and intersectional framework for engaging with disability rights, the Disability Justice movement.

Disability Justice

Before I get into Disability Justice, I wanna give the disability rights movement its tulips, carnations, and roses. The movement opened up opportunities for people with disabilities to participate more fully in society and face less public erasure and discrimination, and brought about legal mandates like curb cuts, closed captioning, and equal access to all things federal. But it left out one teeny, tiny crucial thing: *most disabled people.*

My intersecting identities impact how I see myself, how the world sees and hears me, and where I fit into both the Disability community and mainstream culture. Disability does not discriminate, and its intersection with race, gender, class, sexuality, size, and disability type also jacks up the level of systemic oppression a person faces. For example, a cishet Caucasian male wheelchair user and an Afro-Latina trans wheelchair user may both need a ramp to get into the toga party, but only one of the two would have gotten an invite. Hell, the overweight working-class Caucasian male wheelchair user didn't get an invite, either. Thus, the Disability Justice movement enters, stage left.

Disability Justice is a framework acknowledging that not all disability rights are created equal, and that ableism comes in as many shapes and sizes as humans do. It acknowledges that each one of us is a delicious cocktail of multiple identities, each one equally valid and precious, each affecting how we move through the world. It recognizes that those rocking the most marginalized identities are the ones most impacted by systemic ableism and that their voices and experiences should thus be put front and center. Dr. Sami Schalk puts it very well in *Black Disability Politics*, writing, "Disability is often created and exacerbated by racism, sexism, homophobia, fatphobia, classism, and other forms of oppression. They are inextricably linked."

Imani Barbarin, disability blogger and creator of the viral Crutches and Spice content platform, speaks often on the interconnectedness of systemic oppression and disability, saying in a popular TikTok post, "Every form of marginalization in this country leads to disability." I caught up with her and asked her to expand.

"The best evidence for this is [our] treatment in, and apprehension towards, the medical system," she said during our chat. "When women are dismissed in medical settings, their symptoms worsen, often becoming more pervasive as they wait for treatment. When Black people seek care, they are often brushed off until their ailments become emergent. When trans people are denied adequate intervention, often their mental and emotional health deteriorates.

"This is nothing to say of other institutional impacts," she went on, "like food deserts exacerbating heart and kidney health, and redlining being linked to asthma. Police violence . . . leading to post-traumatic stress. At every turn, institutionalized bigotry wears itself in the bodies of the marginalized."

Disability Justice prioritizes the most historically excluded groups, ensuring that all people with disabilities—including women, Indigenous peoples, people of color, immigrants, people who identify as queer, trans, or fat, and incarcerated or unhoused individuals of all classes, ethnicities, and appearances—can partake fully in their hard-won disability rights with dignity and autonomy.

Another great pop culture expert, disabled, Black, and queer author, journalist, and self-proclaimed cheesecake aficionado Keah Brown (creator of the hashtag #DisabledAndCute), brought the truth when I kiki'd with her on intersectionality and Disability Justice.

"I can't divorce my queerness from my disability or my Blackness from my disability or my disability from my queerness and my Blackness," she said on our call. "I'm all these things, and my womanhood, at once. I'm never not those things. I've said to many people in the movement: If you cannot see me for all that I am while doing the work of Disability Justice, then I'm not interested in your Disability Justice. People are eager to be like, 'Let's not focus on your being Black or your being a woman or your being queer. We just have to focus on disability.' But that's not the real movement. We live in a culture where the face of disability is too white."

Unsurprisingly, the folks insisting we focus on our similarities rather than our differences are the ones who have the luxury to do so. When it comes to matters of Disability Justice, even two chronic jokesters such as Keah and me sit up straight and real-talk.

Disability Justice began when communities of color realized the disability rights movement was leaving them behind. Throughout the 1980s, 1990s, and 2000s, it became clear which demographic was truly benefiting from the fight for disability autonomy. Activists recognized that because of systemic, institutionalized, and often unintentional biases from childhood to working adulthood, there were social and environmental factors that increased hardship for multi-intersectional people, making meritocracy moot. They also recognized that there was bigotry *within* the Disability community: silos, hierarchies, and a lack of focus on sustainable, cross-movement, collective liberation.

In 2005, three queer disabled women of color who were engaged in radical social justice work that did not systemically address ableism—Patty Berne, Mia Mingus, and Stacey Milbern—got together in San Francisco to lay down the foundation for what would eventually become the principles of Disability Justice. Voilà! A movement. But don't take it from lil old me when you can get it from an OG of Disability Justice. I was fortunate enough to sit down with Patty Berne before she passed to describe Disability Justice in her own words.

"Disability Justice is both a theoretical framework and a practice which centers people who are most marginalized by ableism," she said. "That's disabled BIPOC people, that's disabled queer, trans, non-binary, and IA+ people, people with disabilities who have been marginalized from social support the most and are most economically marginalized.

"Is it an identity politic? No, it's actually a movement-building politic," she continued. "It lends itself toward a cross-movement politic, because we're talking about bringing together people from different kinds of social spaces—people in the blind community, people from communities of queers, people from deaf communities, Indigenous communities—and acknowledging that while we all have our various access needs, we are all impacted by the white supremacist ableism that is essentially dominating all of our movements."

Patty was also the cofounder and executive director of Sins Invalid, a Disability Justice performance project that incubates and celebrates artists with disabilities, centering artists of color and queer or gender-variant artists. The Sins Invalid website lays out ten guiding principles for operating within a Disability Justice framework, the Bill of Rights for true disability liberation. I encourage you to dig into the Ten Principles of Disability Justice and take them in in a way that fits your processing, but here they are in my own words.

At the top of the list is *intersectionality*, which acknowledges that every human is a collage of interconnecting identities, like a figure made of different-colored Lego blocks. Each identity can lead to both privilege and oppression, like how being a blind woman often lets me cut the line but also keeps me from finding it.

Next is having an *anti-capitalist politic*. Any person is free to pursue a productive career in their own way, outside of the "sleep is for earners" work ethic we idolize. This politic doesn't mean don't go out and earn bank. It means that when you make that bank, you take it and spread the wealth. It means don't buy the lie that any one body-mind is less valuable because their cog doesn't fit perfectly in the capitalist machine.

"We need resources to live, and at the same time, how we generate and where we distribute those resources is another conversation," Patty said during our chat, telling me that Sins Invalid received $1.2 million from MacKenzie Scott—Jeff Bezos's ex-wife—and that after paying bonuses to their staff of queer and disabled employees, they used the rest to pay reparations to descendants of enslaved people. "It's about what we do with our resources," she finished. "It's a choice whether or not we support our communities financially."

The next principle, *leadership of those most impacted*, says that the people most affected by oppression should be the leading voices in promoting change, something RAMPD takes very seriously. Many disability organizations are the brainchildren of well-meaning nondisabled mothers, fathers, and Beckys, but again, the only real experts on what people with disabilities need are the people living with those disabilities day-to-day.

Cross-movement solidarity calls on disability organizers to collaborate with other social justice movements like a mutual bad-assery power-up. Racial justice organizations, Indigenous rights movements, women's rights groups—they're force multipliers helping each other challenge long-held biases, unjust laws, and outdated stereotypes.

Sustainability comes next. Staying power should be the goal when building any movement or practice promoting long-term change.

Collective access says that everyone should have equal access to all aspects of culture, from computers to concert halls to

Congress, together with the swanky tech and other creative solutions that enable everyone to enjoy the modern and natural worlds without impairment.

Recognizing wholeness acknowledges that disabled people are whole people with unique inner desires, passions, intellect, and emotions that deserve appreciation.

According to *cross-disability solidarity*, every subcommunity under the Disability umbrella is equally important and valuable, and all have a role to play in creating a better future.

Collective liberation insists that all groups experiencing oppression—not just the Disability community—should walk, roll, or shimmy arm in arm toward equality, dignity, and freedom. No one is free until we are all free.

Last comes arguably the most important principle, *interdependence*. People within and outside the Disability community need to depend on and help one another without judgment and with a greater degree of understanding, respect, and grace. The goal is to create a culture where everyone freely supports one another and everyone feels empowered to let others know how they'd like to receive that support. Everything is founded on dignity, autonomy, empathy, and respect for each person's unique needs, situation, and preferences.

Even if we haven't always lived up to every one of them, these ten principles represent a standard toward which all social movements, including RAMPD's Disability Culture movement, must strive. If disability rights concern us all (and they do), then we're all Disability Justice warriors.

"Our communities are not something to be overcome; they are something to be invested in and given back to," Patty continued. "My hope is that there's more attention on how we can ensure that Disability Justice does not evolve in an anti-Black way . . . We need to make sure that we are resourcing ourselves and our community so that we can survive when—I'm not even saying *when* shit hits the fan—but *as* shit continues to hit the fan."

Pathologizing Identity as a Weapon

Now y'all know I'm a disciple of "Judyism," but here's what I want to know: When it comes to the 504 sit-in, why do we only know the white lady instead of the Black dude who *did* the dang thing? Is it because saying "We have federally mandated curb cuts because of the Black Panthers" doesn't fit our narrative of what American heroes look like? Why don't people talk about Brad Lomax with the same reverence and gusto they give Judy "Mother of the Disability Rights Movement" Heumann or widely recognized disability rights activist Ed "Father of the Independent Living Movement" Roberts?

A young, blind, Black man from San Francisco named Dennis Billups gave an interview to a Black Panther Party reporter at the sit-in. The transcript of what he said is like a lyrical, eloquent piece of found poetry. Here's a bit of it:

"To my brothers and sisters that are Black and that are [disabled]: Get out there, we need you. Come here, we need you. Wherever you are, we need you. Get out of your bed, get into your wheelchair. Get out of your crutches, get into your canes. If you can't walk, call somebody, talk to somebody over the telephone; if you can't talk, write; if you can't write, use sign language; use any method of communication—all of it is open . . ."

Why don't we know more about Dennis Billups? The heroic narrative of disability rights has been severely lacking in color, sauce, and Yaaas Queen Energy since its inception. Why is disability so not Black, Brown, or gay? Like anything with some added spice, grit, and soul, wouldn't the Disability movement be less . . . bland?

Well, throughout the eighteenth, nineteenth, and twentieth centuries, pathologizing an identity was used as a weapon to excuse unequal treatment of immigrants, women, and low-income people, as well as the dehumanization of Black people. A lot of this is highlighted in the article "Disability and the Justification of Inequality in American History" by Dr. Douglas Baynton. Hold on to your butts as we dip a toe in the boiling cauldron of America's history of weaponizing disability as a tool of oppression for a hot second.

Baynton starts by speaking on how the common antebellum argument in favor of enslavement was that the impaired intelligence of the African mind, as decreed by medical authorities of the day, rendered Black people unequal to other Americans. For instance, doctors said that enslaved people prone to escape had a laundry list of psychological disorders and that they would be further disabled by freedom. In fact, drapetomania was a fictional mental illness used to describe the tendency of enslaved people to try to escape captivity. Digging deeper, enslavers considered enslaved people who'd been subject to abusive conditions and malnourishment to be mentally or physically disabled, along with enslaved women who were infertile. Enslaved disabled people were subject to harsh punishments or neglect because of their inability to keep up, or were sold to doctors as subjects for medical experiments. It's no wonder Black Americans have mostly kept their distance from Disability identity.

Moving to the late nineteenth century, opponents of women's suffrage pointed to women's supposed "physical and temperamental disabilities"—citing frailty, intellectual inferiority, irrationality, and emotional instability—as evidence that they were incapable of equality and that things like voting and unnecessary education would place an undue mental and physical burden on them. Bayton points out that, like the antislavery writers, suffragists didn't challenge the view that disability justified inequality, but rather denied that women had disabilities and thus deserved equality. Suffragists asked why women should be classed with "idiots, lunatics, persons under guardianship, and felons."

Immigration laws, leading up to the Immigration Act of 1907 and subsequent regulations, directed inspectors to keep anyone with a mental or physical defect out of the country, with possible reasons for exclusion being arthritis, asthma, flat feet, poor eyesight, and other, more apparent disabilities. The commissioner general of immigration stated that "the exclusion from this country of the morally, mentally, and physically deficient" was the sole point of immigration laws. Bayton gets into the quota system initiated in 1924, which limited the number of immigrants from what were seen as "defective races" who could be allowed in. This was rooted in the widespread notion that certain ethnicities were more susceptible to congenital defects. Bayton quotes a sociologist of the time, who said, "The physiognomy of certain groups unmistakably proclaims inferiority of type . . . the polar opposite of our pioneer breed."

Ableism is classist, too. Throughout the first half of the twentieth century, the state of Virginia was a leader in the systemic eugenic sterilization of rural and lower-class white Americans. In her book *Pure America*, Elizabeth Catte discusses how eugenicists believed the forced sterilization of poor whites would pave the way to a better American society. The state passed the Virginia Sterilization Act of 1924, intended to limit the reproduction of the poor, disabled, and "feebleminded." The Supreme Court later struck down a challenge to the law, which led to more than seventy thousand sterilizations across the nation. Virginia didn't repeal the law until 1974, with the last sterilization under that program occurring in 1979.

Throughout the early twentieth century, America is also littered with examples of pathologizing Indigenous Americans. Insane asylums specific to Indigenous Peoples were federally sanctioned, the most notable being the Hiawatha Asylum for Insane Indians. "It's also referred to as the Canton State Hospital and is an example of the labeling of hundreds of natives with diagnoses like 'horse stealing mania,'" Vesper Moore explained over a Zoom call. Vesper is a mental health and disability rights activist and a tribal member of the Taíno Yukayeke. "When we talk about things like horse stealing mania," Vesper said, "it's the association of being violent, being fast. It was described like a compulsive urge to steal horses that came from a place of having a lack of profit—a criminal behavior that you can't help because you are lesser."

In 1952 The American Psychiatric Association (APA) deemed homosexuality a mental disorder under "sociopathic personality disorder," a classification that also included sexual deviance. This led to institutionalizations, electric shock aversion therapy, and lobotomies. After the 1969 Stonewall riots and the gay liberation movement, gay rights activists challenged the classification of homosexuality as a mental disorder because of the prejudice and inequality it invoked. The result was a panel discussion with the APA titled "Gay is Good."

With our rich history of pathologizing identities in order to classify them as undeserving of human rights (a.k.a. using medical model disability attribution as a tool for oppression), I can see why different historically oppressed groups have separated themselves from disability. They were busy trying to fight their own fights for dignity and autonomy. Some neurodivergent folks, d/Deaf folks, little people, folks with chronic conditions, and people with low access needs separate themselves from disability for the same reason.

There is the sense that a person with a disability *does* deserve oppression, so instead of saying "What's wrong with disability anyway?" it's easier to say, "Hold up, I'm not *them*, so I deserve dignity and rights." We see this tactic of weaponizing disability in the rhetoric of politicians today, who use disability as a tool to claim their opponent unfit for leadership.

But the APA itself says in the *Diagnostic and Statistical Manual of Mental Disorders, Fifth Edition,* "Judgment that a given behavior is abnormal and requires clinical attention depends on cultural norms that are internalized by the individual and applied by others around them." Culture defines disability. Because society can ascribe disability to whomever it wants whenever it wants, I'm like, *Okay, I proudly identify as disabled. And you can't bring me down, 'cause your ultimate kryptonite don't work no more. So now what?* (Sticks out tongue.)

Society can label me however it wants, but either way I'm deserving of the same air, water, and discounts; the same rights, the same opportunities, and the same space as the next guy. I deserve to be treated like everyone else. You know what? No, I actually deserve to be treated better than you treat everyone else, because if I have to say it, then you probably ain't treatin' people right.

I may navigate differently, see differently, date differently, and wear my hair differently, but treat me with dignity and respect my autonomy. Period.

The Intersection

"Because disability has been shunned by entertainment and pop culture, people tend to learn from me because I'm the first Muslim they're aware of meeting—because they don't realize their doctor was a Muslim—and then I'm the first disabled person they didn't get freaked out by or feel bad for," said Maysoon Zayid, a globally touring Palestinian comedian, actress, and author with cerebral palsy, who met up with me to chat.

"I literally became a comedian because my dream in life was to be on television," she said. "TV shunned disability. I saw Richard Pryor. He shook, he was Black. I shook. I was Brown. I was like, 'Let me become a fucking comedian.' That's the kind of hubris a twenty-one-year-old has."

Representation matters. Maysoon paints the perfect picture of how seeing figures in mainstream media who represent a similar story to yours can spawn the next generation of dope and different. For this reason, I'd like to amplify a few cultural icons, past and present, who intersect and have influenced my Black disabled story.

I've mentioned Tom Wiggins and Brad Lomax (who should hold the official title "Godfather of Disability Rights," by the way). Let's lay down some others. I'll start. First up, we have the queen herself, Harriet Tubman,* who we all know led dozens of enslaved families to freedom as the "conductor" of the Underground Railroad and who fought for women's suffrage after the

---

* I consider Harriet Tubman my ancestor in disability. She had charisma, led a bold movement, took heavy risks, never took no for an answer, and just kept on winning. Now them's my type of people!

Civil War. She acquired lifelong epileptic seizures and vision impairment after receiving a traumatic brain injury from her enslaver. Pity? She was like, "No, thanks, I'd rather change the world."

Legendary "High Priestess of Soul" and civil rights activist Nina Simone had bipolar disorder. Calypso icon, civil rights activist, and MLK Jr. confidant Harry Belafonte sported dyslexia. Afrofuturist writer Octavia Butler also had dyslexia. Voting and women's rights activist Fannie Lou Hamer rocked polio. Renowned hitmakers BB King and Bill Withers both stuttered. Rock & Roll Hall of Famer Curtis Mayfield, one of the most influential musicians in soul and socially conscious music, became paraplegic later in life.

Shout-out to present-day colleagues like Missy Elliott, who I was honored to meet up with at a White House gala (Graves' disease), Stevie Wonder, who I finally met up with in person at NAMM 2025 (blindness), Solange Knowles (neurodivergence), Whoopi Goldberg (dyslexia), and some artists I've had the pleasure to collaborate with, including *RuPaul's Drag Race* winner Yvie Oddly (chronic bone condition) and Apl.de.ap of the Black Eyed Peas (low vision, like yours truly). I can't forget Bridgit Antoinette Evans and Nikki Brown Booker, two Black women with disabilities working tirelessly to find, fund, and champion some of the most impactful disability narrative change projects.

I asked Maysoon if representation has gotten better in the media, in terms of comedy, for disability. "If you're a white man or Ali Stroker," she said, laughing. "There's some really incredible voices out there that I'm just blown away by, like Lauren Ridloff, Natasha Ofifi, and Ryan J. Haddad. But I don't see enough. Like Keah Brown says, 'Disability so fucking white, dude.'"

Each identity intersection in the pan-disability spectrum has a different set of stories that deserve representation. From queer disabled to Black or Brown disabled, to deaf or neurodivergent women, and not excluding straight white men (as class, size, age, and nationality also factor into systemic oppression), Disability Justice is a voice for every culture infiltrating from the margins.

Let's start with LGBTQIA+. First off, being disabled is uniquely different from being queer disabled. Living on both the LGBTQIA+ spectrum and the disability and neurodivergent spectrums, folks may have to hide two major parts of themselves for their own safety, but they also have the opportunity to rep twice as much identity pride within two rich communities.

A mix of systemic, cultural, and institutional ingredients combine to make it more likely for a queer person to develop a disability or mental health condition. The 2019 Movement Advance Project found that three to five million LGBTQIA+ Americans have a disability. The self-reported level of disability in the Queer community is approximately 36 percent, much higher than the general population, and includes mental health conditions like anxiety and depression that often come from being forced to self-isolate at a young age.

As for trans folks, this is a complex, nuanced conversation, and I am not trans, so it is certainly not my area of expertise. But here goes. Being trans is not a disability. However, there are some in the trans community who feel that the ADA makes gender-affirming care more accessible. Given that such care can be life-saving, and that the ADA may be the only way some people can access it (see "busted-ass healthcare system"), this is a valid point. OTOH, others believe that classifying gender dysphoria as a disability equals pathologizing the trans identity.

I think the only concrete conclusion here is that folks should be free to define their trans identity and, if they so choose, their Disability identity as they see fit, and that everyone should have access to the care they want without the burden of stigma or having their identity up for debate.

Disability Justice makes space for candid conversations about LGBTQIA+ disabilities, mental health, and body dysmorphia, especially among people of color. But community building, social platforming, and research into the queer/disabled intersection will only come with an increase in cultural representation. Visibility is the starting point for reducing isolation and promoting pride. The larger LGBTQIA+ movement has been wildly successful at this, incorporating cultural movement work with rights movement work, infiltrating TV, film, and media in order to change mainstream perceptions while advocating for legislative change.

While queer activists like artist Frida Kahlo (who, as I mentioned, had polio) and poet Audre Lorde (who had low vision and dealt with cancer) did not live during a time when they felt they could celebrate their Disability identity, activists of today like attorney Lydia X. Z. Brown, Deaf actor Nyle Dimarco, and former Lady Francesca of Drag Syndrome (a drag collective featuring queens and kings with Down syndrome) have been shedding a light and celebrating this fierce, bold intersection.

Let's pull up to the next intersection: disabled men of color. Being disabled is uniquely different from being Black disabled or Brown disabled. In fact, it's way—and I mean *way*—easier for me to be blind in America than to be Black in America. Again, the international symbol of accessibility is literally an upper-middle-class, skinny white dude in a wheelchair. You're like, *Lachi, again with the symbol argument?* Hear me out. I get that the symbol was made by a young woman, Danish art student Susanne Koefoed, sixty years ago. I also get that white paint shows up well on a blue background, but y'know what also pops? Black on yellow. I see you rolling your eyes, like, *C'mon, Lachi, it's just a symbol,* but symbols matter.

The symbol may also suggest that disability is purely physical and that only physical access needs should be met. But non-apparent disabilities are a big reason that 50 percent of Black disabled men are arrested by age twenty-eight, according to 2017 research published in the *American Journal of Public Health.* Black people experience disability through a Black lens, through the consummate non-model minority lens. Many Black autistic men, like Reginald Latson and Matthew Rushin, are hypersensitive, requiring care and patience when meeting their access needs. However, some law enforcement officers have been known to misinterpret their behavior, and they can end up in prison, which is a terrifying place for anyone, especially a nonspeaking person with sensory or developmental disabilities.

Black deaf men like Tyron McAlpin, Ricardo Harris, and Brady Mistic end up in prison for not being able to hear and follow police commands, and they're often not provided with adequate interpreters when brought in for questioning. They're tossed in prison because of lack of communication accommodations, and they are unable to functionally assimilate in an environment where assimilation is a matter of survival. The Innocence Project highlighted reasons why people with disabilities could be wrongfully convicted, including communication barriers, misrepresentation of behavior, inadequate accommodations, suggestibility, limited access to legal representation, memory and perception issues, and general prejudices and biases. It's a severely stacked deck.

Now, I have tons of friends who risk their lives in law enforcement every day, so no disrespect to any uniform. But intersectional bigotry against disabled Black men is real, systemic, and reinforced across all institutions. Also, a lot of Black and Brown men acquire disabilities and mental health conditions as a result of social circumstances like gang violence and the anxiety and grief that comes with it. Thug or not, they have a disability and need services—mental health and otherwise—that they don't get.

Few disabled Black male characters are featured in the media, and when they are, they're often portrayed in disploitative ways, as if the only way to make a Black character sympathetic and less threatening is to make him intellectually or developmentally disabled. Second, the Black man with intellectual or developmental disabilities is usually not a three-dimensional person, and is usually played by Cuba Gooding Jr., for some reason. The character is often an object of pity, allowing a white affluent family, community, or coach to be inspired, gain empathy, and learn a lesson. Everyone grows, or the case is thrown out, or the team wins, and we all ride off into the sunset.

But we never quite find out what happens to the disabled guy. Does he get married? Does he graduate from high school? Nobody knows. Receipts? Got 'em. *Radio*, with Cuba Gooding Jr., *Men of Honor*, also with Cuba Gooding Jr. (Author's note: Cuba, what up, my guy? Everything alright? You eatin' good?) *The Soloist*, with Jamie Foxx. *The Green Mile*, with the late Michael Clarke Duncan.

I asked Lateef McLeod his thoughts on the representation of Black disabled men in the media. Lateef, a nonspeaking augmentative and alternative communication (AAC) user, is a Black writer and intellectual with cerebral palsy, widely known for his searing poem "Why Are You Scared of Me?" "I think the media portrayal of Black men with disabilities has been harmful," Lateef said. "We have been portrayed as dangerous and out of control, or as helpless victims. So it puts us in these unwanted boxes in people's conceptions of us . . . Mainstream media needs to fully understand the Disability community has a vibrant culture."

Popular culture drives the narrative, and the narrative is that Black men are threatening, and that they particularly threaten American exceptionalism. Black disabled male characters are seldom fully realized human beings. Instead, they're neutered when portrayed in the media and neutralized when apprehended in real life.

To quote Keah Brown, "Representation saves lives." I want to see Black disabled men authentically represented in the media, living the reality of an actual Black disabled man with main character energy and a main character life, accomplishing main character dreams.

The Intersectional Feminist

Let's carve out space to talk about disability and women of color, because that's where this girl lives. It is also where the most self-expressive hairdos and the flyest AF outfits live. But it's also where misogynoir, the gendered racism I mentioned before that uniquely affects Black women, thrives.

Misogynoir is why I don't really get down with feminists. I've broken bread with Gloria Steinem in her home, so I know what a real feminist looks like. If you believe you're a feminist but you are not an intersectional feminist (or haven't heard the term), then you may not actually be a feminist. An intersectional feminist operates within a framework that recognizes the unique challenges faced by non-white and nonconforming women.

Black and Brown women with disabilities are held to an impossible triple standard. You're supposed to be a woman, which to many people means "be attractive but do nothing to attract attention." You're supposed to be Black, but not *too* Black, as you walk the tightrope between self-confidence and perceived aggression. You're also disabled and simultaneously navigating being ignored while being a burden, and being marginalized while being in the way. Does that not sound exhausting?

The Brown American identity generally includes some South Asian, Southeast Asian, Middle Eastern, North African, some Indigenous, Latin American, and some non-white immigrant cultures, and faces its own unique set of culturally driven challenges. These communities experience heightened fatal profiling, like John T. Williams, a deaf member of Canada's Nuu-chah-nulth tribe, who was shot and killed by Seattle law enforcement in 2010 for not responding to directions. These communities also experience heightened erasure due to an ingrained fear of bringing shame upon their families.

SukhJeen Kaur, creator of the nonprofit Chronically Brown, puts the power of shame within the Brown disabled population into perspective in a 2020 *Huffpost UK* interview. "It comes from that mentality of 'What will they say?' There's so much shame around illness that they can't talk about their illness," she says.

"So many people have had to ignore symptoms and have made it worse for themselves . . . I always wanted to make people know that your illness isn't a bad thing and you're not alone in this."

Many Black and Brown women with disabilities spend their lives fighting against the ever-bright gaslight, receiving very little space and grace from their counterparts. It's the gaslight that convinces us not to be proud, not to raise our hands, or not to feel pretty. It's the gaslight that tells us we need to straighten our hair or alter the way we speak or dress. It's the gaslight that demands perfection or it will be happy to escort us back home before we've even gotten to the party. I felt the gaslight at the U.S. Army Corps of Engineers. I feel the gaslight as I navigate music industry politics. I feel the gaslight every time someone tells me I'm intimidating or whenever I catch myself before apologizing for no reason. I recognize this cultural gaslighting to be a direct result of how Black women are misrepresented in the media. This misrepresentation leads to a lack of empathy for and understanding of the true and whole Black woman experience.

In television, film, advertising, and music we see the Black female character reduced to three tropes: the Mammy, the self-sacrificing quintessential Black mother who's usually portrayed as a maid; the Sapphire, the angry or aggressive Black woman who is generally combative, sassy, or ratchet; and the Jezebel, the oversexualized vixen whose power lies solely in her promiscuity. These caricatures have been around since the transatlantic slave trade, when such imagery was used to pimp out, upsell, or devalue enslaved females. The caricatures were popularized throughout nineteenth-century minstrel shows and are still going strong today.

With complex, authentic Black female stories being the exception, not the rule, the reductive depictions of Mammy, Sapphire, and Jezebel ignore the depth of a Black woman's complex lived experience and emotions. They say to audiences and society as a whole, "This is Black women" and to us Black women, "This is you. This is how we see you."

What these stereotypes tend to leave out is that Black mothers have the highest labor force participation rates of all American mothers, that Black women are considered the most educated subgroup of all Americans, that more than two thirds of Black women turn out to vote, that Black women can be attorneys general, House representatives, senators, and vice presidents, and that Black-owned businesses are the fastest-growing sector of women-owned businesses, including this here girl's business.

Personally, I often feel reduced to the Sapphire. Mainly because a good part of my advocacy requires confidence and ambition, and there is nothing that pushes society's "mad Black woman" buttons like an ambitious, confident Black woman. In 2013, *Essence* surveyed more than twelve hundred Black women and found that they had a resoundingly negative reaction to the portrayal of Black women in the media. Navigating life as a Black woman is like walking against strong winds; add disability into the mix, and it's a full-blown hurricane.

"One thing to know about Keah Brown," Keah said on our call, "she is pop-culture obsessed. I consider myself an aficionado. It's this thing that I love deeply, but it does not love me back. We live in a culture where people of color are supposed to say 'things are better and are slowly making the change,' and maybe they are, but I still don't feel represented as a Black, disabled, queer woman in pop culture . . . The idea that a disabled person, Keah, is happy or joyful, or can experience those things, still makes people uncomfortable. And so, I don't think that we are anywhere near giving disabled people, specifically disabled people of color, their full lived experience on-screen."

She continued, "I think one of the best things we can do is live a life we're proud of for ourselves and each other and call it a day."

Culture: Vibrant Not Silent

Here's why we need color, spice, and Yaaas Queen Energy in the Disability movement if we want to infiltrate the mainstream: Black Culture, Brown Cultures, Latin Cultures, and Queer Culture are what define the best of American pop culture, and pop culture sets the narrative.

When you think of Black Culture, you probably think of home-cooked food, witty slang, the downright swag, but mostly the trendsetting music, a global celebration of soul. Black folks are the paragons of resilience and resistance and have upheld a rich heritage of unbreakable spirit since before we got here. That's why teens keep turning to Black music and Black culture for identity during their rebellious years. Let's face it, Black is the new black.

For those suburban moms looking up tween slang in order to connect with their rebellious kid, here's the 411: Tween slang is what hip-hop was saying three years ago. Rock, pop, country, electronic music, K-pop—every genre of popular music came from Black traditions. Pretty much anything popping in pop culture got its start in Black culture. Creative, entrepreneurial Black folks are still out here shaping the culture, remixing the narrative ocean, and shaping the culture to our advantage, despite being discriminated against, despite appropriation.

When you think of Latin Cultures, you probably think of the food, the spice (I personally think of the drinks, but that's just me), the rhythms of rapid-fire Spanish, the close families, and the music and dance styles that celebrate a rich heritage that traces back to the Maya, Aztec, Taíno, and Inca civilizations, mixed with the Spanish and African histories of colonization and enslavement.

When you think of immigrant cultures in general, you might think of the importance of family, of ancient tradition, of education, and a proud work ethic. But what gets me is the food. Can't none of y'all beat authentically prepared food. We all know it, so let's stop playing like we don't.

Then there's Gay Culture, Queer Culture, or as it's now known for max inclusivity, the LGBTQQIP2SAA* community. When you think of Queer Culture, you think chic couture and bright, experimental style, sexual liberation, body positivity, finger-snapping empowerment, and radical self-acceptance. Queer identity has become iconic, having used culture and collective voice to drive one of the fastest cultural shifts on record.

From toxic stereotypes to outright violence, we've had to overcome horrific representation of Queer Culture across all forms of media. But once everyone in the 1990s realized they had a gay cousin, tunes changed, and queer concepts like the chosen family flourished.

What do Black, Brown, and Queer cultures have in common? Hold on, I want to say this deep into the mic: *unbreakable spirit!*

---

* LGBTQQIP2SAA stands for: lesbian, gay, bisexual, transgender, queer, questioning, intersex, pansexual, two-spirit (2S), androgynous, and asexual. FYI, "two-spirit" refers to an Indigenous person who embodies both masculine and feminine qualities. I love me some alphabet soup, and I'm here for every last letter!

Black folks are the definition of it, Queer folks wield it with surgical prowess, and immigrants wouldn't even be here without it. Cultures that don't inherently possess that spirit, that soul, would do anything to grab onto, claim, and harness it for their own.

We recognize the ongoing legacies of slavery, the continued abuse of trans and queer folks, and the xenophobia faced by immigrants, but the celebration and power of these cultures surpasses all of it. These communities are resilient, while still working overtime to dismantle oppression. Attaining civil rights is step one, but the real liberation comes in cultural work—in showing that our spirit and our pride in who we are is and will remain unbroken. This all supports my deep-rooted belief that the best way to change an oppressive system is to get the folks benefiting from it excited to be a part of the movement.

But why is it that when the general observer thinks about Disability Culture, they think either grievance, trauma energy, compliance training, or—at its most basic—broken? In *I Am Celine Dion*, though Celine struggles to adjust to her new life as a disabled woman, she emerges victorious, embracing her truth, and not allowing social pressures to keep her silent, saying in the film, "My spirit is unbroken." So what is the unbreakable spirit of disability?

Here's what I want the typical person to think when they hear the phrase *Disability Culture*, as I have laid out to everyone from my 2023 TEDx Talk audience to any local barista who'll listen. Disability Culture exemplifies the vast and diverse intersectionality of the disability experience, and includes the rich contributions, perspectives, and creative genius of our different minds and bodies. It is the music, words, and worldviews birthed from the oppression and erasure we've faced, and it is rooted in the problem-solving, ingenuity, and creative thinking that we use to navigate the world differently. It is unapologetic, adaptable, innovative, and resilient, and it deserves to be celebrated.

If we want mainstream culture to recognize the next-level guts and greatness of Disability Culture, we're gonna have to add some color, spice, grit, and style. I call upon the Disability community to lift up our Black, Brown, and Queer artists, storytellers, creators, and innovators, with their brilliant ideas and perspectives. I also call on Queer communities, immigrant communities, feminists, trans futurists, climate justice warriors, and most important, the Black community to seek out and lift up the disabled, neurodivergent, and those with chronic conditions within your community.

If we want to see radical change, mainstream acceptance, and Disability Justice in our collective futures, then we must recognize that every community has (and every individual is) a Brad Lomax. The Brad Lomax within all of us deserves to be celebrated, too.

Chapter Ten

A Declaration of Interdependence

It was February 28, 2023. Judy Heumann and I were chatting on the phone, as we'd been doing all that week, celebrating RAMPD's success at ramping up the 2023 Grammys and helping set the future of Disability Culture. This particular Tuesday, she was also trying to puzzle out what my speaking fee had been for a conference I'd keynoted the previous year. They were trying to book her for this year, and she wanted to ensure she wasn't getting screwed. Classic Judy.

Before we hung up, I said, "Hey, Auntie Judy." (It tickled her when I called her this, for some reason.) "Can you connect me to any dope Black leaders I should be connected with?" At the time, I was struggling to find other Black disabled females to kiki in community with. Judy would often call me up—at any random hour—and ask me to sing to her friends on speakerphone, and in return she opened up her Rolodex.

"I have the perfect intro for you," she said, and placed me on hold while she made a brief call, then came back only to keep me on the line while she sent an email to Keah Brown that read,

Keah, I just left you a voicemail re Lachi who lives in NY City and is a fabulous blind woman who is a musician, a storyteller, and a leader. I do hope the two of you can link up and let me know what mischief you will cook up. Seriously, I know you will both benefit from knowing each other and lending support to your visions. Send.

That's just who Judy was. When she was done clicking away on her smartphone, we said we were proud of each other, and that we loved each other. Little did I know that conversation would be the last with my mentor and friend.

Four days later, on March 4, Judy passed on at the age of seventy-five.

On that day, the constant force of New York Aries that is Lachi came to a complete halt. Several folks in the community received the news of Judy's passing from me, and I strong-friended folks through it, not quite ready to grieve myself. Other than the passing of my manager, Gary, from COVID, I haven't had a lot of death in my life, so I wasn't quite sure what to do or how to mourn. Why wasn't I crying? Was I in shock?

Not long after Judy's passing, I let a few friends know about my inability to mourn, and I was encouraged to write my feelings down in a song. It took a few days of aimlessly walking around the apartment, staring at walls, and loitering on park benches before I finally sat down at my keyboard, hit the voice memo record button, and started playing. I didn't realize I was in tears until I felt drops sprinkle onto my fingers. I began singing lyrics from my heart directly to Judy:

You would call me in the morning just as I woke up.
You didn't care for it when I mumbled, so with you I spoke up.

We would laugh about our dreams, and the world we wanted to see.
And who I needed to be, for the world I wanted to see.

It all began to come together spontaneously, because I was talking to my friend, and I knew my friend was listening.

The next day James Ian and I were on the phone comparing fun Judy anecdotes, and it felt good to laugh about her again. I asked James if he would join me in writing the song to continue the beautiful spirit of our conversation. James, another Judy disciple, is part of the RAMPD community and advocates for people with spinal muscular atrophy like himself. It was only fitting that we would collaborate on a musical tribute.

You know those moments when some cosmic Lego pieces click together, but you don't really know it happened until after the fact? That was that moment for us. Word spread that James and I were writing a tribute song for Judy, and other folks from RAMPD began expressing interest. Gaelynn Lea got involved. April Rose Gabrielli, a songwriter and producer living with epilepsy who's signed with BMG and is also part of the RAMPD community, caught wind of the song and jumped on board as a cowriter to give the track some pop edge.

Jacob Kulick, April's partner, a half-deaf producer who's done work for Sony, was down to mix and master the recording for us. And we were off, virtually constructing this new, powerful song called "Lift Me Up." As we were making the track, it was already clear that this project had evolved far beyond just us.

Then one day, during a Zoom writing session, we came to a consensus: *We should release this song in July with a music video!* Of course! It was already late March, and July 2023—Disability

Pride Month as well as the fiftieth anniversary of the Rehabilitation Act—was approaching fast, but I was determined that we would have a finished song and a finished music video ready to go by July. Even though we had no budget, no business plan, and no release partners, I was like, "Judy, take the wheel." And she did.

Day Al-Mohamed, the disabled filmmaker and another one who was close to Judy, had just left her gig as the White House's director of disability policy, so she was a free agent. Before the White House doors shut behind her, I jumped in her path and exclaimed, "Boy, do I have your first post–White House project right here!" I told her what it was. As if this were the *Rick and Morty* heist episode, she was like, "You son of a bitch, I'm in!"

It really was like building a crew for a heist—Lachi's Eleven, except that instead of cat burglars and con artists, we had award-winning, authentically disabled artists and crew. Catriona Rubenis-Stevens, an acclaimed short-film director who I'd met through the 2022 Easterseals Disability Film Challenge, jumped on board as a director-producer, and brought invaluable crew members from up and down the disabled, neurodivergent, and queer spectrum, including director of photography Caroline Mariko Stucky. We were also fortunate enough to snag Genevieve Ramos, a Chicago sketch artist with cerebral palsy, to create the cover art for the song.

I was adamant about having sign language performers portraying James, Gaelynn, and me, and having them front and center, not in a box in the corner. The team was like, *hell to the yes.* So we found and cast three viral and authentically Deaf/hard of hearing ASL performers—Aurnell Russell, Otis Jones, and Amber Galloway (who doubled as director of artistic sign language)—to sign for the three of us out in front. Both Gaelynn and Amber just happened to be in New York when we needed them, so things were all lining up for us to shoot this thing and record final vocals in the beginning of May.

Somehow, Arthur had jiu-jitsued a clear plate for me, so I was ready to work magic. I was flying folks in, paying dailies, renting spaces and equipment, and purchasing insurance policies, all using the stash of cash under my mattress. I approached a few labels about partnering for support, but got the same message: *A song and video revolving around disability? We don't get it.* But I wasn't even pressed. With Judy at the wheel, I knew the money would come. This thing was hurtling downhill at high speed, and stopping it was no longer an option.

We shot the "Lift Me Up" video at the historic Gymnopedie, a Brooklyn space famous for gymnasium video shoots, and recorded final vocals at Quad Recording Studios in Midtown Manhattan. The love in the air at both the shoots and the sessions was palpable.

The goal was to make a high-quality, competitive video celebrating intersectional disability and accessibility. We wanted to add a brief audio description at the top of the video, which would allow blind people to enjoy it, so we brought on Ali Stroker, who played Judy in that *Drunk History* episode where I first learned about her, to voice it. When I asked Ali, she also said, "You son of a bitch, I'm in!" Perfect synchronicity.

We then added captions and transcripts on YouTube. The final "Lift Me Up" track and video was authentic, beautiful, and most important, so professionally polished that labels, brands, and folks with a few dollars immediately began to sniff around the project.

Meanwhile, back at the Batcave, we had been talking up the project, releasing snippets, and getting the community involved. We brought on Rosemary McDonnell-Horita of Crip Camp's Impact Campaign and she helped us put together a fifteen-day countdown to the premiere, which got the community fired up and buzzing. Disability community leaders like Jim LeBrecht, Haben Girma, Tiffany Yu, Keri Gray, Mandy Harvey, Keith Jones, Judy's brother Rick Heumann, and so many more were incredibly supportive.

As we got down to the final hours, Facebook, LinkedIn, and the blogosphere were ablaze, and the powers that be at Google finally said, *You know what, you son of a bitch, I'm in!* Google jumped in and sponsored the project, and we were off.

We dropped "Lift Me Up" on July 25, 2023, to a tumult of fanfare and excitement. MTV.com premiered the video. It played on BET Soul. It played on terrestrial radio, peaking at number twenty-nine on the adult contemporary charts. We got written up in *The Hollywood Reporter*. We got release-day support from Google, Android, and our friends Coldplay, who really helped blow the thing up. The video went viral, scoring millions of views on TikTok and hundreds of thousands of streams across music platforms in our first week. The song became the 2023 Disability Pride anthem.

Before long, the White House was buzzing about "Lift Me Up," thanks to some strings Jim LeBrecht was pulling in the background. The project ended up winning Best Music Video at Diversity in Cannes in association with the Cannes Film Festival, won a Bronze Shorty Award, and had screenings across the globe, including at Deaf film festivals.

Like me, Judy was a *connectrovert*, someone who's all about community, connectivity, and power building, and our tribute reflected that. People from all across the spectrum lifted each other up—behind the camera, in front of the camera, and across the internet, creating a vibrant ripple of love, power, and legacy. We showcased women directors and Black, Brown, Deaf, disabled, neurodivergent, and LGBTQIA+ artists and crew, with everyone, top to bottom, operating out of love.

I caught up with Ali Stroker and asked her how she enjoyed the experience, and as I suspected, her answer made my heart smile. She said, "Working with you on this was an absolute dream. You are a professional and a creative genius, and I am so excited to see where that voice takes you next." Right back at you, Ali!

Judy was also about mainstreaming disability, and that's exactly what "Lift Me Up" set out to do. We created a work of commercially competitive art good enough to rival other mainstream tracks and music videos, but with a beating heart of pure Disability Pride. We lifted up Disability Culture with authentic representation, accessible art, community culture, impact, and purpose. It was a groundbreaking, transformative experience and the first of many such projects. Best of all, I knew I had Judy by my side the entire time, cheering me on—and up there somewhere playing the whole thing on speakerphone.

That's community. That's working pop culture to amplify disability narratives to mainstream discussion. We did that. Us. The Disability community. The more we say no to the "crabs in a barrel" mentality, the more control we have over our own cultural narrative.

You know the analogy. You put a bunch of crabs into a barrel, and when one starts to climb out, the others drag it back down. That's that zero-sum game, the scarcity mindset that says if one person from a group gains an opportunity, the others lose that opportunity. You often find this way of thinking in historically excluded groups. But the other crabs, even the ones trying to pull you down, aren't actually the problem. The problem is the barrel. Who put this barrel here, and how the heck do we get out? The chef and fine-diners outside the barrel—the ones defining and picking the "choice" crabs—create and perpetuate this problem.

The scarcity mentality declares that everyone's competing for a tiny slice of the same shrinking pie, so there's never enough to go around. But scarcity is the greatest con in human history. There are as many opportunities as there are ideas, but we've been prevented from thinking big by oppressive systems that have told us we can't—or shouldn't. But we *can* and *should*. When people ask me, "Lachi, how do you find all these opportunities?" I tell them I just have a ton of big ideas (thanks to the ol' ADHD) and the compulsion to carry them out (muchas gracias, OCD). To an entrepreneurial mind, where there's talent, big ideas, bigger cojones, and a dive right into the trenches, the sky's the limit. We know the entrepreneurial spirit is baked in for hustlers with disabilities, so why the scarcity mentality?

Before I go there, it's important to honor the fact that, due to social barriers and a history of exclusion and erasure, being disabled or neurodivergent is really tough for a lot of people. No one has the right to tell anyone else how to hurt, or what to do about that hurt. For some people, every day is a bare-knuckle brawl just to get bare-bones accommodation and a little bit of human dignity. I understand the natural inclination to envy the haves when one feels they are a have-not.

An abundance mindset is the fix. An abundance mindset opens our doors to each other, allowing us to compound our ingenuity, problem-solving skills, and drive. It allows us to push for change through our ideas, resilience, and collective voice. An abundance mindset says *more is more*, and everyone was born to contribute their "more."

So how can we overcome ableism, our urge to keep each other in the barrel, and achieve this culture of collective difference? Well, because I firmly believe every one of us intersects with the Disability identity, I also believe that not only is it up to us to make that paradigm shift, it is *because of* us that shift *will* happen.

It comes down to one thing: *interdependence*. With interdependence, all individuals in a system recognize that when we collaborate to meet each other's needs, we're stronger, we're better, and we all win.

How could we possibly achieve that utopia, you ask? Well, thankfully, there's a formula:

$$Interdependence = (Allies + Community) - Social\ Barriers$$

My interpretation of this equation is a sexy, disability-centric update of its original 1959 debut in *The Social Psychology of Groups*. You get interdependence when *a community* and its *allies* collaborate to overcome *social barriers*. Now, let's deconstruct this bad boy.

Breaking Down Social Barriers

Social barriers are engineered conditions that limit everyday functioning. I'm talking about everything from employment, healthcare, and educational barriers to the literal physical barriers that keep people with disabilities from accessing employment offices, hospitals, and university lecture halls. This is where intentional inclusion, accommodation, and accessibility join the convo, because the more you clear away barriers for one person, the more you create momentum to include all people.

This is that curb-cut effect again doing its thing. Email, elevators, closed captions, Hue lights, home devices like Alexa, family-size restrooms, text-to-speech, speech-to-text, captions, remote controls, and, well, curb cuts are all great examples. When job seekers with disabilities get what they need to nail an interview and do their jobs effectively, people without those disabilities also benefit from having those more convenient, less strenuous options. Bonus, they also come into contact with a larger pool of dope-ass fellow humans with dope-ass stories who can enrich their lives in dope-ass ways.

Often when talking about accessibility and accommodation, people focus on physical wheelchair access. And that's valid. But it's mainly because the only interaction most folks have with disability is the parking spot, bus seat, or bathroom stall they're not supposed to use. But that's just the pretty, hand-scrolled foam on top of the tasty latte that is accessibility.

First, when it comes to social barriers, accommodating someone could just be a trust signal or vibe. Even if it's a struggle to enter a space, you can tell if the people trying to help you get in have inclusive, "We serve your kind here" energy. Second, accessibility and accommodation are different, but intersecting, concepts. The University of Wisconsin–Madison puts it really well: "Accessibility is proactive and strives to remove barriers during the design stage . . . Accommodation is reactive and strives to remove barriers for individuals caused by inaccessible design." Good accessible-first design is smart design, but because there is no accessibility checklist that could cover all needs, having a mindset that's always down to accommodate is the name of this here game.

Certain accommodations can be beneficial across disabilities. For example, something that makes things easier for people with vision loss could also be beneficial for neurodivergent people, such as special lighting, self-descriptions, consent before touch, and clear directions. Also, raise your hand if you wouldn't benefit from consent before touch or clear directions! Audiobooks, originally designed for the blind, also empower people who learn or read differently.

The ultimate goal is *universal* design, products, and environments that are usable to the widest range of people right from the start, lessening the need for individual accommodations and expensive add-ons. For that to happen, we'll need more "We serve your kind here" buy-in from society as a whole. Dr. Josh Miele, the blind MacArthur Genius I talked about earlier, says this accessibility utopia starts with ending ableism.

"Accessibility, the technical side of disability inclusion, is something that we can do, but it's not enough," he said on our Zoom call. "You can't really have complete disability inclusion until you have accessible systems, whether it's a classroom, a computer, or a workplace. But the real giant to be slain here is ableism, the assumption that people with disabilities are not as valuable, don't contribute as much, and are not as human as people without disabilities."

Josh went on, "The Americans with Disabilities Act drives the conversation forward, but is not the endgame. The endgame is that while we need accessibility, we need the tools to make sure people can participate. What we really need is to shift the culture. That's the same struggle that everybody who isn't at the pinnacle of privilege is fighting."

Exactly. It's about changing attitudes, opening minds, and getting more people saying "Oh snap, I get it now!" Access is belonging is inclusion is love. It's fostering an "I want you here" culture.

I want to feel good about the culture in which I live. When I see that culture accommodating everyone equally, with dignity and respect, even if I'm not benefiting at that moment from that accommodation, I feel better about that culture—about where I work, live, go to school, hang out with my friends, or get my nails did. When we see someone else being valued *for* their differences, not in spite of them, we assume that's how we'll be treated when it's our turn. We feel seen, heard, understood, and connected. We work harder, contribute more, and show up fully for each other. We lift each other up.

The Allyship Question

Now, let's move on to the *allyship* portion of our interdependence formula. In her book *Please Don't Sit on My Bed in Your Outside Clothes*, the gorgeous and talented Phoebe Robinson (full disclosure: she's the founder of the imprint that published this book, and totally a Dope Queen regardless) has a brilliant essay called "We Don't Need Another White Savior" that slices through the performative fiddle-faddle that often stains allyship. I encourage you to read the whole essay, but in part she writes:

> The revolution cannot and should not be
> Karenized. That vibe wants fast results, placation,
> and constant positive reinforcement, and
> recontextualizes easy wins as major victories, so
> that when the wins don't quickly happen or happen
> at all for the weightier and messier issues,
> disappointment and frustration settle in,
> threatening to dissuade future efforts.

Phoebe was speaking in the context of racial allyship, but the concept could be applied to all oppressed groups, including the disabled population.

Those who aren't in tune with the Disability community or their own Disability identity are often afraid of overstepping, saying the wrong things, or acting on the wrong assumptions, mainly because they've been taught to reduce Disability Culture to grievance culture. If this is you, it just means you're not quite an ally yet, but don't fret, we'll get you there.

Being an ally to the Disability community starts with accepting the Disability identity within you. Ask yourself, "Where does my experience intersect with disability, neurodivergence, or chronic or mental health conditions? Who in my immediate family or community can I relate to on those levels? Is there a larger community outside of this that I can connect with on any of these levels? If so, where are they, and how do they talk, navigate, and view themselves?"

I'm an ally. I'm not a d/Deaf person or a wheelchair user, and I don't have Tourette's, but I do know what it's like for an aspect of my physical and psychological identity to be viewed as too far from Reference Man perfection to deserve equity or respect. That understanding came after some heavy introspection. Even though I was born legally blind and was diagnosed with both OCD and general anxiety during my time at the Corps, I didn't accept that I had a disability or neurodivergences until much later. Accepting my Disability identity led me to seek out and listen to the Disability community and eventually join it. Now I staunchly (and stylishly) advocate for my Disability family, which includes people with disabilities, nuerodivergences, and other chronic conditions that aren't my own.

Whatever part of the Disability community we intersect with, we all know what it's like to fight for accessibility and accommodation, persevere through discomfort, dodge shame and stigma by any means, face down stereotypes without apologizing, and try to make a decent living and be treated like sexy-ass, intelligent, independent adults. Some people have higher-access needs than others, but that doesn't make anyone "more disabled" than anyone else. Everyone has a personal relationship to disability, and once you recognize yours, you're on your way to being a true ally. You will be more comfortable approaching, speaking to, and learning from a person with a disability because you will see and recognize the "you" in them.

Suppose you see someone with a disability in an airport looking confused or stressed. First, recognize your apprehension for what it is, then set it aside. Think to yourself, *How would I want a Good Samaritan to approach me, if I was that person?* You might then approach the person, armed with this mindset, and say something like, "Excuse me, is there anything I can do to help you?" If they're an adult, you would speak directly to the disabled person, not their handler, and face them, not their interpreter, if they have one. Because that's what you would want. You would acknowledge their *crip time*—the time it takes for a disabled person to communicate or complete a task—with patience and empathy. The person might respond verbally, via text, or via their interpreter, with a polite decline of your help. You may then be like, *Aight, later, Boss.*

Or they may say, *Actually, which way is gate five?* To which you could respond, *It's ten gates down and to the left. I can go with you halfway, but then I gotta peace out to my own gate. Is that cool?* The person might smile, thank you, and now y'all are off like two buddy cops. You didn't do it for thanks (though a "Good looking out, my friend" send-off might brighten your plane ride a little) but because of empathy. You did it because you're both people and that's just what people do.

There's a great quote cowritten by the members of a 1970s aboriginal rights collective in Queensland, Australia: "If you have come here to help me, you are wasting your time. But if you have come because your liberation is bound up with mine, then let us work together." Allyship is no more complicated than that. It doesn't need to be combative, burdensome, or full of anxiety or guilt. Just a little patience and some "I see you" understanding. But if you do feel that anxiety or guilt 'cause you're not there yet, my advice is not to check your privilege, but to use it. Educating yourself by following, listening to, and learning from creators and leaders across the Disability community is a good toe dip. You'll see a clearer reflection of yourself in the person who provoked that anxiety, and you might find the key to the growth needed to address it.

Allies are not lifeguards, reaching a hand down to pull someone up. Allyship is a handshake from equal footing. It is listening, empathizing (not sympathizing), and giving space. It is recognizing the value of and opportunity in someone else. It is recognizing yourself in someone else. Allyship begins within.

The Disability Community

Let's dig into *community*. In some instances the term *Disability community* is used to refer to the full disabled population in order to contextualize the blanket concept to a nondisabled public. But they are very different groupings, and since it's just you and me, I'll give you the real tea. The disabled population is just anyone who reports having a disability. Those who ascribe to the Disability *community* and those who identify with a disability-specific subsect share a sense of solidarity and pride and wouldn't be caught dead uttering *differently abled*.

We tend to value working with other people who identify as disabled to improve life and autonomy through advocacy, impact campaigns, creative collabs, or simple gatherings. We embrace our Disability identity with pride and purpose, and build or are part of everything from Disability Pride parades to cultural centers and resource groups. We take bold action to eliminate stigma and shame. Finally, we embrace the social model of disability, which says that disability is a natural difference between people and that it is societal barriers and social exclusion, not our differences, that truly impair us.

(Sidebar: I was putting together a joke about how the disciples of the social model, those who are all about reclaiming disability words, like *crip*, should be called Crips, while medical model people, those who believe in cures and blood work, should be called Bloods. My white friends didn't laugh. My Black friends didn't laugh. My Crip friends didn't laugh. My Blood friends didn't laugh. Comedy is brutal.)

Truth is, the different disability-specific community subsects are still working on what it would look like to fully coexist, claim space, and grow resources. Sometimes, we cooperate for the betterment of everyone in the broader community. Sometimes, we don't get it quite right. But that's okay. Disability power-building is a radically new concept, never mind pan-disability power building.

The widely divergent physical realities of daily life for people with different disabilities, whether we're talking accessibility, communication, or health and safety, also mean sometimes we don't have a common cause to unite behind. Neurodivergent folks might advocate for workplace designs that accommodate sensory processing, while people with chronic muscle pain work to fight against medical gaslighting.

So what are our shared interests? Disability justice. Equity. Accessibility. The end of ableism. As our collective definition of disability and Disability identity takes shape, so will our collective goals. We can all come together as a community and work toward those goals, which benefit everyone, while each subsect still strives independently toward fulfilling whatever disability-specific mission is most important to its members. For me, as long as one subsect ain't out there like, "We're not the freaks, they are," then we're on our way.

I asked my friend Lacey Henderson, a Paralympian, model, and sports psychology professional who lost her right leg to cancer, about Disability community and identity on our call. The Paralympics is an international Olympic-grade sports competition for athletes with disabilities that's been going strong since 1948. With the U.S. taking home 105 medals in 2024, the games have been a great example of a mainstream-penetrating, disability-centered event that is inspirational, yet anything but a traumady.

Lacey told me that the world of disabled athletics, where the "walkies" and the "wheelies" converge to compete at the elite level, has fostered in her a deep sense of pride. "I've joked for a long time that disability has had terrible marketing," she said. "But I loved my experience at the Paralympics because there's something so special about doing what it takes to become a professional athlete, achieving these really high performance results, while also knowing what it's like to experience being disabled in a society that does not see you as a meaningful, contributing member."

I asked Lacey when she began to feel Disability community pride. "It was a variety of things, like when my frontal lobe finally fucking formed at twenty-eight and I felt my head get removed from my own ass, which was really life-changing," she said, laughing. "I was self-involved for a really long time. When I joined parasports, I had no idea there were hot disabled people other than me. What a shocker. But I didn't understand what it truly felt like to belong until I was in a Disability community like that. And I mean, it was an evolution of me starting to give a shit about other people outside of myself. I started seeing more fundamental issues that affected me, but also affected a lot more people."

She went on, "Disability has done a lot historically to move things forward. But we have a hell of a lot more work to do. And the only way we can do that is if we do it together. If we bring everybody with us and everybody gets heard."

So our community still has some growing to do to set its differences aside, lift each other up, and eventually achieve the collective, radical change we hope to inspire. But we don't have to be in lockstep. We don't have to give up our individual causes. In fact, we don't have to give up anything. We can stay ferociously independent, with the understanding that because we all bring something to the table, we're stronger when we're united.

Here's a perfect example. Molly Burke, who I've mentioned, was one of the first dozen creators with disabilities I came across in my pre-COVID search for community, and my silent rejection of her tagline at the time, "I happen to be blind," eventually led to where we are now—you and me, on this page, claiming our mutual Disability identity. Molly and I have since become good friends, so I felt completely comfortable asking her the big question.

I asked her, "Why do you like to say, I *happen* to be blind, as opposed to identifying as blind?"

"I think especially early on in the industry, everything was because I'm blind," she said on our Zoom call. "So I was either succeeding because I'm blind or I wasn't successful because I'm blind. Somehow, everybody seemed to pick and choose whichever one they thought felt right at the time. So 'She's only getting views because she's blind.' But also, 'You're not going to succeed because you're blind, and there's no room in this industry for people like you.' How can it be both? How is everything I do about my blindness and not my talent or my work? Every headline was 'Blind YouTuber does XYZ.' I was just like, 'Yes, I'm proud of it, and it's a huge part of my identity.' But when you remove the human from me, you dehumanize the community."

I asked her if that was why she eventually settled on: "I'm a YouTuber. I'm a model. I'm a speaker. I am also blind."

"Correct," Molly said. "These are the things that I do that are important and meaningful, but also, I'm blind."

As our light, spirited conversation went on, we agreed that both self-representations, "identify as" and "happen to be," are valid and can coexist in an empowered space, mainly because we've felt both at a visceral level. I'd felt the exact same way Molly did after I signed with the EMI label. We, like all other individuals in the disabled population, are on a journey toward our own definition of identity, acceptance, and pride, and no one is a monolith. There is no one-size-fits-all solution to oppression. There is only community.

Universal accessibility. More accurate representation in popular culture, behind the camera, in the boardroom, and in public office. Greater economic opportunity. Education that wipes away the stigma of disability. That's our rising tide. We can all agree on those. But let's start with something basic: letting people know the Disability community exists. We out here! Many have no idea that there are creators, authors, organizations, online forums, a whole pride month in July, year-round events, and people who understand what they're going through, who they can listen to and learn from as they work toward accepting their own Disability identity. Let's let the world know we exist, and that they're welcome. That'll do for a start.

If the idea of Disability community could penetrate mainstream discussion, someone like Dave Grohl, Nirvana drummer turned Foo Fighters frontman with ADHD, would not have blamed himself for his troubles at school and for dropping out. Actor Mark Ruffalo, who has ADHD and dyslexia, told the Child Mind Institute that he felt "unique and freakish, like I didn't fit in anywhere," while Channing Tatum, who has the same diagnoses, told *The New York Times* he, too, had trouble fitting in. Journalist Lisa Ling found out she had ADHD through her own reporting on it, while Daniel Kwan, codirector of *Everything Everywhere All at Once*, says he realized he had ADHD after staying up all night in tears conducting research on it for the film.

Right there, there's a whole ADHD community of wildly successful people in the same industry. But are they navigating the social trials or triumphs of their neurodivergence as a community? Ruffalo said he would tell his younger self, "There's help and there are ways to deal with it and to manage it and to overcome it."

I would tell his younger self, "You are not alone. We got you."

We All Need Somebody to Lean On

Now for the final variable in our formula, *interdependence*. That's when a person with a disability and an ally mutually benefit from navigating a social barrier together, with the understanding that every identity intersects with disability and that everyone, whether accepting of their Disability identity or not quite there yet, can be an ally. Coming together to create beautiful art celebrating Judy, locking arms as allies, integrating accessibility from the jump, building a community that unites while maintaining its individuality . . . it's all interdependence.

Interdependence rejects the narrative that disability equals scarcity and that we need to trip the kid scurrying next to us in the rat race so we can get ahead. Interdependence recognizes that like a Phil Jackson–led basketball team where every player plays an important role—looking at you, Muggsy Bogues—everyone's differences have value and contribute to the whole. It recognizes the strength in asking for support and the gain in providing it. There's a reason we are social beings. We all need each other, and we're better when we're working together.

When I woke up blind that June morning in New York and did my first-ever Strut down to the eye clinic on Fourteenth Street, interdependence got me there. Being bold enough to ask for help got me there. The catcaller on the street corner walked me to the bodega. The transit workers walked me to Strawberry. The retail workers helped me get a new, non-kombucha-stained shirt. And the cabbie got me to the clinic, skipping the line and all.

To many in the Disability community, interdependence means viewing people not as opponents but as opportunities. That's true allyship. I don't need you to save me, but I do want you to be on my team. True interdependence sees no distinction between the person with a disability and the ally, because we all have needs, and we all have something to offer. Here's what I mean. One day, while I was working on this book in a coworking space—rocking my nondescript hoodie, baggy jeans, Glam Cane, and seven-inch heels ('cause I can't really be nondescript)—I went around the corner to a Starbucks. I walked up, placed my order, and the barista began making the latte.

A bit peckish, I started digging around the snack section looking for some of that Starbucks butter popcorn, because does anyone really go to Starbucks for the coffee? The barista asked me what I was after, and I smiled and said something ridiculous like, *One hundred and fifty calories of butter in a bag.* He laughed, came around the counter, picked out the popcorn for me, rang it up, and told me where to insert my card. No fuss, muss, or drama. I got my drink and snack and started maneuvering around for a table. A young woman came up, complimented my heels, and then indicated a table that was unoccupied, so I thanked her and took a seat. End scene.

That might seem like a mundane, routine interaction, and that's the point. It was ordinary. I wasn't burdening anyone. In fact, I offered respite from the burden of monotony to a young woman, and made an otherwise bored barista smile. No one sacrificed their dignity. No one felt patronized. No one felt obligated. No fanfare. We were just New Yorkers being courteous to each other on a Tuesday. That's why I love my city: Interdependence is second nature. It's amazing how far a touch of charm and a smidge of diplomacy can get you. You might be saying, *Well, now that's just pretty girl privilege,* to which I say, *Why, thank you!* But they would have never even encountered this pretty girl if we still had the ugly laws.

I was going through a small sliver of my day and two other New Yorkers were going through small slivers of theirs. Those days intersected for about a minute and a half, everyone did their individual thing together, and the world was a smidge better for it.

The difference between interdependence and grievance culture is a radiating acceptance of Disability identity. But is the world really ready for an interdependent utopia, where each individual values everyone else's space, creativity, access needs, and dignified autonomy as much as they value their own? Some people across the disability spectrum fear this may water down their identities or that their priorities will be put on the back burner if everyone begins to embrace their Disability identity. But when we treat everyone with dignity according to their needs—not just people who identify as disabled—*all* accommodations can be taken more seriously, including ours. We definitely have work to do and trust and alliances to build. We bring resilience, entrepreneurial passion, intellectual rigor, adaptability, leadership, and creative genius to the table. First thing, we've got to go beyond viewing disability as just diversity and see it for what it really is: a shared social identity.

Social identity is a construct. It's the "we" and the "us." It's the belonging that defines our relationships with each other, with the world around us, and with ourselves. Identity is taking individual pride in the community you've claimed and helped to build. It's choosing how you wish to be seen, heard, and held. It's resilient when challenged, but open to growth. It's protective but open to change. Identity is power, acceptance, individuality, and community.

I took a chance in discovering, embracing and eventually celebrating my disability. And my disability is exactly that. *Mine.* That is identity.

Lifting Each Other Up

When identity and community come together, great things happen. Here's what that looks like:

I wanted to write a book. When one wants such an audacious thing, one first pitches a short book proposal to potential literary agents, and once an agent accepts the proposal, they then begin the journey pitching to publishers. I linked up with Tim Vandehey, and when we were nearing the finish line with the book proposal for *I Identify as Blind*, Tim said something like, *We'll get a major publisher down to tell this story. But that starts with us getting a top-tier agent down to sell this story.* I don't think it rhymed when he said it, but I nailed his casual confidence.

I remember thinking, *Bruh, publishing industry so white and I am so Black disabled.* I then asked, "How do I get an agent?" knowing full well the query-rejection-rinse-repeat hell that is the agent search.

Tim responded with something like (though he still didn't rhyme), *Turn to your community, and ask with impunity.*

My community? For a Black woman, daughter of immigrants, and artist who came to accept my Disability identity later in life, the idea of asking anyone who wasn't Judy for help, let alone asking someone from the Disability community, was daunting. I almost preferred cold-call-query hell. But I was tryna write a book on Disability Culture, community, and power, so I had to walk my walk and trust in my community.

I started by writing to exactly three trusted friends, Judy Heumann, Haben Girma, and Emily Ladau. I said, "Heyyy . . . how are we? Miss you! Can you hook a sister up with your agent? Miss you for real! But the agent though . . . hugs and kisses!" All three friends, in different ways, said *Sure.*

Emily had gotten back to me first, so I looked up her agent's website only to find she was not accepting submissions (the subtext read *ever again*). I queried anyway, because screw it, that's how I got signed at South by Southwest. Within forty-eight hours I received this response back from Laura Lee Mattingly: "Well, receiving this note made my morning. I've been following you on Instagram for quite some time now." Apparently Laura Lee, who also identifies as blindish, knew a friend of mine, Will Butler, another fellow blindish, and he'd turned her on to my content celebrating identity pride. Huzzah!

Generally I'm known out on the street for #MakeUpAddiction photos, so this was a happy surprise. Before long, Laura Lee was knee-deep in the *I Identify as Blind* proposal and nabbed us the perfect partner in Phoebe Robinson's Tiny Reparations Books, an imprint that's hyper-focused on amplifying unique, diverse voices. The company is a part of Penguin Random House, the largest publisher in the country. Now, here we are. That's community.

"I'm the expert on my story, not the expert on disability," Emily said when I asked her how she'd felt about my asking for a connection to her agent. "Even in my book, I point people to other people's work, writings, and resources, because if you read one book, you're still only scratching the surface on disability. So for me, if somebody is saying, 'I want to also share my story,' I want to help you broaden that landscape, because I'm not the sole owner and proprietor of Disability, Incorporated."

Emily continued, "The other thing I think is important to mention, is that my book deal also came because of the Disability community lifting each other up. One of my friends who has a disability invited me onto a podcast. Laura Lee heard me on the podcast and recognized that she'd read some of my writing previously, so she reached out. So, again, it's like, why wouldn't I pay that forward?"

For my community, I am grateful. For my many identities, I am grateful. For this time you've spent with me, getting to know me, I am grateful. Just know that to know me is to love audacity, honesty, and change. Some see change as frightening, but change is life, and life is always a gain. So I offer you my hand in collective difference. Together, let's render shame powerless. Let's celebrate our unapologetic deviance from the oppressive and mediocre standard of the Reference Man.

You wanna win? Let's flex our perceived flaws. Let's take that thing that makes us most unique—that thing we're most afraid or ashamed of—and wear it on a T-shirt. That's how we win.

Last Word

Underestimated, so overachieves
Pearl-clutching stares, so drapes finest beads
Uninvited by the flowers, so empires among bees
Where the doors and windows lock, every knock
    is given key

Once too high to reach, now near
Once too hard to teach, now clear
Climbing towers, once at nadir
Finding power, where once lay fear

Now a beacon where once unclean
Now a river where once un-streamed
Now achievements where once undreamed
Now a movement where once unseen

Together, we build a world even
Liberated from shame and upheaval
Where dreamers don't have to build movements
For dreamers would get to be people

                    —LACHI, "WHERE ONCE UNDREAMED"

In October 2024, I sat up, excited and pumped, at my first meeting of the Recording Academy's National Membership Committee, a forum that works to develop the criteria and goals for new membership processes globally. I'd just gotten off a raucous week of gallivanting at a White House gala, a TEDNext conference, and a Women in Innovation Awards ceremony, and now here I was in L.A. with the bigwigs.

My folded Glam Cane at my side, I took a deep breath, inhaling the massive energy of some of the most powerful people shaping the music industry, and had the strangest thought: *Lachi, you belong here.*

That thought unleashed a rush of humility and gratitude so intense that I had to work to regain my focus. Little did I know, I would become a full-blown, card-carrying trustee—one of the most prestigious elected positions in the music industry—only seven months later. It was a far cry from the feeling I'd had only five years earlier, when I was petrified to show up to my first Grammy mixer holding a cane. But now my cane symbolizes my embrace of my Disability identity. Because of my cane, where I walk in with fear, I walk out with friends.

I didn't get into that room because of masking, squirreling, camouflaging, or hoping. I earned my seat at that table because I went all in à la Disability, front and center. Was it always easy? No. Is it always worth it? *Absolutely.* Disability activist and my good friend Anastasia Somoza once said something to me that echoed in my head while I sat there among the greats. "The pressure is a lot. The pressure is real," she said. "But the pressure to do right by my community is a privilege."

That's exactly it. The work, the doubt . . . it's all a *privilege.*

My Disability identity has fueled my successes, my strongest relationships, and my Big Dis Energy. Where folks see a glass half full, I see a bottomless brunch (someone get this girl a mimosa, stat). It has allowed me to recognize and understand the stigma, the exclusion, and the erasure I and so many others face, as well as the small, stylish, musical, dad-jokes-riddled part I can play in switching up the narrative.

Until people hear my story, what they make up about me is just a piece of *their* story. I wrote this book because I decided I would no longer contribute to my own erasure or perpetuate the exclusion and isolation that my eight-year-old self felt. I told the stories that little girl wanted to hear, built the organization she wished would've popped up during her Google searches, shot the music videos and media content she longed to see, conducted the research studies she wished she could reference, glammed her canes, and gave her a loud, proud voice. I live in the world she should have lived in, and it wouldn't be possible without my fearless identity, my Disability community, and a touch of pure Disability joy.

As I hope you know by now, Disability identity is everywhere—including in you. Its biggest source of erasure is you not recognizing that fact. So eyes open and eyes up! Disability identity is all around you, threaded throughout pop culture, from the celebrities you love and the tech you use to the places you go, the films you watch, and the feelings you feel.

Disability is a condition, but Disability identity is about acknowledging how that condition leads you to experience the world in a different way from everyone else. It reveals your adaptability, resilience, and drive, wakes up your empathy, stokes your interdependence, and welcomes you into a community. Who *wouldn't* want that?

Disability identity is a measure of one's access needs along a big-umbrella spectrum of disability, not an on-off switch. My gender identity is woman, my racial identity is Black, and my

Disability identities are Blind and neurodivergent with a touch of general anxiety and a pinch of PTSD. There is just so much competitive advantage in embracing the parts of yourself people have historically tried to cut down as flaws. It's the ultimate kryptonite to any -ism.

It's okay to have a complicated relationship with your Disability identity, just like you have a complicated relationship with your hair, your cat, and your cat's hair. But open yourself to that relationship. Find that sweet spot, and when shame and ableist conditioning make you feel like you should back away, lean in. That's where the power is.

As for me, I'm out here fired up and doing way too much, and if you feel energized to get out here and renaissance along with me, that's the ultimate knock on the clubhouse door. There *is* space for you inside. Just be sure that you walk in with five extra folding chairs.

Still, the average person within the disabled population just wants to live a decent life and navigate the world with dignity and autonomy, without having to be a loud proud advocate but also without having to mask. That's Big Average. That's recognizing that Disability identity isn't about trauma tropes and inspiration porn, but about a human being doing their best to get by while being a good friend, parent, child, sibling, and partner.

So, armed with this perspective, what can you do? First, no more pretending. Whether you identify as disabled or not, you've taken the red pill. You're unplugged from the Matrix, and you can see the social barriers, the attitudes, the shaming, the mimicry, and the Big Trauma . . . and you can stop giving them power. How? With your wallet, with your viewing habits, with your content diet.

When you see inspiration porn, don't support it.

When you see Big Trauma, don't fall for it.

When you come across Disability mimicry, change the channel.

Instead, loudly support and elevate the voices of leaders, talent, innovators, creators, executives, and everyday people who are open about disability. Do what you can to help them tell their stories or just to join the party. That could be as simple as finding an accessible bar to hang in so John the wheelchair user can finally grab that IPA, or as significant as investing in a disabled director's film project based on a disability-centered script written by a disabled screenwriter and featuring a cast of authentically cast disabled talent.

If you see exclusion, call it what it is, *exclusion*. Someone else's access is your access. Someone else's inclusion is your inclusion. Whether someone has high-access needs, has low-access needs, or their access needs are met, whether they identify as disabled, have a state-defined disability, or don't know where they fit, we all live on the Disability identity spectrum. When someone breaks a leg, sustains a head injury, experiences joint pain, anxiety, or light sensitivity, or ages into disability, they are literally you. See your Disability identity in them. That is your first step in dismantling ableism. That's how you stop fearing Disability.

Claiming my Disability identity has been the single most powerful thing I've done in my life. I am proud to identify as Blind.

Acknowledgments

This project could not have been completed without the support of my best friend, partner in crime, and other half, Arthur Gwynne, and everyone at Team Lachi and Team RAMPD who picked up the slack while I dove in, way over my head, to complete this manuscript.

I cannot express enough thanks to Tiny Reparations Books for believing in my story and bringing it to life—including executive editor Emi Ikkanda; book designer Kristin del Rosario (for finding lovely accessible fonts); the Dope Queen herself, Phoebe Robinson; and my full Penguin Random House team. To my cowriter, Tim Vandehey—thank you for seeing what no one saw and jumping in headfirst. Thanks to my fearless agent, Laura Lee Mattingly, and to Emily Ladau for introducing us.

Finally, to all the interviewees, to those whose stories I was able to share, and to my Disability community—thank you for the poignant contribution you have made to my life and to future generations.

Ask Me Anything

Q: You look like you can see. Are you actually blind?

A: I have low vision and am legally blind. Only 15 percent of blind people are totally blind.

Q: Do all blind or low-vision people use a cane or dog?

A: About 2 to 8 percent use a cane or dog. The rest are out here free-balling it.

Q: Do blind people have supernatural senses?

A: Nope. Still tryna win the lotto.

Q: Is it rude to say things like "See what I mean?" to a blind person?

A: Some may take offense, but I personally don't see a problem with it . . . See what I did there?

Q: Is it offensive to say the word *disability*?

A: Many in the Disability community prefer the terms *person with a disability* and *disabled person*. Euphemisms like *handicapable!, differently abled!,* and *special* stopped working for most of us by the time we were eight. Let's talk like adults.

Q: Do you find blind jokes funny?

A: When I tell them, yes! For nondisabled comedians who punch down on disability for a cheap laugh, I feel sympathy for their unwitting internalized ableism and encourage them to acknowledge and embrace their Disability identity.

Q: You overcame your blindness. How did you become so brave and courageous?

A: Adjusting to disability is a lifestyle, not an inspirational feat. I did not overcome my disability; I work every day to overcome *inaccessibility*. The courage to stand up against ableism is a necessity, not a compliment.

Q: If I hire a disabled person, won't I have to buy a bunch of equipment?

A: If you hire anyone, they're gonna need equipment. I've yet to successfully send an email by typing into the air! Getting someone the proper tools and training to succeed is just smart business.

Q: I don't know any people with disabilities or neurodivergence.

A: Yeah, you do. There are folks with non-apparent, cognitive, sensory, psychological, and undiagnosed conditions all around, and at any given moment one of them might be you.

Q: Why should I care about Blindness Awareness?

A: Blindness is a natural part of the human experience, and many will transition from sighted to blind as they grow older. More than fourteen million Americans have vision loss, a number that will double by 2050. As a society, it's up to us to make the world more welcoming for those who will eventually join our ranks.

Q: If I go blind or become disabled, will my life be over?

A: Since I began losing my vision I've achieved everything on my bucket list and more, won dozens of accolades, frequented the White House and the Grammys, toured the world, and got the book deal that led to this very book. So you tell me! The best part is, I don't fear disability.

Q: How can one "identify" as Blind? You're either blind or not.

A: I am aware of, accepting of, and proud of my Disability identity. I embrace the art, perspectives, and contributions of Disability Culture. I stand in solidarity with my Disability community. Claiming one's Disability identity is different from just "having" a disability.

Q: You're not disabled, you can do anything!

A: I am disabled. I can do anything.

Glossary

Able-bodied / Abled

Some people use these words to mean not physically disabled; how-ever, they imply that people with disabilities don't have an "able body." I'm blind and I'm pretty fit. So I prefer the term *nondisabled.*

Ableism

Most people define *ableism* as "discrimination against people with disabilities." I go further and say it's the general act of being a jerk—believing you are more worthy than another for whatever reason—whether intentional or not.

Access Check-in

Done before a shoot, production, or meeting, an access check-in is the practice of checking in on the access needs of everyone pres-ent as well as sharing information about the accessibility features of the production or event.

ADA

The Americans with Disabilities Act is a federal law signed in 1990 that prohibits discrimination based on disability in employ-ment, public accommodation, and more. It establishes a legal definition of disability that is often reduced to its benefits implications. For this reason, some people feel they can't claim or acknowledge Disability identity if it doesn't neatly fit into the legal or medical definition.

Adaptive Fashion

Apparel and accessories centered on the needs of (and often celebrating) people with varying body types, sizes, and degrees of mobility.

Aging into Disability

The process of developing age-related physical, mental, or sensory disabilities. Just as one naturally grows from toddler to teen, one can transition from sighted to blind.

ATP

Ask the Person: An acronym that encourages respectful communication with people about their identity and needs, and is a practice preferred by the Disability community. It encourages asking someone their preferred language or whether they need help, rather than assuming.

Big Average

A term I use to counter the narrative that disabilities are either trauma tropes or inspirational tropes. Big Average says that most people with disabilities, neurodivergence, or other chronic conditions fall into a third, "average person" lane. And the average person has some form of Disability identity, whether it's visible or not, requires accommodation or not, or they recognize it or not.

Big Dis Energy

A term I use to describe the innate ability to problem-solve, adapt, innovate, and think creatively, thanks to the built-in drive and sense of self-determination that come from a life of navigating the world differently.

Big Trauma

Think along the lines of Big Pharma or Big Tobacco. Big Trauma is a term I use to refer to any enterprise that exploits the disabled population as objects of on-demand sympathy to manipulate an audience into parting with money.

Big-Umbrella Disability Identity

An all-inclusive, wide-tent take on Disability identity that goes beyond the physical, intellectual, and sensory to include chronic conditions like arthritis and asthma; mental health conditions like generalized anxiety disorder and depression; diseases like MS and epilepsy; neurodevelopmental disorders like ADHD and Tourette's syndrome; learning conditions like dyslexia; and many other conditions—one of which you might identify with.

Blindish

Someone who is legally blind, partially blind, or identifies as blind but is not totally blind.

Blindness Spectrum

Only 15 percent of blind people in America are totally blind. Someone could be high partial, low partial, deafblind, legally or registered blind, have central vision loss, peripheral vision loss, night blindness, light sensitivity, and so much in between. Only 10 percent of legally blind people in the U.S. read Braille.

Curb-Cut Effect

This term, coined by Angela Glover Blackwell, describes when features originally designed to be accessible to people with disabilities are used by and beneficial to a wider group of people.

Curism / Cure Chasing

Terms I use to describe an obsession with "finding a cure" for disability, neurodivergence, mental health, or chronic conditions.

d / Deaf

A term used to refer to both people who are deaf and people who identify as Deaf. Generally, when referring to someone who is deaf, a lowercase *d* is used, and when referring to someone who identifies with Deaf Culture, an uppercase *D* is used. Deafness is a spectrum. For those with hearing loss, the phrase *hard of hearing* is widely accepted. Those who are not d/Deaf or hard of hearing are referred to by the Deaf community as "hearing."

Differently Abled / Special Needs / Handicapable

Patronizing euphemisms for disability that reinforce shame and avoidance and are just plain corny.

Disability

The ADA offers a legal definition of *disability* that is, by its nature, a measure for benefits or discrimination. After hanging with and learning from leaders who I deeply respect within the Disability community, I've come to define *disability* "as a condition of the body or mind that increases the level of difficulty one has in navigating a social construct or barrier unaided." That's my definition. Your definition of *disability* and how it integrates with your identity may be different, and that's okay.

Disability Community vs. Disabled Population

The Disability community (or DisCo) is a kindred of people who share a sense of Disability identity and belonging, who view the disability experience from a place of unity and power-building, and who thrive on collective difference. "Gooble gobble, gooble gobble" and all that. This should not be confused with the "disabled population," which includes any human with a disability (generally referenced in big-data statistics). You can be a part of the disabled population without being a member of the Disability community.

Disability Culture

Disability Culture (as defined by RAMPD) exemplifies the vast and diverse intersectionality of the disability experience and includes the unique art, stories, perspectives, contributions, and creative genius that come from our different body-minds. It is the shared identity, self-worth, and evolving language born of social oppression, erasure, and being chronically underestimated. It is rooted in the problem-solving, ingenuity and creative thinking that we use to navigate the world differently. It is unapologetic, adaptable, innovative, and resilient, and it deserves to be celebrated.

Disability Identity

Disability identity is a person's internal sense of self as it relates to big-umbrella disability. It is a categorical needs identifier. To recognize your Disability identity, you must recognize the part of yourself—any condition of your body, mind, or the way you process emotions—that, if unaided, fits into big-umbrella disabilities. One doesn't need to call themselves disabled to acknowledge their Disability identity.

Disability Joy

A form of resistance and self-acceptance, challenging the notion that the Disability identity solely encompasses grief or grievance, as opposed to joy. It is an unapologetic celebration of Disability Culture, pride, community, and expression.

Disability Justice

A framework originally conceived in 2005 by queer, disabled activists Patty Berne, Mia Mingus, and Stacey Milbern that aims to challenge ableism by recognizing its connection to other forms of oppression. There are ten principles of Disability Justice: intersectionality, leadership of those most impacted, sustainability, interdependence, anti-capitalist politic, recognizing wholeness, cross-movement solidarity, cross-disability solidarity, collective access, and collective liberation.

Disability Pride

A celebration of the Disability community's experiences and achievements while honoring each individual's unique Disability identity as a natural part of human diversity. Disability Pride month is celebrated in July.

Disability Tax

The extra costs people with disabilities incur in order to live with the same quality of life as people without those disabilities. The irony is that many people with disabilities often have a cap on how much they can earn in order to receive healthcare and other benefits, which leads to institutionalized dependency on low-income Social Security checks.

Disploitation

A term I use to describe when third parties try to capitalize on the disability experience by portraying it as trauma or an inspirational trope.

Empathy Blockage

A term I use to describe any emotional armor that protects you from the guilt that comes with witnessing ableism and realizing you're part of the problem. It's when you come across a person with a disability and part of you whispers to yourself, *Thinking about you and how we as a society have failed you is exhausting, and I don't want to think about that anymore.*

Eyeglass Concession

A term I use to describe the selective social acceptance of certain disability accommodations, like eyeglasses and casts.

Grievance Model of Disability

A model of disability I coined, in which someone views a person with an apparent disability or who is open about their Disability identity as someone who will, sooner or later, file a complaint or legal grievance of some kind. For example, a restaurant owner sees a person on a scooter approaching her restaurant and thinks, *Oh no, if I let him in, he's going to complain about something not being accessible*, while praying he zooms past.

Handicapped

An outdated term no longer acceptable to many in the Disability community. Instead, consider saying *person with a disability* or *disabled* when describing a person, and saying *accessible bathroom* or *accessible parking* when describing an accommodation.

Handler Complex

A need (usually by a parent, guardian, aide, or caregiver) to speak on behalf of or to accomplish tasks for a person with a disability because of the assumption that they cannot speak or accomplish the task for themselves. We also see this when others choose to address the disabled person's "handler" or aide instead of the disabled person themselves. This results in the loss of power, dignity, and skill-building autonomy for disabled people. One example would be a helicopter parent.

Hollywood Tropes

The harmful and misguided ways Hollywood consistently stereotypes their limited characters with disabilities, neurodivergence, and other conditions. I've named a few of the main tropes, which include the victim edit, the villain edit, tragical but magical, the super crip, and inspiration porn.

Impairment

A person is only impaired if their access needs aren't met. With my cane, zoom text, and screen-reading tools, I am blind but not impaired. The Deaf community generally prefers *d/Deaf* or *hard of hearing* as opposed to *hearing impaired* for similar reasons.

Inspiration Porn

The exploitation of people with disabilities as an inspirational prop—usually in social media, news stories, or film and TV—for the feel-good benefit or gratification of spectators.

Interdependence

When a person with a disability and an ally mutually benefit from navigating a social barrier together, with the understanding that every identity intersects with disability and that everyone, whether accepting of their Disability identity or not quite there yet, can be an ally.

Malingering

Pretending to have a disability you do not have. It includes everything from saying "I'm so ADHD or OCD" when you truly aren't, to faking a disability or neurodivergence for clicks, to get a gig, to get out of school, work, or service, or for government benefits.

Masking or Camouflaging

Terms to describe the maneuvers people use in trying to pass as "normal," typical, or socially acceptable.

Mental Health Condition vs. Mental Illness / Disorder

Some organizations, like the National Institute of Mental Health and the National Alliance of Mental Illness, use the terms interchangeably. Others feel the term *mental health condition* is more inclusive, as it can encompass everything from mild to severe mood, behavioral, and psychiatric disorders.

Mimicry

The acceptable term for when a nondisabled actor portrays a disabled character. Terms like *cripface* and *cripping up*, or comparing disabled mimicry to blackface, are considered cultural appropriation.

Misogynoir

The unique, racially enhanced gender discrimination faced by Black women.

Models of Disability

Ways of thinking about disability that can affect how people feel about and respond to it. Some models include: social model (viewing disability as a result of social barriers), cultural model (viewing disability as a collective identity), medical model (viewing disability as a biological problem that must be cured), charity model (viewing people with disabilities as objects of pity), and a model I've coined, the grievance model (viewing people with disabilities as an eventual complaint or lawsuit).

Neurodivergent / Neurotypical

A colloquial (i.e., nonmedical) term used to describe the experience of not being neurotypical. Have you ever considered someone and thought, *There's no way anyone can be that well-adjusted?* That guy's neurotypical. Neurodivergence generally includes autism, ADHD, dyslexia, Tourette's, and other sensory, processing, or cognitive conditions. I include it under big-umbrella disability.

Non-apparent Disability

A physical, mental, or neurological condition that is not easily seen or detected by others. It's sometimes referred to as invisible or non-visible; however, non-apparent is more inclusive because some conditions can waft in and out of being detectable.

Nondisabled

I believe everyone interfaces with Disability identity, so for the purposes of this book, I refer to people who don't yet identify with or acknowledge their Disability identity—perhaps because it is non-apparent or requires little outside accommodation—as non-disabled (recognizing there are exceptions). For short, I call these folks "Endies." ND—get it?

RAMPD

Recording Artists and Music Professionals with Disabilities is an organization that equips the music industry with the tools, programming, and resources needed to support working music creators and industry professionals with disabilities, neurodivergence, and chronic and mental health conditions, while fostering career and networking opportunities.

Reference Man

The theoretical model of a standard "normal" individual. Many use the Reference Man to define what success and beauty look like. However, I've found that the more I un-normal, the more I embrace my deviations from the Reference Man, the more successful I become and the more love I experience in my life.

Self-Description / Visual Description

Sometimes referred to as a visual description, a self-description is when people describe visual aspects of themselves to help include blind people (it's often done at the top of a meeting or event). It generally consists of one's ethnicity, gender identity, and one pop of visual flair, and should take no more than ten seconds. This should not be confused with audio description, which is a separate audio track that describes the key visual elements of a video.

Stim

Self-stimulating or self-soothing repetitive movements or vocalizations, like rocking, jumping, biting nails, or humming, that neurodivergent people use to cope with emotions or environmental stimuli.

"Thank You Doctor"-isms

A term I use to describe a form of concern trolling or unsolicited advice concerning someone's disability. Offender: "Have you tried healing potions? I know a guy who can fix your problem." Me: "So, you know a guy who can get you outta my face?"

Touch Tours

A guided experience that allows people with visual disabilities or neurodivergence to explore the set, props, and costumes of a performance by touch, usually before the show.

Traumady

A term I use to describe the heartstrings-plucking, trauma-focused disability narrative often appearing on film, TV, and social media.

Ugly Laws

A colloquial term used to describe the collection of laws common throughout the nineteenth century (but continuing up to the 1970s) that prohibited people with apparent disabilities from being in public.

Weaponizing Disability

The assignment of disability as a means of oppression. For example: stating that women are fragile or hysterical or that people of color are not as intelligent as their counterparts. These statements are used to justify the idea that said groups should not enjoy the same level of dignity and rights as others.

Notes

I've done my darndest to bring you into my world—the Disability identity / "Gooble gobble" part, and the glammed-up, six-inch stilettos, couture-with-a-side-of-spice-and-soul part—but that means we got some housekeeping to do. And while these nails do not get anywhere *close* to a mop bucket or one of those scrubby pads, I do want to make it clear from whence I got my dope facts. So, some notes. By the way, every quote I use came from a real-life interview with a real-life disabled person, either face-to-face or virtually, unless I say otherwise. Shall we?

Introduction: I Identify as Blind

5 **I'd found, Molly Burke:** YouTube. https://www.youtube.com/chan nel/UCwf9TcLyS5KDoLRLjke41Hg.

9 *USA Today* **Woman of the Year:** Kramer, Peter D. "Blind Singer-Songwriter Lachi Makes Her Name by Raising Canes as an Activist." *The Journal News. Rockland/Westchester Journal News.* February 29, 2024. https://www.lohud.com/story/news/local/new-york/2024/02/29 /singer-lachi-usatoday-women-of-year-nominee-ny-raised-cane-voice -disabled-musicians/72107217007/#gnt-frnt=women-of-the-year.

10 **coined by scholar Kimberlé Crenshaw:** Crenshaw, Kimberlé. "Mapping the Margins: Intersectionality, Identity Politics, and Violence Against Women of Color." *Stanford Law Review* 43, no. 6 (1991): 1241–99. https://doi.org/10.2307/1229039.

Chapter 1: The Day I Woke Up Blind

21 **a high AQ—adversity quotient:** Stoltz, Paul. *Adversity Quotient: Turning Obstacles into Opportunities.* New York; Chichester: Wiley, 1997, 7.

22 **late Hawaii senator Daniel Inouye:** "U.S. Senate: Daniel K. Inouye: A Featured Biography." United States Senate. December 3, 2019. https://www.senate.gov/senators/FeaturedBios/Featured_Bio_Inouye.htm.

22 **dancer Clayton "Peg Leg" Bates:** "Clayton 'Peg Leg' Bates." South Carolina African American History Calendar. n.d. https://scafricana merican.com/honorees/clayton-peg-leg-bates/.

22 **William Henry "Chick" Webb:** Nicholas, Alice. "Chick Webb, the King of Swing." African American Intellectual History Society. November 22, 2023. https://www.aaihs.org/chick-webb-the-king-of-swing/.

23 **nonprofit Attitude Is Everything:** Garner, George. "New Survey by Attitude Is Everything Reveals the 'Hidden Barriers' Faced by Disabled Musicians and Artists." *Music Week.* May 9, 2019. https://www.musicweek.com/media/read/new-survey-by-attitude-is-everything-reveals-the-hidden-barriers-faced-by-disabled-musicians-and-artists/076130.

23 **Def Leppard drummer Rick Allen:** WEEI Boston Sports Original. "Def Leppard Drummer Rick Allen Joins the Greg Hill Show!" YouTube. March 11, 2024. https://www.youtube.com/watch?v=j_nbe yos1jE.

23 **American Psychological Association defines resilience:** "Resilience." American Psychological Association. 2024. https://www.apa.org/topics/resilience.

29 **older adults experiencing vision loss:** Boerner, K. "Adaptation to Disability Among Middle-Aged and Older Adults: The Role of Assimilative and Accommodative Coping." *The Journals of Gerontology Series B: Psychological Sciences and Social Sciences* 59, no. 1 (2004): 35–42. https://doi.org/10.1093/geronb/59.1.p35.

29 **A University of Kansas study:** Krings, Mike. "Study: Students with Disabilities Show Resilience That Could Guide Post-Pandemic Education." *KU News.* May 11, 2021. https://news.ku.edu/news/article/2021/05/11/study-students-disabilities-resilience-can-lead-way-post-pandemic-education.

Chapter 2: Just Say the D-Word

35 **"they make bad decisions":** Harari, Yuval Noah. "AI Is Already Able to Manipulate People." *Morning Joe*. September 6, 2024. https://www.msnbc.com/morning-joe/watch/-ai-is-already-able-to-manipulate-people-expert-warns-of-growing-ai-power-218767941746.

36 **"largest minority in the world":** Carr, Katie. "The Harmful Reality of Disability Euphemisms: Why You Shouldn't Use Phrases like 'Special Needs.'" The Nora Project. June 16, 2023. https://thenoraproject.ngo/nora-notes-blog/the-harmful-reality-of-disability-euphemisms.

36 **In 2025, the CDC revealed:** "Disability Impacts All of Us Infographic." Centers for Disease Control and Prevention. April 14, 2025. https://www.cdc.gov/disability-and-health/articles-documents/disability-impacts-all-of-us-infographic.html.

36 **live with a disability:** World Health Organization. 2024. https://www.who.int/health-topics/disability#tab=tab_1.

37 **Latin prefix meaning "apart":** "Dis Definition & Meaning." Dictionary.com. n.d. https://www.dictionary.com/browse/dis.

38 **University of Wisconsin:** Gernsbacher, Morton Ann, et al. "'Special Needs' Is an Ineffective Euphemism." *Cognitive Research: Principles and Implications* 1, no. 29 (2016). https://doi.org/10.1186/s41235-016-0025-4.

38 **Center on Disability and Journalism:** "Disability Language Style Guide." National Center on Disability and Journalism. 2018. https://ncdj.org/style-guide/.

42 **Comedy Central's *Drunk History*:** Waters, Derek, et al. "Review of *Drunk History* Television." Comedy Central. YouTube. https://www.youtube.com/watch?v=y505KwHp4O4

43 **2020 documentary *Crip Camp*:** *Crip Camp: A Disability Revolution*. Cripcamp.com. 2020. https://cripcamp.com/.

45 **"but we are disabled people":** Langtree, Ian C. "Disability or Disabled? Which Term Is Right?" Disabled World. n.d. https://www.disabled-world.com/definitions/disability-disabled.php.

50 **Invisible Disabilities Association reports:** "Invisible Disability Definition." Invisible Disabilities Association. 2010. https://invisibledisabilities.org/what-is-an-invisible-disability/.

50 **"is statistically pretty high":** "Judith Heumann—Defying Obstacles in 'Being Heumann' and 'Crip Camp,'" *The Daily Show*. YouTube. March 10, 2020. https://www.youtube.com/watch?v=ybcQbpSVo3c.

Chapter 3: Main Character Energy

54 **my 2021 YouTube series:** Lachi. "*Off Beat—Going Blind & Staying Fabulous in NYC* | Episode 14—Skydiving Blind!" YouTube. September 17, 2021. https://www.youtube.com/watch?v=Ta4Q69ckY8U.

54 **Disability Data Report from Fordham:** Mitra, Sophie, and Jaclyn Yap. *The Disability Data Report 2021*. Disability Data Initiative 2021. https://disabilitydata.ace.fordham.edu/wp-content/uploads/2021/05/The-Disability-Data-Report-2021.pdf.

58 **"I'm not your inspiration":** Young, Stella. "I'm Not Your Inspiration, Thank You Very Much | Stella Young." *TED*. July 9, 2014. https://www.youtube.com/watch?v=8K9Gg164Bsw.

59 **Jacob Stolworthy's article:** Stolworthy, Jacob. "*Run* Director Says Some Actors Faked Disability to Audition for Wheelchair User in New Film." *The Independent*. November 22, 2020. https://www.the-independent.com/arts-entertainment/films/news/run-wheelchair-disability-kiera-allen-sarah-paulson-b1759896.html.

59 **by the Ruderman Family Foundation:** "The Ruderman White Paper on the Challenge to Create More Authentic Disability Casting and Representation on TV." Ruderman Family Foundation. September 2017. https://rudermanfoundation.org/white_papers/the-ruderman-white-paper-on-the-challenge-to-create-more-authentic-disability-casting-and-representation-on-tv/.

60 **The 1932 horror film *Freaks*:** Mureda, Angelo. "One of Us: Tod Browning's Freaks, Disability Culture, and the Criterion for Inclusion." Disability Visibility Project. October 8, 2023. https://disabilityvisibilityproject.com/2023/10/08/one-of-us-tod-brownings-freaks-disability-culture-and-the-criterion-for-inclusion/.

61 **on *Code of the Freaks:*** *Code of the Freaks*. n.d. https://www.codeofthefreaks.com/.

61 **Hollywood's pre-Code period:** "Awards & Festivals: *Freaks*." Mubi. 2024. https://mubi.com/en/films/freaks/awards.

61 **example of history-making:** Ebert, Roger. "The Home Front Is Not Without Its Casualties." December 29, 2007. https://www.rogerebert .com/reviews/the-best-years-of-our-lives-1946.

62 **"stigma around disability in Hollywood":** Hayes, Patrick. "The Powerful Story of the Only Actor to Win Two Oscars for the Same Performance." MovieWeb. February 1, 2023. https://movieweb.com/actor -won-oscars-same-performance/.

64 **Runway of Dreams 2023:** Kim, Irene. "Victoria's Secret Makes Its Adaptive Fashion Debut on the Runway of Dreams During NYFW." *Vogue*. September 16, 2023. https://www.vogue.com/article/victorias -secret-makes-their-adaptive-fashion-debut-on-the-runway-of-dreams -during-nyfw.

65 **self-identified as having a disability:** "Rio 2016 Paralympic Games." International Paralympic Committee. 2016. https://www .paralympic.org/rio-2016.

68 *American Masters* **series called** *Renegades:* "*American Masters*: Kitty O'Neil." PBS. 2023. https://www.pbs.org/wnet/americanmasters/mas ters/kitty-oneil/.

69 **New York City Board of Education:** "How Judith Heumann Became the 'Mother of the Disability Rights Movement.'" NYC Public Schools. n.d. https://www.schools.nyc.gov/learning/subjects/social -studies/hidden-voices/contentdetails/hidden-voices/2024/05/20/how -judith-heumann-became-the-mother-of-the-disability-rights -movement.

72 **increase documentary programming:** "*American Masters* Announces Visibility, Inclusion and Accessibility (VIA) Initiative | American Masters | PBS." *American Masters*. November 2, 2023. https://www.pbs.org /wnet/americanmasters/american-masters-announces-visibility -inclusion-and-accessibility-via-initiative/30212/.

72 *America's Got Talent:* Goalcast. "Mandy Harvey: How a Deaf Singer Earned Simon's Golden Buzzer | Goalcast." YouTube. December 11, 2021. https://www.youtube.com/watch?v=96Sh_gwoxuk.

74 **Christopher Reeve's iconic speech:** Oscars. "Christopher Reeve at the Oscars®." YouTube. July 1, 2009. https://www.youtube.com/watch? v=ffSy3-PJ5QI.

Chapter 4: Am I Them? Are You Us? The Identity Question

78 **historian David M. Perry:** "Disabilities and Identity—Spectrum, Not Binary." *This Is David M. Perry.* September 16, 2014. https://www.david mperry.com/disabilities-and-identity-spectrum-no/.

81 **physical or mental impairment:** U.S. Department of Justice Civil Rights Division. "Guide to Disability Rights Laws." ADA.gov. February 28, 2020. https://www.ada.gov/resources/disability-rights-guide/.

81 **with disabilities don't receive benefits:** "What 2024 Could Bring for Working-Age Adults with Disabilities." KFF. January 4, 2024. https://www.kff.org/medicaid/press-release/what-2024-could-bring-for-working-age-adults-with-disabilities/.

82 **"typical daily activities and interactions":** "Disability." *Merriam-Webster.* 2019. https://www.merriam-webster.com/dictionary/disability.

82 **"Ability + Barrier = Disability":** Horton, Sarah, and Whitney Quesenbery. *A Web for Everyone: Designing Accessible User Experiences.* Brooklyn, NY: Rosenfeld Media, 2013.

82 **"Disability is a Spectrum":** Barnett, Steve, and Nicola du Toit. "Disability Is a Spectrum, Not a Binary." *24 Accessibility.* December 8, 2018. https://www.24a11y.com/2018/disability-is-a-spectrum-not-a-binary/.

87 **into disability, but just aging:** Kahana, Jeffrey, Timothy Goler, and Lawrence Force. "Aging into Disability: A Conceptual Challenge for Gerontology." *Innovation in Aging* 5, supplement 1 (December 17, 2021), 541. 10.1093/geroni/igab046.2067.

89 **most important and striking works:** Smith, Jean Kennedy, and George Plimpton. *Chronicles of Courage: Very Special Artists.* New York: Random House, 1999.

91 **sensory, cognitive, and processing disorders:** DO-IT. "What Do 'Neurodiverse' and 'Neurodivergent' Mean?" University of Washington. 2023. https://www.washington.edu/doit/what-do-neurodiverse-and-neurodivergent-mean.

98 **Christina Applegate came out:** Christina Applegate. August 10, 2021. https://x.com/1capplegate/status/1424982406180704259?lang=en.

98 **"scared to be around me":** "Christina Applegate Says 'Dead to Me' Helped Her Cope with MS Diagnosis: 'It Was Cathartic.'" YouTube. December 8, 2022. https://www.youtube.com/watch?v=4XrkRUoPR6c.

98 **"host of neurodevelopmental disorders"**: Garvey, Marianne. "Rob McElhenney Shares He Was Diagnosed with Neurodevelopmental Disorders and Learning Disabilities at 46." CNN. July 12, 2023. https://www.cnn.com/2023/07/12/entertainment/rob-mcelhenney-diagnosed-health-wellness/index.html.

98 **Women in Film dinner:** "Selena Gomez Tells Haters to 'F*** Off' After Revealing She Can't Carry Kids." TMZ. September 20, 2024. https://www.tmz.com/2024/09/20/selena-gomez-responds-bipolar-fertility-negativity/.

99 **"they find in the end":** Cincotta, Craig. "How I Put My Mental Health First (and How You Can Too)." *Entrepreneur.* May 5, 2016. https://www.entrepreneur.com/living/how-i-put-my-mental-health-first-and-how-you-can-too/275103.

100 **Australian wellness guru Belle Gibson:** Donelly, Beau, and Nick Toscano. *The Woman Who Fooled the World: Belle Gibson's Cancer Con, and the Darkness at the Heart of the Wellness Industry.* London: Scribe, 2017.

100 **dubbed her a *bad influencer*:** "BBC Three—Bad Influencer: The Great Insta Con." BBC. n.d. https://www.bbc.co.uk/programmes/p09ln51v.

101 **as old as Black America:** Pérez-Peña, Richard. "Black or White? Woman's Story Stirs Up a Furor." *The New York Times.* June 12, 2015. https://www.nytimes.com/2015/06/13/us/rachel-dolezal-naacp-president-accused-of-lying-about-her-race.html.

Chapter 5: Vice, Spice, and Everything Nice

107 **commercial for L'Oreal Paris:** Coleman, Claire. "'Because I'm Worth It' Galvanised Generation to Put Themselves First." *Mail Online.* March 28, 2021. https://www.dailymail.co.uk/femail/article-9412075/Because-Im-Worth-galvanised-generation-women-first.html.

113 **"Gratitude to @glamcanes by @lachimusic":** Andrew Barkan: "'Cane I kick it?' So I came out as a cane-user at the #Grammys. I thought it would help make my disability visible and support @ramped_up i.e. be mostly symbolic (and stylish!)." Instagram. February 12, 2024. https://www.instagram.com/andrewbarkan/p/C3RUsWXrH9T?img_index=1.

114 **There's Something About Mary:** Ramisetti, Kirthana. "Peter Farrelly Remembers the Late Danny Murphy, Quadriplegic Actor in 'There's Something About Mary': 'He Was the Bravest Guy I Ever Knew.'" *New York Daily News.* August 8, 2014. https://www.nydailynews.com/2014/08/08/peter-farrelly-remembers-the-late-danny-murphy-quadriplegic-actor-in-theres-something-about-mary-he-was-the-bravest-guy-i-ever-knew.

116 **"consenting adult, honey, you're fuckable":** "Make Your Day." TikTok. 2024. https://www.tiktok.com/@peacock/video/7330725750586363179.

116 **2023 #IHaveThisAbility campaign:** "Durex's #IHaveThisAbility Campaign Redefining Disability and Sexuality." Campaign softheworld.com. August 29, 2023. https://campaignsoftheworld.com/tv/durex-i-have-this-ability/.

118 **"I was completely unaffected":** Grace, Paris Campbell. "'Y'all like bats? #Standupcomedy #Standup #Autism #Autisticadults #Neurodivergent #Comedy.'" Instagram. 2020. https://www.instagram.com/pariscampbellgrace/reel/CnX9I83qRjb/.

121 **"for and by Disabled People":** Smith, S. E. "The Beauty of Spaces Created for and by Disabled People." *Catapult.* October 22, 2018. https://magazine.catapult.co/column/stories/the-beauty-of-spaces-created-for-and-by-disabled-people.

123 **accessible festival with friends:** "Austin's Story." Accessible Festivals. October 11, 2021. https://accessiblefestivals.org/austins-story/.

124 **provide access for disabled customers:** "Americans with Disabilities Act Title III Regulations." Americans with Diabilities Act. March 8, 2012. https://www.ada.gov/law-and-regs/regulations/title-iii-regulations/.

125 **A 2022 Harris poll:** Bounfantino, Giusy. "New Research Shows Consumers More Interested in Brands' Values than Ever." *Consumer Goods Technology.* April 27, 2022. https://consumergoods.com/new-research-shows-consumers-more-interested-brands-values-ever.

126 **"Your assumption becomes reality":** Holohan, Meghan. "Viral Ad Challenges Stereotypes About Down Syndrome: 'Assume I Can Drink a Margarita.'" *Today.* March 15, 2024. https://www.today.com/health/assume-that-i-can-ad-down-syndrome-rcna143618.

128 **and a myriad of others:** Blatt, Ruth. "What Do Neil Young, Kurt Cobain and Other Disabled Rockers Teach Us About Working with Disability and Chronic Illness." *Forbes.* July 29, 2014. https://www.forbes .com/sites/ruthblatt/2014/07/29/what-do-neil-young-kurt-cobain-and -other-disabled-rockers-teach-us-about-working-with-disability-and -chronic-illness/.

128 **"I hobble when I wobble":** "'Spasticus Autisticus': The Day the BBC Banned Ian Dury." Dangerous Minds. December 9, 2012. https://dan gerousminds.net/comments/spasticus_autisticus_the_day_the_bbc _banned_ian_dury.

128 **"society that wasn't available":** Blatt. "What Do Neil Young."

129 **she developed Functional Fashions:** "Functional Fashions." *Milwaukee Art Museum Blog.* May 7, 2019. https://blog.mam.org/2019/05/07 /functional-fashions/.

130 **Ukraine's 2024 Fashion Week mid-war:** "War in Focus as Ukrainian Fashion Week Returns." Reuters. October 28, 2024. https://www .reuters.com/pictures/war-focus-ukrainian-fashion-week-returns -2024-09-04/.

132 **"experience adverse socioeconomic outcomes":** "Economic Inclusion of Persons with Disabilities." International Finance Corporation. n.d. https://www.ifc.org/en/what-we-do/sector-expertise/gender/eco nomic-inclusion/persons-with-disabilities.

133 **trillion in annual disposable income:** Milis, Brenda. "Disability: Accessibility and Representation | Adobe Blog." *Adobe.* August 14, 2024. https://blog.adobe.com/en/publish/2024/08/14/disability-acces sibility-representation.

133 **A 2015 Disability Belongs report:** "United States." 2015. https://www .disabilitystatistics.org/StatusReports/2015-PDF/2015-StatusReport _US.pdf.

133 **have the highest net worth:** DeVon, Cheyenne. "Here's Americans' Net Worth at Every Age—for People under 35, It's Up 142%." CNBC. October 28, 2023. https://www.cnbc.com/2023/10/28/americans -median-net-worth-by-age.html.

133 **and up have a disability:** "Disability in USA." Global Disability Rights Now. n.d. https://miusa.globaldisabilityrightsnow.org/info graphic/disability-usa/.

136 **book, *The Anti-Ableist Manifesto*:** Yu, Tiffany. *The Anti-Ableist Manifesto*. London: Souvenir Press, 2024, 172.

Chapter 6: Innovating 'stead of Waiting

139 **swing at $10,000 for RAMPD:** "RAMPD | Recording Artists and Music Professionals with Disabilities." RAMPED. https://rampd.org/.

146 **"network of talent and industry":** White, Abbey. "How the Recording Academy, RAMPD Expanded Accessibility and Disability Inclusion for the Grammys' L.A. Return." *The Hollywood Reporter.* February 6, 2023. https://www.hollywoodreporter.com/news/music-news/grammys-2023-recording-academy-accessibility-disability-inclusion-1235314953/.

147 **A BBC Bitesize article:** BBC. "Characteristics of an Entrepreneur—the Role of Business Enterprise and Entrepreneurship—OCR—GCSE Business Revision—OCR." BBC Bitesize. 2023. https://www.bbc.co.uk/bitesize/guides/zdqvf4j/revision/2.

147 **2020 Harvard Business School article:** Miller, Kelsey. "10 Characteristics of Successful Entrepreneurs." Harvard Business School. July 7, 2020. https://online.hbs.edu/blog/post/characteristics-of-successful-entrepreneurs.

149 **"that's why I love them":** "Read Our Q&A with Daymond John." *Starkey.* January 29, 2020. https://www.starkey.com/blog/articles/2020/01/Daymond-John-QandA.

152 **"father of the internet":** "Official Biography: Vint Cerf." Internet Hall of Fame. n.d. https://www.internethalloffame.org/vint-cerf/.

153 **Coined by Angela Glover Blackwell:** "The Curb Ramps of Kalamazoo: Discovering Our Unrecorded History." Independent Living Institute. n.d. https://www.independentliving.org/docs3/brown99a.html.

154 **Herr, is a double amputee:** Trafton, Anne. "A Prosthesis Driven by the Nervous System Helps People with Amputation Walk Naturally." MIT News | Massachusetts Institute of Technology. July 1, 2024. https://news.mit.edu/2024/prosthesis-helps-people-with-amputation-walk-naturally-0701.

154 **"Entrepreneurship Among People":** Rosenblum, David, and Christopher McLaren. "Business Ownership, Self-Employment and Entrepre-

neurship Among People with Disabilities." *U.S. Department of Labor Blog.* May 14, 2024. https://blog.dol.gov/2024/05/14/business -ownership-self-employment-and-entrepreneurship-among-people -with-disabilities.

156 **"shouldn't be allowed to work'":** "Why Are Disabled People Treated with Hostility Surrounding Work?" Reddit. 2023. https://www .reddit.com/r/NoStupidQuestions/comments/18q4777/why_are_dis abled_people_treated_with_hostility/.

156 *Stories from the Stage:* "Lachi's New Attitude: Head Up, Work Hard, Smile (Only If You Want To)." *Stories from the Stage.* YouTube. March 5, 2024. https://www.youtube.com/watch?v=p673-eX_Ulk.

158 **Kauffman Foundation published:** Capital Access Lab. "Approach." Ewing Marion Kauffman Foundation. 2022. https://www.kauffman.org /capital-access-lab/approach/.

158 **Disability & Philanthropy Forum:** "Fact Sheet: Why Fund Disability Rights and Disability Justice?" Disability & Philanthropy Forum. October 31, 2023. https://disabilityphilanthropy.org/resource/fact -sheet-why-fund-disability-rights-and-justice/.

160 **Democratic senator Jeanne Shaheen:** 118th Congress (2023–2024). "S.3528—Supporting Disabled Entrepreneurs Act." Congress.gov. 2023. https://www.congress.gov/bill/118th-congress/senate-bill/3528 /text.

162 **SSI Savings Penalty Elimination Act:** 118th Congress (2023–2024). "S.2767—SSI Savings Penalty Elimination Act." Congress.gov. 2023. https://www.congress.gov/bill/118th-congress/senate-bill/2767.

162 **Supplemental Security Income:** 118th Congress (2023–2024). "H.R.7138—Supplemental Security Income Restoration Act of 2024." Congress.gov. 2023. https://www.congress.gov/bill/118th-congress /house-bill/7138.

162 **2022 Social Security Administration:** Social Security Administration. "Annual Statistical Report on the Social Security Disability Insurance Program, 2022." https://www.ssa.gov/policy/docs /statcomps/di_asr/2022/di_asr22.pdf.

Chapter 7: The Drama with Big Trauma

169 **"Dining in the Dark":** "Dining in the Dark: A Unique Tasting Experience." Dining in the Dark. n.d. https://dininginthedarkexperience.com/.

169 **"Dialogue in the Dark":** "Dialogue in the Dark." Dialogue Social Enterprise. 2019. https://www.dialogue-se.com/what-we-do/dialogue -in-the-dark/.

172 **"efforts to live independent lives":** Kemp, Evan Jr. "Opinion: Aiding the Disabled: No Pity, Please." *The New York Times*, September 3, 1981. https://www.nytimes.com/1981/09/03/opinion/aiding-the-disabled -no-pity-please.html.

172 **leadership of the MDA:** "The Story." The Kids Are All Right. n.d. https://thekidsareallright.org/story.html.

173 **wheelchair as "a steel imprisonment":** "The Infamous Parade Magazine Article." Crip Commentary. 2024. https://www.cripcommentary .com/parade.html.

173 **raised $2.45 billion in donations:** Carson, Kevin. "Jerry Lewis' MDA Labor Day Telethon #OneMinuteMondays." September 2, 2024. https:// kevincarson.com/2024/09/02/jerry-lewis-mda-labor-day-telethon -oneminutemondays/.

174 **$10.8 billion in assets in 2023:** "Financials." Love to the Rescue. July 25, 2022. https://lovetotherescue.org/about-us/financials.

175 **"hospitals instead financed temple":** Strom, Stephanie. "In Shriner Spending, a Blurry Line of Giving." *The New York Times*, March 19, 2007. https://www.nytimes.com/2007/03/19/us/19shrine.html.

175 **"money raised for the hospitals":** Strom, Stephanie. "Report on Shriners Raises Question of Wrongdoing." *The New York Times*. July 25, 2008. https://www.nytimes.com/2008/07/25/us/25shrine.html.

175 **"premises and fund its activities":** "Shriners Exposed: Reports of Animal Exploitation, Misogyny, and Cultural Appropriation." PETA. September 20, 2023. https://www.peta.org/blog/shriners-exposed/.

177 **going home with a statue:** Thompson, Anne. "Here Are 59 Actors Who Landed Oscar Nominations for Portraying Characters with Disabilities." *IndieWire*. September 25, 2017. https://www.indiewire.com /awards/industry/actors-oscar-nominations-disabilities-afflictions -1201879957/.

179 **"My SO is visually impaired":** The Alchemyst. Reddit.com. 2025.

"My SO is blind and I do her makeup, here's her annual Grammy Carpet look! Serving African Mermaid realness." https://www.reddit.com/r/MakeupAddiction/comments/1ih57c2/my_so_is_blind_and_i_do_her_makeup_heres_her/.

181 **sideshow popped up in 1738:** "Sideshows." Lynchburg Museum System. n.d. https://www.lynchburgmuseum.org/sideshows.

181 **a nineteenth-century painter:** "Charles B. Tripp, Armless Wonder." *Travalanche.* July 6, 2013. https://travsd.wordpress.com/2013/07/06/charles-b-tripp-armless-wonder/.

182 **end of slavery in America:** Townsend, John. "Thomas 'Blind Tom' Wiggins." Klinkhart Hall Arts Center. n.d. https://klinkharthall.org/guest/thomas-blind-tom-wiggins/.

185 **"disability is my normal state":** Ladau, Emily. "The Complexities of 'Curing' Disabilities." Emily Ladau. August 15, 2013. https://emilyladau.com/2013/08/complexities-of-cures/.

188 **"is not a prayer request":** Kenny, Amy. *My Body Is Not a Prayer Request.* Ada, MI: Baker Books, 2022.

195 **"weirdest story while working?":** "Escort Helps Man Improve Stutter." Reddit. September 9, 2022. https://www.reddit.com/r/MadeMeSmile/comments/x9j70l/escort_helps_man_improve_stutter/.

196 **Chris Martin developed tinnitus:** "Chris Martin About His Tinnitus." ColdplayDaily. October 16, 2018. https://www.youtube.com/watch?v=eh0Xq9t-HcA.

Chapter 8: Shame on Who, Exactly?

200 **than live with a disability:** "Americans Would Rather Be Dead Than Disabled: Poll." Reuters. July 11, 2008. https://www.reuters.com/article/lifestyle/americans-would-rather-be-dead-than-disabled-poll-idUSN7B320259/.

201 **My maladaptive daydreaming:** Dolan, Eric W. "These Four Factors Predict Maladaptive Daydreaming in Neurodivergent Individuals." *PsyPost.* December 25, 2024. https://www.psypost.org/these-four-factors-predict-maladaptive-daydreaming-in-neurodivergent-individuals/#google_vignette.

203 **it means to be normal:** Lewis, Talila. "Working Definition of Ableism—January 2022 Update." Talila A. Lewis. January 1, 2022.

https://www.talilalewis.com/blog/working-definition-of-ableism
-january-2022-update.

203 **"ethos of whole systems"**: Krishnan, Vinay. "The Sick and the Well."
Medium. January 27, 2020. https://vinaykrishnan.medium.com/the
-sick-and-the-well-b6e844ba166.

204 *So Let's Talk About It*: RealLyfe Productions. "Jaguar Wright Joins
the Cast! So Let's Talk About It! Ep. 20 'Delete Your Search History.'"
YouTube. May 25, 2024. https://www.youtube.com/watch?v=NVOc
ZS32NSk.

207 **damaging a professional relationship**: "Attitude Is Everything
Launches Next Stage: Artist Survey." Attitude Is Everything. 2019.
https://attitudeiseverything.org.uk/attitude-is-everything-launches
-next-stage-artist-survey/.

211 **"your whole self is wrong"**: Cuncic, Arnic. "Why Your Whole Self
Feels Ashamed but Only Part of You Feels Guilty." Verywell Mind. Up-
dated June 28, 2023. https://www.verywellmind.com/what-is-shame
-425328.

214 **67 percent of people feel**: "Brits Feel Uncomfortable with Disabled
People." Scope. May 7, 2014. https://www.scope.org.uk/media/press
-releases/brits-feel-uncomfortable-with-disabled-people.

215 **collection of Old Norse wisdom**: "HAVAMAL: The High One's Lay |
Poetic Edda (English Translation)." We Vikings. October 11, 2024.
https://wevikings.com/library/havamal-eng/.

215 **them from place to place**: Marini, Irmo, Noreen M. Glover-Graf,
and Michael Jay Millington. *Psychosocial Aspects of Disability: Insider Perspectives and Counseling Strategies*. New York: Springer, 2011.

216 **Polykleitos sculpted the *Doryphoros***: Recker, Jane. "This Ancient
Roman Statue Embodies the 'Perfect' Man. But Was It Stolen?" *Smith-
sonian Magazine*. May 25, 2022. https://www.smithsonianmag.com
/smart-news/ancient-roman-statue-embodies-perfect-man-was
-it-stolen-180980138/.

216 **Aristotle followed suit, writing**: "Disability History Exhibit: Panel
Content." Alaska Department of Health. n.d. https://health.alaska.gov
/gcdse/pages/history/html_content_main.aspx.

217 **"injurious to the race of"**: Darwin, Charles. *The Descent of Man*. London: John Murray, 1871.

217 **we forget those ugly laws**: Hawthorn, Ainsley. "Illegal to Be 'Ugly'?

The History Behind One of America's Cruelest Laws." *National Geographic*. August 9, 2024. https://www.nationalgeographic.com/history/article/history-of-ugly-laws-america-disability.

217 **U.S. passed the Rehabilitation Act:** "Recruit. Hire. Retain. Advance." EARN. https://askearn.org/page/the-rehabilitation-act-of-1973-rehab-act.

217 **1990 Americans with Disabilities Act:** U.S. Department of Justice Civil Rights Division. "ADA.gov." Ada.gov. 2024. https://www.ada.gov/.

222 **version of the Reference Man:** Epker, Eva. "Stuck in the 70s: Why the 'Reference Man' Needs to Be Replaced as the Standard." *Forbes*. September 3, 2023. https://www.forbes.com/sites/evaepker/2023/08/30/stuck-in-the-70s-why-the-current-reference-man-needs-to-be-replaced-as-the-standard/.

226 **"Be humble, sit down":** KendrickLamar/VEVO. "Kendrick Lamar— HUMBLE." YouTube. 2017. https://www.youtube.com/watch?v=tvTRZJ-4EyI.

Chapter 9: Our Symbol—a White Guy in a Wheelchair

233 **White House lawn photo:** Lachi. LinkedIn. September 29, 2022. https://www.linkedin.com/feed/update/urn:li:activity:6981243842456907776/.

235 **page of the Arts section:** Zornosa, Laura. "A New Coalition Amplifies Disability Culture in the Music Industry." *The New York Times*. January 20, 2022. https://www.nytimes.com/2022/01/20/arts/music/rampd-disability-culture-music-industry.html.

237 **504 of the Rehabilitation Act:** Crowley, Maddie. "Disability History: The 1977 504 Sit-In." Disability Rights Florida. n.d. https://disabilityrightsflorida.org/blog/entry/504-sit-in-history.

238 **a Black disabled man:** "The 504 Protests and the Black Panther Party." Disability Social History Project. December 19, 2021. https://disabilityhistory.org/2021/12/19/the-504-protests-and-the-black-panther-party/.

239 **"They are inextricably linked":** Schalk, Sami. *Black Disability Politics*. Durham, NC: Duke University Press, 2022.

241 **the principles of Disability Justice:** Berne, Patty. "Disability Justice—a Working Draft by Patty Berne." June 10, 2015. https://static1.square

space.com/static/5bed3674f8370ad8c02efd9a/t/6329eb83b478e84b6a
2502ba/1663691651875/Patty_Berne_DJ-Working-Draft.docx.pdf.

242 **for true disability liberation:** "10 Principles of Disability Justice."
Sins Invalid. September 17, 2015. https://www.sinsinvalid.org/blog
/10-principles-of-disability-justice.

245 **"all of it is open":** "Civil Rights & Disability Rights: A Celebration of
Intersectionality." n.d. https://ddi.wayne.edu/possibilitiespodcast
/civil_rights_disability_rights_drm.pdf.

246 **"Disability and the Justification of":** Baynton, Douglas. "Disability
and the Justification of Inequality in American History." Social Welfare
History Project. February 10, 2014. https://socialwelfare.library.vcu
.edu/woman-suffrage/disability-justification-inequality-american
-history/.

246 **to try to escape captivity:** "The Strange History and Career of Drapetomania: The Mania That Caused Enslaved Blacks to Escape and the
Man Behind It." Massachusetts Historical Society. November 7, 2022.
https://www.masshist.org/events/strange-history-and-career
-drapetomania-mania-caused-enslaved-blacks-escape-and-man
-behind.

247 **"persons under guardianship":** Baynton, Douglas. "Disability and
the Justification of Inequality in American History."

247 **commissioner general of immigration:** Kiwan, Dina. "Dis/Abled
Decolonial Human and Citizen Futures." *Citizenship Studies* 26, no.
4–5 (2022): 530–38. https://doi.org/10.1080/13621025.2022.2091236.

247 **In her book *Pure America*:** Catte, Elizabeth. *Pure America: Eugenics
and the Making of Modern Virginia.* Cleveland: Belt, 2021.

248 **"sociopathic personality disorder":** Drescher, Jack. "Out of DSM:
Depathologizing Homosexuality." *Behavioral Sciences* 5, no. 4 (2015):
565–75. https://doi.org/10.3390/bs5040565.

249 **given behavior is abnormal:** *Diagnostic and Statistical Manual of Mental
Disorders, Fifth Edition.* Washington, DC: American Psychiatric Association, 2022.

252 **three to five million LGBTQIA+:** "LGBTQ People with Disabilities." GLAAD. February 21, 2022. https://glaad.org/disabilities/.

254 **Danish art student Susanne Koefoed:** "Koefoed & the International
Symbol of Access." International Sign Association. March 25, 2021.

https://signs.org/industry-news/koefoed-the-international-symbol
-of-access/.

254 **American Journal of Public Health:** McCauley, Erin J. "The Cumulative Probability of Arrest by Age 28 Years in the United States by Disability Status, Race/Ethnicity, and Gender." *American Journal of Public Health* 107, no. 12 (2017): 1977–81. https://doi.org/10.2105/ajph.2017.304095.

254 **Many Black autistic men:** Vargas, Theresa. "A Black Disabled Teen Went Unheard in Prison. People Are Now Listening." *The Washington Post.* February 25, 2023. https://www.washingtonpost.com/dc-md-va/2023/02/25/neli-latson-white-house-disabled/; Vargas, Theresa. "Black, Autistic and out of Prison, Matthew Rushin Becomes an Advocate." *The Washington Post.* April 30, 2022. https://www.washingtonpost.com/dc-md-va/2022/04/30/matthew-rushin-black-autistic-advocate/.

254 **Black deaf men:** Burke, Minyvonne. "Charges Dismissed Against Deaf Man with Cerebral Palsy Who Was Tased and Repeatedly Punched by Phoenix Police." NBC News. October 19, 2024. https://www.nbcnews.com/news/us-news/charges-dismissed-deaf-man-cerebral-palsy-was-tased-repeatedly-punched-rcna176231; "Black Deaf Man Ricardo Harris Says He Was Wrongfully Convicted; Seeks Writ of Habeas Corpus." *The Daily Moth.* June 25, 2020. https://www.dailymoth.com/blog/black-deaf-man-ricardo-harris-says-he-was-wrongfully-convicted-seeks-writ-of-habeas-corpus; Tucker, Emma. "Deaf Colorado Man Who Couldn't Hear Police Commands Says He Was Tased and Spent 4 Months in Jail." CNN. September 30, 2021. https://www.cnn.com/2021/09/30/us/deaf-colorado-man-arrested-jailed-four-months/index.htm.

255 **general prejudices and biases:** Nguyen, Meghan. "8 Ways People with Disabilities Can Be Vulnerable to Wrongful Conviction." Innocence Project. July 31, 2023. https://innocenceproject.org/ways-disabilities-can-be-vulnerable-to-wrongful-conviction/.

256 **"Why Are You Scared of Me?":** Lateef McLeod. "Why Are You Scared of Me?" Poetry Foundation. June 22, 2023. https://www.poetryfoundation.org/poems/159967/why-are-you-scared-of-me.

257 **not responding to directions:** "Police Killing of Native Woodcarver

Results in $1.5 Million Civil Rights Settlement and Changes to Seattle Police Department." MacDonald Hoague & Bayless, Civil Rights and Immigration Attorneys. n.d. https://www.mhb.com/cases/police -killing-of-native-woodcarver-results-in-15-million-civil-rights -settlement-and-changes-to-seattle-police-department.

258 **"you're not alone in this":** "6. How It Feels When People Think You're 'Too Young' to Be Ill." *Chronic by HuffPost.* Acast. December 1, 2020. https://shows.acast.com/chronic-by-huffpost/episodes/6.howit feelswhenpeoplethinkyouretooyoungtobeill.

262 *I Am Celine Dion:* Taylor, Irene, director. *I Am Celine Dion.* Film. Amazon MGM Studios. 2024.

262 **from my 2023 TEDx Talk:** "Dis Education: Flipping the Script on How We View Disability | Lachi Music | TEDxCherry Creek Women." TEDx Talk. YouTube. December 1, 2023. https://www.youtube.com /watch?v=HqNsbAOeNJo.

Chapter 10: A Declaration of Interdependence

266 **age of seventy-five:** Shapiro, Joseph. "Activist Judy Heumann Led a Reimagining of What It Means to Be Disabled." NPR. March 4, 2023. https://www.npr.org/2023/03/04/1161169017/disability-activist-judy -heumann-dead-75.

270 **in *The Hollywood Reporter:*** Hamilton, Xennia. "Legally Blind Singer Lachi Releases 'Lift Me Up' to Raise Disability Awareness." *The Hollywood Reporter.* July 29, 2023. https://www.hollywoodreporter.com /news/music-news/lachi-lift-me-up-judy-heumann-disability -awareness-1235547028/.

270 **thousands of streams across:** Lachi. "Lift Me Up OFFICIAL Music Video - Lachi and James Ian ft Gaelynn Lea." YouTube. July 25, 2023. https://www.youtube.com/watch?v=zmr4H9NpTKk.

270 **Best Music Video at Diversity:** "X.com." Lachi. X (Formerly Twitter). July 3, 2024. https://x.com/iachimusic/status/180860552795126 2196.

270 **won a Bronze Shorty Award:** "Lift Me Up." Shorty Awards. 2023. https://shortyawards.com/16th/lift-me-up.

274 **Accommodation is reactive and strives:** "Accessibility vs. Accom-

modation." Accessibility @ UW-Madison. 2024. https://accessible.wisc
.edu/guides/accessibility-vs-accommodation/.

276 **"Don't Need Another White Savior":** Robinson, Phoebe. *Please
Don't Sit on My Bed in Your Outside Clothes.* New York: Tiny Reparations
Books, 2021, 207.

279 **aboriginal rights collective in Queensland:** "Let Us Work Together." Uniting Church Australia. October 25, 2019. https://unit
ing.church/lilla-watson-let-us-work-together/.

ABOUT THE AUTHOR

Lachi is an award-winning recording artist, public speaker, and the first openly disabled National Trustee of the Recording Academy. Born legally blind, she is the CEO of RAMPD (Recording Artists and Music Professionals with Disabilities), a global network that has partnered with Netflix and the Grammys. Named a *USA Today* Woman of the Year and a "dedicated foot soldier for disability pride" by *Forbes*, Lachi hosted the PBS *American Masters* series *Renegades*, and has been featured in *The New York Times*, *Good Morning America*, and *Time* magazine, and in ads for Google and Mastercard. She has spoken at the White House and the United Nations. She lives in New York City.